I0807321

Preaching Is Worship

The Sermon in Context

Second Edition of Liturgical Preaching: Contemporary Essays

Edited by Paul J. Grime and Dean W. Nadasdy

CONCORDIA PUBLISHING HOUSE • SAINT LOUIS

Copyright © 2001, 2011, Concordia Publishing House
3558 S. Jefferson Avenue, St. Louis, MO 63118-3968
1-800-325-3040 · www.cph.org

First edition published as *Liturgical Preaching: Contemporary Essays*.

All rights reserved. Unless specifically noted, no part of this publication may be reproduced, stored in a retrieval system, or transmitted, in any form or by any means, electronic, mechanical, photocopying, recording, or otherwise, without the prior written permission of Concordia Publishing House.

Unless otherwise indicated, Scripture quotations from the ESV Bible® (The Holy Bible, English Standard Version®), copyright © 2001 by Crossway Bibles, a publishing ministry of Good News Publishers. Used by permission. All rights reserved.

Scripture quotations marked NKJV is Scripture taken from the New King James Version. Copyright © 1982 by Thomas Nelson, Inc. Used by permission. All rights reserved.

The quotations from the Lutheran Confessions in this publication are from *Concordia: The Lutheran Confessions*, second edition; edited by Paul McCain et al., copyright © 2006 Concordia Publishing House. All rights reserved.

Quotations from the Small Catechism are taken from *Luther's Small Catechism with Explanation*, copyright © 1986, 1991 Concordia Publishing House. All rights reserved.

Quotations identified with the abbreviation *LSB* are from *Lutheran Service Book*, copyright © 2006 Concordia Publishing House. All rights reserved.

Quotations identified with the abbreviation *LSB: Altar Book* are from *Lutheran Service Book: Altar Book*, copyright © 2006 Concordia Publishing House. All rights reserved.

Hymn texts with the abbreviation *LW* are from *Lutheran Worship*, copyright © 1982 by Concordia Publishing House. All rights reserved.

The appendix "Liturgy and Spiritual Awakening" by Bo Giertz, copyright © 1950 Board of Publication of the Lutheran Church in America, administrated by Augsburg Fortress. Reproduced by permission.

Manufactured in the United States of America

Library of Congress Cataloging-in-Publication Data

Preaching is worship : The sermon in context / edited by Paul J. Grime and Dean W. Nadasdy

p. cm.

ISBN 978-0-7586-2972-2

1. Liturgical preaching. 2. Lutheran preaching. I. Grime, Paul. II. Nadasdy, Dean, 1947–. III. Title.

BV4235.L58 L58 2001

251—dc21 200100290

---

1 2 3 4 5 6 7 8 9 10 20 19 18 17 16 15 14 13 12 11

PRAISE FOR *PREACHING IS WORSHIP*

Too often homiletics speaks of the sermon as a stand-alone "event." The preachers and scholars in Preaching Is Worship remind us well that the sermon is part of the whole "work of the people." It is Word and Sacrament. It is prayer, praise and proclamation. Readers will find in this collection of essays diverse theological proposals and practical advice for shaping the sermon better in relation to the whole of Christian liturgical practice.

Rev. Dr. O. Wesley Allen Jr.
Associate Professor of Homiletics and Worship, Lexington Theological Seminary

Over the centuries Lutherans have been among those who have been particularly careful to recognize the centrality of preaching to Christian worship. With prayer, praise, and Sacrament, the reading and preaching of Scripture should be at the heart of Christian worship. To be sure, this was one of the major contributions of Martin Luther himself. It is encouraging to discover that this reform is honored even today.

Dr. Hughes Oliphant Old
Erskine Theological Seminary

This remarkable volume succeeds in reuniting preaching and liturgy, two subjects that in recent years have wandered down separate hallways in the academy. Readers from various traditions will benefit from engaging the richly textured theological thought of these Lutheran scholars as they discuss topics from preaching as sacrament and liturgy as Word of God to the visual arts and the church in the world. These essays are insightful and often inspiring for both the theology and practice of worship.

Rev. Dr. Paul Scott Wilson
Professor of Homiletics, Emmanuel College, University of Toronto

Here is a stimulating book of essays and commentary on the proclamation of the Word as an act of worship of the living God. Here we find a most fruitful linkage of the roles of pastor and priest and the church's acts of preaching and worship. Too often we have focused upon preaching as speech delivered to a congregation; in this book we find due consideration to the sermon as an offering to a God who has so graciously offered Himself to us.

Will Willimon
Bishop, the North Alabama Conference of the United Methodist Church

More Praise for *Preaching Is Worship*

In preaching, context is everything. This compilation of insightful essays sheds helpful light on many contexts. From culture to confession, from liturgy to life, these environmental factors can wreak havoc on a sermon, taking it over. Wise is the preacher who tethers himself to the Word of God while being stretched by the demands of the itchy world around him. The authors behind this volume, fellow journeyman preachers all, help us live in the tension without snapping the Gospel's scriptural lifeline.

Rev. Dr. Scott K. Seidler
Senior Pastor, Concordia Lutheran Church, Kirkwood, Missouri

These essays are a treasure for the liturgical preacher. The first essay by Dale Meyer is a gem and is well worth the price of the book. Meyer asserts that while the sermon is framed by the context of the liturgy, the sermon has eyes into the lives of the hearers that the liturgy does not. These essays will open the eyes of the preacher to new pearls for preaching.

Rev. Dr. Gilbert J. Duchow
Retired LCMS pastor, Church Worker Caregiver for the Ohio District
Frequent contributor to *Concordia Pulpit Resources*

Preaching has multiple contexts—the theological tradition, the local congregation, and the wider world among them. The most usual context is liturgical worship. Preaching occurs in an assembly gathered for the proclamation of the Word and the celebration of the Sacraments. In many and various ways the contributors to this volume explore the ramifications of this setting for the sermon. Like the Christian scribe in Matthew 13, the editors have brought out of their treasure contributions that are new and old. The inclusion of the classic essay "Liturgy and Spiritual Awakening" by the late Bishop Bo Giertz adds immensely to the value of this project. The contributors to this book offer worthwhile counsel that should be received gratefully by all who engage in this most essential task of the minister of the Word.

Rev. Dr. Frank C. Senn
Pastor, Immanuel Lutheran Church, Evanston, Illinois

Contents

Abbreviations

AC	Augsburg Confession
AE	*Luther's Works: American Edition*. Volumes 1–30: Edited by Jaroslav Pelikan. St. Louis: Concordia, 1955–76. Volumes 31–55: Edited by Helmut Lehmann. Philadelphia/Minneapolis: Muhlenberg/Fortress, 1957–86.
Ap	Apology of the Augsburg Confession
Concordia	*Concordia: The Lutheran Confessions.* 2nd edition. Edited by Paul T. McCain et al. St. Louis: Concordia, 2006.
CPR	*Concordia Pulpit Resources*
FC Ep	Epitome of the Formula of Concord
HS98	*Hymnal Supplement 98*. St. Louis: Concordia, 1998.
LBW	*Lutheran Book of Worship*. Minneapolis: Augsburg; Philadelphia: Board of Publication, LCA, 1978.
LC	Large Catechism
LCMS	The Lutheran Church—Missouri Synod
LSB	*Lutheran Service Book*. St. Louis: Concordia, 2006.
LW	*Lutheran Worship*. St. Louis: Concordia, 1982.
LWHP	*Lutheran Worship: History and Practice*. Edited by Fred L. Precht. St. Louis: Concordia, 1993.
NKJV	New King James Version
SA	Smalcald Articles
SC	Small Catechism
TLH	*The Lutheran Hymnal*. St. Louis: Concordia, 1941.

Contributors

The Rev. Kent J. Burreson, PhD, is Assistant Professor of Systematic Theology and Assistant Dean of the Chapel at Concordia Seminary, St. Louis, Missouri.

The Rev. William M. Cwirla, STM, is senior pastor of Holy Trinity Lutheran Church, Hacienda Heights, California.

The Rev. Ronald R. Feuerhahn, PhD, is Professor Emeritus of Historical Theology at Concordia Seminary, St. Louis, Missouri.

The Rev. Carl C. Fickenscher II, PhD, is Associate Professor of Pastoral Ministry and Missions at Concordia Theological Seminary, Fort Wayne, Indiana. He is the editor of *Concordia Pulpit Resources*.

The Rev. Bo Giertz was a bishop in the Church of Sweden.

The Rev. Charles A. Gieschen, PhD, is Professor and Chairman of the Department of Exegetical Theology at Concordia Theological Seminary, Fort Wayne, Indiana. He is the assistant editor of *Concordia Theological Quarterly*.

The Rev. Paul J. Grime, PhD, is Dean of the Chapel and Associate Professor of Pastoral Ministry and Missions at Concordia Theological Seminary, Fort Wayne, Indiana.

The Rev. Dale A. Meyer, PhD, is the tenth president of Concordia Seminary, St. Louis, Missouri.

The Rev. Dean W. Nadasdy, DLit, is senior pastor of Woodbury Lutheran Church, Woodbury, Minnesota.

The Rev. John Arthur Nunes has served as president and CED of Lutheran World Relief (LWR), a $35 million global organization, since 2007.

The Rev. David J. Peter, DMin, is Associate Professor of Practical Theology at Concordia Seminary, St. Louis, Missouri.

The Rev. Robert C. Preece, DMin, is senior pastor of Zion Lutheran Church, Dallas, Texas, and first vice president of the Texas District of The Lutheran Church—Missouri Synod.

The Rev. David R. Schmitt, PhD, holds the Gregg H. Benidt Memorial Chair in Homiletics and Literature at Concordia Seminary, St. Louis, Missouri.

The Rev. James A. Wetzstein, MDiv, is University Pastor at Valparaiso University, Valparaiso, Indiana.

The Rev. Kenneth W. Wieting, DMin, is pastor of Luther Memorial Chapel, Shorewood, Wisconsin.

Foreword

Preaching Is Worship. There is not much to argue with there. Given the Lutheran understanding of justification as something spoken and done by God through the Word and the means of grace (AC IV and V), it is natural to affirm that preaching is worship. Yet one has the sneaking suspicion that there are unexamined definitions, unspoken assumptions, and unsettling conclusions embedded in that innocuous phrase. If preaching is worship, then the consequences are significant for the people of God, for their worship, and for the preaching that, in some sense, defines worship. Notice, it does not say *Worship Is Preaching*. There is more to Christian worship than preaching. Forgiveness and reconciliation are worship. The Lord's Supper is worship. Prayer and praise are worship. Fellowship in the Body of Christ is worship. Ritual is worship. Yet other than Baptism and the Lord's Supper, it is difficult to conceive of anything as formative and fundamental to Christian worship as preaching. In preaching, the Body of Christ is addressed by God's Word. In being addressed the people gathered take on identity (flesh) as the living, worshiping Body of Christ. The words of preaching are the words of a Father to His children. As paternal words of rebuke, mercy, and love, they are the very heart of the conversation of the family of God gathered at the Father's supper table. The Word of God fills the worship, and in the preaching it becomes the personal address of God to this gathering of His family. All the other things that are Christian worship are claimed by this gathering through the preaching of the Father through His Son in the power of the Holy Spirit. This is the worship of *God's* people. He has spoken to us. He has preached!

So when one says preaching is worship, one is saying something life-affirming for the people of God. That is why it is important to discuss how the Church preaches in worship and how the Church worships through her preaching. This collection of essays is now, more than ever, a vital contribution to that discussion. Originally published in 2001 by Concordia

Publishing House as *Liturgical Preaching*, it is now reissued in a second edition with two new essays. Why is this collection useful in republication? Much has happened in the ten years since its original release. New hymnals and additional worship resources have been introduced, including the 2006 publication of *Lutheran Service Book* by the LCMS. Issues relative to worship continue to be central points of conversation within many denominations. In a culture often ambivalent to and at times in conflict with the practices of Christian worship, the Church continues to ask how it might best embody its life together before God publicly in worship. Amid these developments the relationship between preaching and worship is still of central importance. The people of God should know what it means to hear the Word preached within the corporate worship gathering. And they should know how to worship in ways that reflect their encounter with the preaching of God's Word. These essays have as much to contribute toward shaping a healthy and holistic relationship between preaching and worship as they did ten years ago. Preaching is worship, after all.

Because preaching is one of the means by which the gifts of God in Christ are given and the Holy Spirit awakens faith, it is fitting that sainted Swedish Lutheran Church Bishop Bo Giertz's classic essay "Liturgy and Spiritual Awakening" is included as an appendix in this second edition. While Bishop Giertz's essay is not directly concerned with the relationship of preaching and worship, it does ground both worship and spiritual awakening in the Word of God. Preaching looms in the background. As Giertz says, "The deepest significance of liturgy lies in the fact that it is a form which the Spirit Himself has created to preserve and deepen the life which He has awakened in the church"—a life awakened through the *preaching* of the Word. Preaching awakens; liturgy preserves and deepens. So, in the same vein, these essays speak to preachers who proclaim the Word in the corporate worship of God's people. Like Giertz's essay, they call preachers to preach the Word that awakens the people of God in the living garden of the liturgy. The liturgy waters the soil into which the Word of God is sown. It is a good place to plant.

The essays in *Preaching Is Worship* till the soil and water the garden of the preacher so that the Word preached may spiritually awaken and strengthen the Body of Christ in worship. The essays divide nicely into three thematic categories: "Preaching in the Divine Service," "Liturgical Context Shaping Preaching and Its Content," and "Liturgical Preaching's Method and Purpose: Preaching *from*, *to*, *within*, and *for* the Church." The various essays explore the interweaving threads of the relationship between preaching and worship.

Five essays contribute to understanding the relationship between preaching and worship in the Divine Service. Dale Meyer's "The Place of the Sermon in the Order of Service" stresses that the sermon does not stand alone. As a living voice it finds its roots in pastoral care relationships in the parish and uncovers the treasures of the liturgy for the hearer to possess them. Such a living voice in worship always proceeds by using Law and Gospel in balance, avoiding negligence or obsession, as David Schmitt contends in his essay "Law and Gospel in Sermon and Service." The worship context demonstrates that the sermon is a living event with different types of discourse, all of which should be honored and kept in balance. David Peter further pursues the shape of balanced preaching in his essay new to the volume: "Balanced Preaching: Maintaining a Theological Center of Gravity." He advocates for preaching that keeps the vertical and horizontal dimensions of preaching in balance, warning against the threats of overextended preaching on the active righteousness plane. He discusses resources from the worship context that can assist in maintaining that balance. Finally, Robert Preece's essay, "Sacramental Preaching: Holy Baptism," and Kenneth Wieting's essay, "Sacramental Preaching: The Lord's Supper," emphasize preaching that takes a baptismal shape and that proclaims the Christ present for His people in the Supper at the center of Christian worship.

Five essays focus on the ways in which the liturgical context can shape preaching and its content. In "Preaching through the Seasons of the Church Year," Charles Gieschen contends that sensitivity to the themes and cadence of the church year can assist the pastor in proclaiming sermons that are Christocentric and consistent with the proclamation of the rest of the service. Attending to the church year involves " 'Working' the Lectionary," as Carl Fickenscher makes apparent. Attending to the lectionary's themes and how it works produces sermons that better reflect the biblical text and its formative impact. The biblical Word is read in the context of the liturgical words, themselves composed of the biblical Word. And, as William Cwirla indicates in "Unfolding the Meaning of the Liturgy," that means the preacher is called to underscore what God is doing for us here and now for our salvation in this corporate worship service. Included in that liturgical context is hymnody, which, as Paul Grime indicates in "Hymnody and Preaching," provides ideas, imagery, and language to enrich the preaching of Christ. Hymnody can paint a visual image of Christ, but so can visual images themselves. In "Preaching and the Visual Arts," Dean Nadasdy calls for the preacher to act as artist and poet, engaging the imagination by employing visual imagery alongside and within the proclaimed Word.

The final essays turn toward the method and purpose of preaching out of the worship context. These three essays elucidate preaching that is *from*, *to*, *within*, and *for* the Church. In "Liturgy as Story," James Wetzstein examines the benefits and pitfalls of an inductive approach to preaching. One of those benefits is that the liturgy provides a source of experiences for proclaiming the meaning of the text through the stories it tells, thereby calling hearers to identify themselves within the salvific story. Further potential for holism in preaching is manifested in John Nunes's essay, "Preaching within the Faith Community." Here the holism and immersive nature of the liturgical context shapes preaching that encompasses the totality of the life of the people of God in public faith and service among the nations of the world. Lastly, Ronald Feuerhahn calls preachers to preach not only *from*, *to*, and *within* the church, but *for* the Church. The liturgical context makes the preacher aware that he preaches a message of death and living hope to the world by the authority of the Lord who will come again.

What, then, are the gifts received from reading these essays? They include a renewed appreciation that the worship of the Church is the arena for the activity of God through His Word and a refined homiletical practice that reflects the conviction that preaching is worship. Unexamined definitions, unspoken assumptions, and unsettling conclusions? Not any longer. For here, in the worship of the Church, God is at work and He is preaching mightily!

Kent J. Burreson
August 18, 2011

Introduction

The preaching task is arguably the most important work of the Christian pastor. Seminary training assumes as much with its emphasis on the study of the biblical languages and the proper interpretation of the Scriptures. The people will expect nothing less as they wonder—even before their new pastor arrives—whether they have received a good preacher. And pastors will demand of themselves their very best as they proclaim the Word of God to their people each week. Preaching is important.

Preaching, however, does not occur within a vacuum. Preaching is contextual. Multiple contexts surround the sermon and impact the sermon, even when the preacher is unaware of them. Homileticians may identify as many as seven preaching contexts: theological, literary, historical, personal, cultural, pastoral, and liturgical. The last of these is the primary focus of this book.

In surveying the literature of homiletics, we find very little that intentionally addresses preaching from the perspective of liturgy. This collection of essays contributes toward filling that gap. All of the essayists in this volume are preachers. Most are parish pastors. A few teach at seminaries. All bring to their preaching a deep love for the broader task of worship.

All these essayists assume that the sermon can never be viewed, either in its preparation or in its hearing, completely apart from its immediate context. Even within Christian traditions that do not follow a "liturgical" pattern of worship, the sermon is surrounded by prayer and song, often in a very organized, if unacknowledged pattern. The sermon is ultimately an act of worship itself. Here God graces the listener with His Word, written in the Scriptures and proclaimed by the preacher. He graces the Table with His presence, the visible Word served by the celebrant. Altar and pulpit are in fellowship. Hence liturgical preaching. While we offer this book to the entire Church, we work from the Lutheran tradition. The essayists locate the sermon within the framework of Word and Sacrament, where exposition of the Word of God, proclaimed to the baptized, leads to feasting on the Bread of Life at the Table of the Lord. We know that in many churches there are unbaptized participants for whom liturgy, symbols, and proclamation can lead to saving faith in Jesus Christ. With the wider Church we assume and promote the use of a lectionary and the observance of the church year.

The context of the sermon is, however, defined somewhat more broadly by several of the essayists. Some explore the Law/Gospel dialectic and its influence on both sermon and service. Others consider new approaches to homiletics in light of the liturgical context. Here is a look at preaching and its relationship to the community and world; there, the place of the visual arts in the preaching task.

As preachers approach the text, they must consider a bewildering number of liturgical influences. How does this reading relate to the other readings? Are there portions of the liturgy to which this text speaks? Where are we in the church year? How will my people "hear" this text? How can I proclaim specific Law and specific Gospel that will both cut to the heart and soothe the soul?

To subject every sermon in its various stages of preparation to the countless suggestions that are contained in the following pages would be frustrating, if not impossible. Our hope is that the ideas that are offered here will stimulate preachers to take up the preaching task with renewed vigor and joy as they proclaim Jesus Christ, whose word is life, who is the Word of life.

The Place of the Sermon in the Order of Service

Dale A. Meyer

"What's Otto doing out there?" I asked.

Glancing out the window of the sacristy door as I vested, I noticed Otto Segelhorst walking toward the cemetery. While some folks were coming at the last minute into the church, Otto was going his own way. He had a knack for doing that. He regularly raised the eyebrows of people who never questioned what we now call "conventional wisdom." There was little conventional about Otto. He thought his own way and did his own thing, so it wasn't at all out of character for him to be going into the cemetery just minutes before the bells would ring.

"Oh, he's going to visit his wife's grave," said Roy, our custodian. "Otto says that the sermon is the main thing; what comes before the sermon isn't as important."

Don't get the wrong idea. Otto was a faithful member, a very faithful member of our church. A retired farmer, he was one for whom the Sunday sermon held a special place. He looked forward to it, made sure he was always there. So it is with God's people; they are there for the preaching. Of course, there are mundane ways to explain their presence: family habits (Otto's family members were devoted churchgoers), community culture (in this little town going to church was the right thing to do), providing moral instruction for the children. These and the like were contributing factors for attending preaching in the 1970s, the decade of this little story. Although times change, there still is nothing new under the sun when it comes to human conduct, so social reasons still account in some measure for church attendance. That said, such earthly explanations are pedestrian compared to the most essential reason God's people come to hear us. They keep coming because they want to hear a good word from the God who has called them to be His own possession. "Whoever is of God hears the words of God" (John 8:47).

That the pulpit has a special place in their hearts is evidence of God's quiet working through the decades. You in your ministry, I in mine—we're not the first through whom God has worked in the lives of His people. There were others before us. When parishioners tell us about old pastor so and so, they're telling us that there were faithful stewards of the mysteries before us, predecessors who were good at speaking Jesus' words of spirit and life. In our tenures we're more like the people who pass out water to runners along the route: we're refreshing the saints and guiding them along their heaven-bound way. So they keep coming to hear preaching—not because of us, but because through us they want to keep hearing that good and compelling word from God that draws them on.

The humbling truth is that even if somehow the hearer in front of you has never heard a clear Gospel sermon, you still are not the first. Through the Word, through the liturgy, through the creeds, through Baptism, God Himself was working in that heart before you ever prepared the sermon, put on your robe, and entered the pulpit. And the Law of God is always at work, whether it's recognized or not. How often the Gospel is spoken by laypeople with no ordained person in sight! That reminds us, our titles aside, that the power is in the Word and not in the speaker. "The Lord gave the word; Great was the company of those who proclaimed it" (Ps. 68:11 NKJV).

We're not the first and—more humility called for—we're not the only ones with messages. In our society every TV, every computer, every radio is a potential pulpit telling people what they should believe. In this media saturation there is no dearth of religious broadcasting. Some media ministries we judge as good; others we find wanting. Whichever, our listeners hear the voices of those religious and secular shepherds too. In our so-called post-modern environment, many have chosen to be spiritual but not religious, to get their Christianity from any place and every place but not exclusively from the local congregation and from the properly called pastor. While the call documents don't tell us how to deal with this pervasive competition, our joy is that people keep coming to hear us, that the pulpit of the congregation is still a commanding place. "I was glad when they said to me, 'Let us go to the house of the Lord!'" (Ps. 122:1).

That is the implicit contract of Sunday mornings. People come to church expecting to be persuaded about some divine truth. They're not hostile as they take their places in the pews (unless the last church meeting happened to be a debacle). They may be lukewarm, but they are still warm enough to come and be roused by the Spirit's sword. With you they have a contract: "Pastor, we've come to be persuaded through you of some truth that is good for our lives and that is from God." Seen through a theological lens, this "contract" is an expression of their baptismal covenant. God claimed them as His own, forgave their sins, and now they come looking for mercies, for words that bring and illumine the loving kindness from the God of their baptismal covenant.

Diplomas on our walls, the jots and tittles of good theological education, expensive vestments, leadership skills and seminars—thank God that a broader perspective than all that comes from aging in pastoral ministry. As a young seminary graduate, I was so enthralled with what *I* was doing in ministry. It is so easy to confuse our egos with God and His work. Rationalizations abound. "Lead us not into temptation." Now I know better, that we shouldn't take ourselves too seriously as we hone our pastoral skills and as we prepare for weekly worship. We weren't the first, aren't the only ones, and won't be the last. You and I are only stewards and that for only a short time. No, we shouldn't take ourselves too seriously, but the work of preaching? Yes, indeed, for sooner or later the faithful come into church looking to that special place, the pulpit, for a good word from God. That's the place where we fulfill our part of the "contract," our call from God through His people to prepare and deliver sermons that inspire them with the mercies of God. It is, indeed, holy ministry.

"Ready?" asked Roy.

"Yup; let's do it."

Roy left the sacristy and went to the steeple where he and brother Earl rang the bells for worship. God's people were present—except Otto, who now was in the cemetery at the grave of his dear wife.

Some years ago I was invited to join in the observance of 150 years of Lutheranism in New Zealand. As one small part of that celebration I was asked to sit on a panel for a general discussion about the life of the church today. The first question put to each of us was the predictable icebreaker "What do you do?" One panel member had a brief and simple answer. A Danish pastor serving a church in Sydney said, "My job is to preach the Gospel."

"Good for you!" I immediately thought. After all, the society in which we minister tries to seduce us from Law and Gospel as we go about sermon preparation. Pop psychology, social action, congregations thriving with activities, entertainment—they all try to replace theological content in our sermons. Not that they don't have some legitimate role in preaching, but meeting felt needs has to be ancillary to the ultimate goal, the salvation of souls. So, when this pastor said, "My job is to preach the Gospel," I reacted with immediate approval.

Then the audience was invited to join in with their own questions and comments. An older woman stood up in the back of the room and told us that she had been born in Sweden but emigrated to New Zealand as a young person. She recently returned to Sweden for a visit and was surprised by a noticeable change in the pastors. "When I was young, they were not especially friendly. When I went back, I couldn't believe the change. The pastors were even greeting the people as they came to worship."

To which the Danish pastor replied with a most dour face, "You may be sure that I will never do that. My job is to preach the Gospel." The audience was incredulous, their eyes wide open in disbelief. I was stunned, too, and have mulled over that incident many times. I venture to say that the Danish pastor didn't fully appreciate the unique place of the sermon in the corporate worship and individual lives of the members of the congregation.

The term *homiletics* comes from the Latin *homilia* ("conversation"). That is the word which was used to describe the theological wrestlings of the Emmaus disciples (Luke 24:14). When Paul preached at Troas, the same word is used in a preaching context (Acts 20:11). Augustine introduced *homilia* into the preaching vocabulary of the Western church. The place of the sermon is more than a bald proclamation of the Gospel truth. There is something going on between preacher and listeners, a conversation, an *antiballo*, a casting back and forth (Luke 24:17). Cicero once criticized Plato for severing *lingua* from *cor*, speech from the heart. I think the Danish pastor was doing the same thing. Homilies should grow out of our keeping company with parishioners in real life.

The history of the word *sermon* tells a similar story. The Latin *sermo*, meaning "conversation" or "discourse," is probably best known as the title of Horace's satires, the *Sermones*. Horace's attitude toward satire is *ridentem dicere verum*: "to speak the truth with a smile," to point out human foibles while acknowledging your own humanity. That's not unlike the sermon. In the order of worship the sermon is unique because it is so human and so divine, at the same time both sacrificial and sacramental. It is sacrificial in that the preacher talks as one of God's people about human life as it is today, not just Horatian foibles but sins, and along with sins he gives voice to the wide range of emotions that he and his audience feel. But the sermon is sacramental because it brings good news of a God who walks with us on the way with His help and hope. It is Jesus "with His skin on."

Most listeners on Sunday morning are the baptized. The Invocation reminds them that they have been claimed by the triune God. Better that I say it should remind them, for most worshipers probably do not draw the connection between Invocation and their own Baptism. Otto might have foregone his cemetery visit had I taught him and the congregation more about the first portion of the Divine Service. Kerygma must be present in the sermon, of course. There can be no true sanctification apart from the Gospel of the forgiveness of sins by grace through faith. Integrating that kerygma into preaching to the baptized will also work on any unregenerate soul that happens to be in the crowd. That said, as the Invocation should remind worshipers that they have been baptized, it should also dissuade us from trite expressions of the Gospel as we prepare and preach to people who are regenerate. If we describe some problem and then offer this sudden revelation, "But God has given you a Savior," we can expect a ho-hum "Yes, pastor, I know that. How does that apply to my divorce, my addiction, my cancer, my . . ." Whatever their level of sanctification in the narrow sense might be, in the wide sense they have been "washed, you were sanctified, you were justified in the name of the Lord Jesus Christ and by the Spirit of our God" (1 Cor. 6:11). The *kerygma* they desire is Article IV of the Augsburg Confession[1] relevantly proclaimed to all facets of their lives so that they may continue to "grow up into salvation" (1 Pet. 2:2).

The other extreme tempts us to see the Sunday sermon as merely teaching the how-to's of Christian living to the baptized, catechesis with a practical bent, ignoring the kerygmatic component. Our Western understanding of preaching comes from Greco-Roman rhetoric, not from Hebraic thought. That's why people read the Sermon on the Mount and think that it is a strange type of sermon. They are right. Sermon content is Hebraic, biblical, but the genre we call "sermon" is Western. The great teachers of classical oratory said that a speech should perform three functions: to please the hearer, to teach, and, finally and most important, to persuade. "What does this mean?" is good pedagogy and good theology. But just as *Christenlehre* was different from the sermon, so teaching practical Christian living is part but not the goal of the sermon. A pastor teaches, in classes, in visitations, in writing, and, yes, in preaching. But in the pulpit: "My job is to preach the Gospel." In that our Danish brother was correct.

What troubled me was not his unwillingness to greet people before church. Technically, that's not part of our call. His refusal seemed to reflect disdain for social intercourse, for rubbing shoulders with the laity. Yet in those daily contacts—some intentional, others casual—the pastor observes the Law at work. You and I are called in significant measure to a ministry of Law. *Homilia* originally described social intercourse. "Bad company [*homiliai kakai*] ruins good morals" (1 Cor. 15:33). *Sermo*, as a title for satire, cannot happen unless you rub shoulders with people in the workaday world. That's where the theologically sensitive pastor sees the Law at work.

I'm of the opinion that one of the greatest problems of preaching today is clumsy and cliché-ridden preaching of the Law. We pound hearers over the head with stereotyped expressions of Law that, true as they are, do not communicate because they've been heard over and over again. And we've left

1 *Concordia*, 33.

the impression that the Law is bad. How can that be? The Law comes from God! "The law is holy, and the commandment is holy and righteous and good" (Rom. 7:12). Even its terrible effects (*lex semper accusat*) are intended by God to bring all to salvation (Gal. 3:24; 1 Tim. 2:4). The more we study the dynamics of the Law in the Scriptures and the Lutheran Confessions, the more our *homiliai*, our rubbing shoulders with laity during the week, will point us to apt preaching of the Gospel. Consider some of the Law's dynamics in contrast to the work of the Gospel.

The Law is innate (Rom. 2:14). You can be absolutely sure that God is working in every heart, saved and lost, through the inborn Law. The Gospel, by contrast, is foreign to us (Rom. 10:14).

The Law is conditional. If you do this, you will be rewarded (Gal. 3:21). Do that and pay the price. Everyone you meet throughout the week, everyone who sits before you on Sunday—even the person in your skin—we are all born with an aptitude for salvation by works. On the other hand, the unconditional Gospel challenges our works-bound way of thinking and living (Eph. 2:8–9).

The Law exposes and even multiplies sin (Rom. 7:7–9; cf. Gal. 3:20). The cookie-jar effect! The Gospel produces the opposite effect: "Are we to continue in sin . . . ? By no means!" (Rom. 6:1–2).

The Law produces wrath (Rom. 4:15). Ever notice this when someone has left your church in a huff because you and the congregation have taken a biblical stance? Ever notice this when someone correctly criticizes you? The Gospel, on the other hand, works through faith (Rom. 4:14).

The Law imprisons (Gal. 3:22) and kills (Rom. 7:10). "Who will deliver me from this body of death?" (Rom. 7:24). "Pastor, what am I going to do? What am I going to do?" The Gospel frees (Gal. 5:1).

In short, "Is not My word like fire, declares the Lord, and like a hammer that breaks the rock in pieces?" (Jer. 23:29). In the Bible you may come across a threat. That passage is Law. The Gospel, on the other hand, does not contain any threats. It offers only comfort and consolation.

Most important, the Law performs God's alien work on faithful and unregenerate alike so that we might be led to Christ (Gal. 3:24).

Good sermons are born from *homiliai*, planned and unplanned contacts, pastoral and social interactions with your people wherein you see and hear firsthand the effects of the Law. In hospitals and nursing facilities, in homes and in office sessions, at wedding receptions and funerals, at sports events, the health club, parties—everyone has a story to tell. They'll tell where they're hurting. They'll let us know if they have Pharisaic pride. They'll show us if they have Epicurean indifference. They love to tell their stories, and the church has trained us to listen spiritually. Out of those conversations, out of *homiliai*, comes an appropriate, tailored preaching of the Law on Sunday mornings. "We believe, teach, and confess that the preaching of the Law is to be encouraged diligently. This applies not only for the unbelieving and impenitent, but also for true believers, who are truly converted, regenerate, and justified through faith."[2]

The sermon is unique among all the elements of the Divine Service in the way it applies the Law. God's Law is present explicitly or implicitly throughout the ordinary and the propers, but in the sermon the pastor makes the Law hands-on. There is no better way to engage your hearers than with the Law, to discuss with credibility where they're at spiritually because you've heard them tell their stories. Just as Nathan's parable of the sheep didn't register with adulterous King David until the prophet said, "Thou art the man," so the constant and variable elements of the liturgy may not register until you preach it. Unlike the liturgy, the sermon is the time to bring it home, to be prophet as well as priest.

The need for suitable preaching of the Law might be even more imperative now. The great mark of our so-called postmodern time is the abandonment of absolute truth. Ask your congregational members if they can recite the Ten Commandments, and their reaction will tell you that they've been influenced by the subjectivism of our time. If they can't recite those ten absolute truths, how can they keep them? And should someone say, "Well, I can't recite them, but I know what I should and shouldn't do," you have evidence of a massive shift from revealed truth to subjectively chosen truth. Gutenberg is dead, and the centuries-old belief that truth is in books and especially that one Book uniquely reveals "the way, the truth, and the life" has eroded even in our faithful listeners. And biblical literacy in those who don't worship? Forget it! "Thus says the Lord" does not carry the weight it did a few decades ago. The sword of the Spirit might be dulled, even sheathed on their side, but not on ours. We have been trained in rightly dividing the word of truth, and a significant part of ministry is the ministry of the Law. From *homiliai* throughout the week to *homilia* on Sunday mornings, the sermon's place in the order of worship is for you to bring into clearer focus the Law at work.

Roy and Earl rang the bells. Hymns, Invocation, Confession and Absolution, Introit, Kyrie, Gloria, Readings—all without Otto. But now the sermon hymn was ending, and I climbed the five steps into that old pulpit. There was Otto in the balcony with the older men—a custom from the days when men and women sat apart in church. Otto's eccentricities never bothered me. I was glad to see him in his accustomed place. Through *homiliai* I had come to know him as one of the dear faithful.

---

2 FC Ep VI 3 (*Concordia*, 486).

Obviously, I knew where they sat because I looked out at the crowd Sunday after Sunday for the seven years I served St. Salvator, Venedy, Illinois. Not so obvious and most important in the relation of sermon and liturgy is that the liturgy can't look but the preacher can.

Augustine tells about a sermon that almost failed. He was in northern Africa speaking to Christians who had retained a custom from their pagan past. The custom was called *caterva*, the Latin word for "crowd" or "troop." As he tells the story in his book *On Christian Doctrine*, the Christians in Mauritania would regularly reenact an ancient civil war and in the reenactment people would be killed. So the bishop came to deliver a "Brothers, these things ought not so to be" sermon. Augustine recalls that he was fulfilling two of the three purposes of a speech. He could see from their smiles that he was pleasing them with his message. Their faces also showed that they were receiving his teaching. However, he saw no tears in the audience as he preached. He was not getting through to them with a message of repentance and amendment of life. So Augustine changed his preaching plan on the spot, trying different approaches until he saw tears throughout the audience. Then he knew he was succeeding. The murderous reenactments were stopped.[3]

That raises this important question: where lies the *persuasive* power of a sermon? The answer is not a facile: "The Gospel!" The tears came because of the power of the Law, and that power—*nota bene*—would not have worked repentance had Augustine not adapted his presentation, had he not adjusted the plan of his sermon. A sermon plan (*rhetoric* in the true sense of the word and not the current connotation of speech that is untrue, the craft of spin doctors) seeks verbal and visual ways that give maximum room for God to do His convicting work through the Law.

The same distinction is true with the *divine* power of a sermon, the best power of God, the only power to salvation, the Gospel of Jesus Christ. Through the means of grace, God gives the Holy Spirit, who "works faith, when and where it pleases God [John 3:8], in those who hear the good news."[4] "Hear the Gospel" assumes that the listeners understand what they hear. If real dialogue is not happening in the sermon and if the preacher is not using good rhetoric (vocabulary, figures of thought and speech, arguments, and illustrations that are readily understood and that prompt the audience to participate in the dialogue through their engaged thoughts), then even an otherwise well-prepared sermon may not communicate.

---

3 Augustine, *On Christian Doctrine*, trans. E. B. Pusey et al. (Chicago: Encyclopedia Britannica Great Books of the Western World, 1952).

4 AC V 2 (*Concordia*, 33).

So there are these two powers at work in an effective sermon: persuasive power and divine power, rhetoric and Word. We use the first to make room for the second, that God's Word may not be bound but have free course and be preached to the joy and edification of Christ's holy people.

The *caterva* speech would not have been effective had Augustine not been watching his audience. The sermon has eyes that the liturgy does not. In the ordinary and propers are aged formulae filled with rhythms and words that don't automatically interact with worshipers. Because of society's sensory overload, people in the pews are often numb to the themes and rich nuances of each Sunday's liturgy. And because we are so hurried, so rushed, so "ASAP" that we cannot tarry as we do liturgy, we feel compelled to "keep the service moving." For me these are not arguments to abandon the various forms of historic liturgy. Our liturgy may be set in printed words and memorized forms (diction and themes not immediately communicative in a biblically illiterate society and among biblically diminished individual Christians), but this does not guarantee dialogue between worshipers and the Word. Its form is fixed; the preacher can improvise. The sermon has eyes that the liturgy does not.

It is a shame, therefore, when a manuscript or notes pull our eyes away from face-to-face dialogue as we preach. The ancients (not the church fathers but the ancient Greco-Roman audiences and orators who perfected the speaking craft) thought that the orator who spoke from a manuscript was *deinos*, "terrible," not to be trusted, a slippery spin doctor. Their ideal speaker was *vir bonus dicendi peritus*, "a good man experienced in speaking." To attain that ideal obviously required preparation, and so the last great teacher of antiquity, Quintilian, advised his students to write out a manuscript if they had time and then commit it to memory. However, the ancient prejudice against crafted speeches never went away, and the great orators, though they prepared and memorized their speeches ahead of time, seldom let paper detract their eyes from reading the faces in the audience. And when those faces looked back and said, "You're not getting through," they'd shift their plan. Augustine, who set the stage for Christian homiletics, was thoroughly classical in his preaching technique. We have lost that ancient discipline of scrutinizing the crowd as we deliver our Sunday sermons. Academic papers read from the pulpit promise to pull our eyes away from true dialogue. The people may not shout "Amen," but they speak with their faces.

That brings us back to the Danish brother. Perhaps he read 1 Corinthians 2 as a renunciation of rhetoric and an advocacy of merely speaking correctly formulated Gospel words. Even if he doesn't, many do.

> And I, when I came to you, brothers, did not come proclaiming to you the testimony of God with lofty speech or wisdom. For I decided to

> know nothing among you except Jesus Christ and Him crucified. And I was with you in weakness and in fear and much trembling, and my speech and my message were not in plausible words of wisdom, but in demonstration of the Spirit and of power, that your faith might not rest in the wisdom of men but in the power of God. (1 Cor. 2:1–5)

Reading that as a renunciation of rhetoric doesn't fit. Paul was a master orator and his Epistles reveal his expertise in that religiously neutral craft. Paul was reacting not to the genuine and beneficial rhetorical skill that every preacher must master. He was specifically criticizing the set speeches of what is called the Second Sophistic, a time when oratory was largely meaningless because the Roman Empire controlled all. Traveling orators hawked their skills, promoted their wisdom and schools of philosophy, and entertained the crowds, much as we let ourselves be entertained by the manipulations of television. Christianity is not opposed to emotions as long as the emotions are secondary and based on the objective Word. Paul's preaching sought to root faith in the power of God rather than in anything human. "Don't lump me with itinerant sophists," he was saying. "A man who delivers such set speeches is, why, he's *deinos*!"

Wherever the sermon is placed in the order of service, the preaching and the listening must finally be focused on the objective Word. Delaying the sermon until some later time is not wrong but not as helpful as some think. Madison Avenue used to say that an advertiser had to make seven impressions before the customer became aware of the product. That suggests that ministry is more about *homiliai*, about repeated pastoral interaction with your people, than about where you place the sermon. Back in the days when Lutherans carried hymnals to worship, my mother had the habit of keeping the Sunday bulletin and putting it in her hymnal. From time to time through the week she would look at that bulletin and perhaps review the hymns, readings, and prayers of the previous Sunday's worship. Impressions. Should I return to parish ministry, I'll be more focused on impressions than on tinkering with the order of worship. A church home page, e-mail devotions, phone calls, notes, visits to members, a "buddy system" among the members—these are impressions, *homiliai*, all climaxing in the Sunday sermon and the living voice of the Gospel.

In the liturgy, treasures are hidden in a field. The sermon uncovers those treasures so that the hearer might own them. "Invocation, confession, absolution, mercy, glory, creed, proclamation, intercession, sacrament, benediction . . ." Without the sermon this is not intelligible talk in our postmodern society; but the ancient words remain precious, pearls of great price, not to be discarded. The sermon, seeing God's people as the liturgy cannot, climaxes the life of the congregation in the Word and affords the Spirit room to put the pearls into the hearts and lives of the faithful.

Now to that lingering matter of Otto, who says that the sermon is the main thing and what comes before it isn't as important. While the liturgy may not "see" as the sermon does, the liturgy lifts our sights beyond our own peculiar place and time. I think that Otto's instincts were right, though his follow-through was unconventional, typical Otto. In his own peculiar way, he was communing with God together "with all the company of heaven" in general and with one very special member of that company in particular. In a sense, he was entering the most holy place in preparation to hear God's Word.

What did he miss when he didn't hear the Invocation? He didn't miss some archaic call to order, some "We make our beginning in the name of the Father and of the Son and of the Holy Spirit." Invocation is not a beginning; Baptism was the beginning. The Invocation is a continuance. When the triune name is invoked, the faithful are lifted beyond the here and now of time and space to the ongoing fact of their Baptism into Christ. "We were buried therefore with Him by baptism into death" (Rom. 6:4). Paul didn't write: "It's like you were buried" or "Let Baptism symbolize your relationship with Jesus." No, we actually were buried. Fact. Lifted out of present time and space. Mystery. That is balanced in the future by the hope of resurrection. "If we have been united with Him in a death like His, we shall certainly be united with Him in a resurrection like His" (Rom. 6:5). This forward-looking hope is sure and certain fact, lifting our sights out of present time and space to eternity. Invocation takes us beyond a visit to the cemetery. "Here we have no lasting city, but we seek the city that is to come" (Heb. 13:14).

This does not deny the present. As a continuance of the eternal in our lives, the invocation of the triune name at a regular time and place, Sunday in the congregation's place of worship, also calls upon God to meet us again in the Gospel of Jesus Christ. " 'Let us go to His dwelling place; let us worship at His footstool!' Arise, O Lord, and go to Your resting place" (Ps. 132:7–8). But for this encounter with the Holy One to happen, the present must be acknowledged. We're not on a New Age fantasy escape from old Adam realities. So we rush to confess. "Lord, to whom shall we go? You have the words of eternal life" (John 6:68). After Absolution come Introit and Kyrie, Hymns of Praise, Collect, Readings, Creed. These all affirm and enlighten our time-and-space-bound present and yet lift our sights to the Church universal, the Church on earth and in heaven, one Church, not two, the one Body of Jesus Christ. Always there is this back and forth in worship, this movement from present to eternal, from sin to forgiveness, from despair to hope, from the imperfect to love, from earth to heaven.

Isn't that what Otto was doing when he visited his wife's grave, yearning for the eternal? And when he joined Edmund and Omer and Walter and the other old men up in the balcony, he was yielding to the action of God upon his present life, time-and-space bound as it is for us all. Pastoral oversight means that someone has been called not only to lead the liturgy but also to be with Otto and the other faithful in the *homiliae* of daily life outside of the church building. The result? In the sermon that shepherd, that overseer, knows where to pour in the balm of the Gospel. "I will set shepherds over them who will care for them" (Jer. 23:4).

Always this back and forth in worship, "body here yet soul above." But the balance between present and eternal should not be equal. Through pleasant speech, through instruction, and through persuasive technique, earthly things for earthly people, the preacher strives to open the hearts and minds of hearers so that God can do a supernatural work, bestowing and nurturing faith in what is unseen. I pray also that "having the eyes of your hearts enlightened . . . you may know what is the hope to which He has called you, what are the riches of His glorious inheritance in the saints" (Eph. 1:18). The how-to's of Christian living that are so popular today are important and ought to be treated in the pulpit, but they are not the goal of the sermon or the goal of the Gospel. The time-specific sermon rings the changes of the ageless liturgy and says to the baptized: "You believe in Him and rejoice with joy that is inexpressible and filled with glory, obtaining the outcome of your faith, the salvation of your souls" (1 Pet. 1:8–9).

That movement toward eternity is confirmed to us by our Lord's Supper, timeless body and blood in, with, and under very temporal elements. Like the *antiballo* of the Emmaus disciples as they talked with the Stranger on their way to Emmaus, the back and forth of liturgy and sermon warms the heart of the faithful in anticipation of the Supper. Otto was faithful in receiving that foretaste of the feast to come; today he shares the eternal feast in the New Jerusalem that we and all the faithful still await.

> Not to us, O LORD, not to us, but to Your name give glory, for the sake of Your steadfast love and Your faithfulness! (Ps. 115:1)

Law and Gospel in Sermon and Service

David R. Schmitt

Without the aid of cinematic technique, life passes rather routinely. Moments of holy recognition are rare, and people constantly overlook God's gracious care in daily living. On television, cinematic technique can emphasize that life is a gift. Camera angles frame the vision, close-ups point out the unnoticed, and musical crescendos alert one to the fact that daily events, such as the hand of a child clutching the hand of a parent, are sacred times to be remembered: the parent has only a moment to hold on before the child grows up and pulls the hand away. With the television off and the routine of daily life constantly playing, however, such cues are absent. Dinner is eaten without close-ups of the food (one's daily bread), conversation stops and starts without musical crescendo (during graceful speech), and children routinely let go of the hands of their parents without any sign that another day has passed (another time to be numbered rightly that one might gain a heart of wisdom). Moments of holy recognition, moments in which one draws near to contemplating God's grace in daily living, are rare.

The scarcity of these moments makes people treasure them all the more, dragging video cameras into churches at weddings and into hospitals at births, hoping to capture and preserve what otherwise would certainly pass them by: a moment of knowing that life is a gift from God. People invent ways to remind themselves that life is to be treasured as a gift. A magnet holds shopping lists, household chores, and dance class schedules onto the refrigerator, punctuating all of these human activities with the announcement: "Every morning is Easter morning—Alleluia!" Supervisors command shipping clerks to rush orders, penciling their commands on Post-It notes stamped with the mass-market wisdom "Treasure the moment." Yet rush and routine triumph over these feeble acts of human intervention. The world is too busy to stop and engage in holy reflection. Chores are done. Appointments are kept. Commands are followed. Yet, all the while, people remain blind to God's gifts. Life passes with a rush and a routine that makes moments of holy recognition rare in everyday living.

Jesus, however, had a way of bringing such moments to light. Without the advantage of film technology, without close-ups and musical crescendo, without video cameras and mass-market magnets, Jesus came and worked simply. He used His hands, His glance, and His word. In His hands, a blade of grass revealed the providence of heaven, a bird in flight the care of a heavenly Father, and a loaf of bread the kingdom come in a desert. With His glance, disciples would stop and take note of the unnoticed: a widow dropping her life's pittance into the treasury, a disciple losing faith in a courtyard, and Zacchaeus catching a glimpse of heaven from a tree. By His word, Jesus opened the Passover table to be a foretaste of heaven and the rough wood of a cross to be the tree of life. In Jesus, the world was never out of the reach of its Savior. His hands, His glance, His word brought death and they brought life, and the good news is that they went everywhere. Jesus placed Himself at the ends of life in this world so that life in the kingdom of God might begin. At a well in Samaria, at a fishing site on the Sea of Galilee, at a Pharisee's home where guests were reclining at dinner, even at a place of execution outside of Jerusalem where all of life brought a criminal to this end, God was there. He opened the eyes of the dying to see in Himself, the God-chosen yet God-forsaken, a life that never ends. Jesus had a way of bringing about such moments of holy recognition precisely because in His life, death, and resurrection the work of God promised for ages was finally, faithfully, and most fully known.

His work continues to this day. Into a world blind with rushing and dead with routine, God continues to come. He comes and brings about life in moments of holy recognition. That is the heart of Christian worship. God awakens His people to the gift of life that they have been given. In the Divine Service, God Himself comes to visit His people in the midst of their daily routine and through Word and Sacrament brings them life, both now and forever, as a gift. What does it mean to speak of Law and Gospel in sermon and service? Nothing other than this: God graciously intervenes in a sin-sick world to speak a word and by that word to awaken the dying to life everlasting. Within the walls of the church, therefore, no human reminders are needed, no human punctuation of life, calling people to stop and recognize the moment. Worship does not need to be cluttered with entertaining techniques to awaken the people. God Himself comes. With a voice that can startle the storm and yet is as common as the pastor's, He names the sinner's burden and sets the sinner free. Christian worship is this work of God, this Word of God bringing moments of holy recognition into a world dead in sin. At the font, with skin and a splash of water, His Word breathes life. He creates sons and daughters. At the Table, where ancient words are spoken, strange comfort lies in His body that is broken. In the pulpit, where human speech humbly serves divine purpose, His Word goes forth. It enters the world. It stops the rush for a moment only to reveal within the routine of daily living the living grace of God.

This is liturgical preaching: God working through the preacher's labor, God speaking through the preacher's words, and God doing what He has promised to do with His words. These divine activities work faith through the preaching of repentance and the forgiveness of sins. By God's design, the preacher speaks and, by God's grace, the world is awakened to moments of holy recognition. For example, Jesus is none other than the promised Messiah, this is none other than the house of God, these are none other than the people of God, and life is nothing other than a gift from God. Liturgical preaching, therefore, is rightly concerned about the proper distinction of Law and Gospel in the sermon, for through His Word, rightly divided, God intervenes in the daily affairs of this world and brings people to life. There is a difference, however, between godly concern for the proper distinction of Law and Gospel in liturgical preaching and what one might call the two errors of human negligence and human obsession in these matters. In faithful proclamation, the preacher seeks to maintain a godly concern for the proper distinction between Law and Gospel in preaching while avoiding the errors of negligence or obsession in these matters.

Law/Gospel and the Tapestry of Preaching

What constitutes godly concern for the proper distinction between Law and Gospel in preaching? It begins with a recognition of the complex dynamics of the sermon and the appropriate place of the Law and Gospel distinction within those dynamics. The sermon is an event of God's gracious intervention into the affairs of this world. God has so ordered His work in this world that, through the office of preaching, His Word goes forth and by that Word the Spirit creates and sustains faith among people. In liturgical preaching, this proclaimed Word is based upon the texts appointed for that day. Through the appointed texts, the church remembers the life of Christ and His Church in a yearly cycle; through liturgical preaching, the sermon proclaims the good news of such remembrance for a particular people on a particular day. As the preacher proclaims that good news, the text and the hearers are joined together in the continuing historical intervention of God. God, who has intervened in the past to work salvation for all people in the life, death, and resurrection of His Son, continues to work through the public proclamation of His Word, forgiving sins and strengthening faith, and promises to do so until Christ returns. The sermon, therefore, recognizes God's historic intervention as recorded in the biblical text but also confesses God's continuing intervention through the public proclamation of His Word and hopes for God's final intervention in the fulfillment of all that God has promised. As the preacher proclaims God's gracious work in Christ, he draws together the text and the people. He remembers God's past work, proclaims God's present work, and hopes for God's future work, all most fully known in Christ. In doing this, preachers employ what has been called a Lutheran hermeneutic[1] and through such interpretation create a tapestry of four types and functions of discourse in preaching.[2]

In the crucible of the Reformation, a Lutheran hermeneutic was defined. As James Voelz has demonstrated, such a hermeneutic involved complementary principles of interpretation: the Scriptures are to be interpreted according to principles appropriate to literary texts inspired by the Holy Spirit; the Scriptures are also to be interpreted Christocentrically as they testify of Christ.[3] Interpreting the Scriptures according to their status as literary texts gives rise to one of four types or threads of discourse in the tapestry of preaching: textual exposition. *Textual exposition involves reading and interpreting passages of Scripture.* Passages of Scripture are to be read and interpreted in their context.[4] While the lectionary severs passages from their immediate context and arranges them with other severed passages from other books in a set of readings, the interpretation of these passages in preaching is to remain consistent with their original context. Through textual exposition, the preacher communicates the intended meaning of the text in its historical context to the hearers. Such exposition is not comprehensive but limited to that which is pertinent for the preaching occasion. Through such discourse, the preacher awakens the hearers to God's historic intervention in many and various ways and makes the hearers witnesses in the present of God's work in the past.

Interpreting the Scriptures according to their status as texts inspired by the Holy Spirit gives rise to a second thread of discourse in the sermon: *theological confession.* Throughout Scripture the same God is speaking, offering a revelation that is not self-contradicting but part of a unified whole. In

1 For a fuller discussion of what is meant by the Lutheran hermeneutic, see Edward Schroeder, "Is There a Lutheran Hermeneutic?" in *The Lively Function of the Gospel*, ed. Robert Bertram (St. Louis: Concordia, 1966), 81–97; and James Voelz, *What Does This Mean? Principles of Biblical Interpretation in the Post-Modern World* (St. Louis: Concordia, 1997), 347–61.

2 For a fuller discussion of what is meant by the tapestry in preaching, see David Schmitt, "Reaching Out as a Lutheran," in *Reaching Out to the People*, Symposium Papers 9 (St. Louis: Concordia Seminary Publications, 1999); and Schmitt, "The Tapestry of Preaching," *Concordia Journal* 32, no. 2 (Spring 2011).

3 Voelz, *What Does This Mean?* 353.

4 Voelz describes this as the principle of integrity, *What Does This Mean?* 353.

interpreting and proclaiming God's work as recorded in Scripture, passages of Scripture may be read in light of one another, working together within a framework that constitutes the teachings of the faith.[5] The lectionary highlights this theological coherence of passages by the way in which readings, severed from their immediate context, are grouped together diachronically in seasons and synchronically in propers of the day. In the sermon, the preacher offers hearers theological confession of these teachings of the faith. Like textual exposition, this thread of discourse is not comprehensive but is limited to what is pertinent for the preaching occasion. For example, in Christmastide, the preacher might offer hearers theological confession of the incarnation and, in Eastertide, the resurrection of the body. Through theological confession, the preacher confesses a framework within which one interprets individual passages of Scripture and through which the hearers understand the nature and work of God and of people in the present day.

Finally, interpreting the Scriptures Christocentrically gives rise to the third and fourth threads of discourse in the sermon: *evangelical proclamation* and *hearer depiction*. Christocentric interpretation involves defining and maintaining a proper distinction between Law and Gospel in interpretation. Without a proper distinction between Law and Gospel, Scripture remains a closed book and God's work of salvation through the proclamation of His Word is hindered.[6] It is through such a proper distinction that textual exposition and theological confession are opened for the hearers so that God might create and sustain faith in the present time through the proclamation of the Gospel. Such interpretation recognizes God's saving work in the past and brings the benefits of that work to the hearers in the present. In evangelical proclamation, the preacher proclaims a Christocentric interpretation of the text and brings that interpretation to present fruition. He opens textual exposition and theological confession to speak of Christ and then brings such speaking to the lives of the hearers in present-tense discourse.[7] Thus God works in the midst of His people through the office of preaching: through evangelical proclamation in the sermon, the preacher calls sinners to repentance and proclaims the forgiveness of sins on account of the death and resurrection of Christ.

Such present-tense discourse also involves hearer depiction. Things written in the past are proclaimed in the present, to and for those whom God gathers and the world in which they live. Hearer depiction captures this contemporary life experience of the hearers. It names the sin and the salvation

---

5 Voelz describes this as the principle of integrity, *What Does This Mean?* 353.

6 FC Ep V (*Concordia*, 484–85).

7 Gerhard Forde, "The Word that Kills and Makes Alive," in *Marks of the Body of Christ*, ed. Carl Braaten and Robert Jenson (Grand Rapids: Eerdmans, 1999), 5–6.

now present. Such depiction avoids simplistic caricature, abstract generalization, and overly sentimental representation.[8] Instead, the preacher offers realistic depiction naming this present world as a place of God's working, the people here gathered as God's holy people, and their lives as a wonder of His creating. The hearers are thereby brought into company with those who have gone before and with those who will follow after. All are recipients of God's continuing gracious work, and the preacher thereby faithfully serves in the office of preaching as God comes and works salvation in that place through the public proclamation of His Word.

As one can see, while godly concern for the proper distinction of Law and Gospel lies at the heart of Lutheran preaching, it is not the whole of Lutheran preaching. The sermon is more than simply an articulation of Law and Gospel. It is a careful interweaving of four threads of discourse through which the preacher creates the tapestry of preaching through which God does His work. When pastors handle the Word of God rightly in preaching, they use these four threads of discourse. In handling the Scriptures as literary texts inspired by the Holy Spirit and pointing to Christ, pastors use textual exposition, theological confession, evangelical proclamation, and hearer depiction in their sermons. On each preaching occasion, preachers are faced with creating a tapestry of these four forms of speech. They do this through concrete definition, appropriate emphasis, homiletical movement, and internal coherence.

Through *concrete definition* in each thread of discourse, preachers avoid general and generic preaching: they open a specific text and specific teaching to a specific proclamation of Law and Gospel to the hearers who are gathered that day. As beginning preachers soon learn, one does not need to cover all of a text and all Christian doctrine in a single sermon and, as experienced preachers know, if one does not have concrete definition that varies each Sunday, all sermons begin to sound the same. Concrete definition addresses these matters.

By having *appropriate emphasis* in each thread of discourse, the preacher offers the development that is needed with that text and teaching so that the Gospel might be proclaimed to those people that day. Hence different preachers in different communities will treat the same text differently as they fashion the tapestry of a sermon appropriate to their community on that day. Sermons published in homiletical resources and even sermons retrieved from years past rightly seem inappropriate. They do not honor the complex dynamics of the living event of preaching and the art of creating a

8 Walther offers a partial overview of such problems in his seventh evening lecture. C. F. W. Walther, *The Proper Distinction between Law and Gospel*, trans. W. H. T. Dau (St. Louis: Concordia, 1928), 50–58. Cf. C. F. W. Walther, *Law and Gospel: How to Read and Apply the Bible*, trans. Christian C. Tiews (St. Louis: Concordia, 2010), 57–64.

sermon that is needed for that particular community on that day. In addition to concrete definition and appropriate emphasis in these four threads of discourse, the preacher also attends to appropriate movement and internal coherence among these four threads of discourse.

Through *appropriate movement*, the sermon avoids remaining solely in one thread of discourse but moves among all four, and through internal coherence these four threads of discourse work together rather than at odds with one another. The hearers are not left wondering what the text has to do with the teaching of incarnation, how the pastor moved from the text to the Gospel, or how the reference to last week's drive-by shooting fits in. Instead, appropriate movement and internal coherence work together to create what is known as the organic unity of the sermon.

The sermon, therefore, is a living event and the metaphor of weaving a tapestry of preaching reflects its organic nature. As an enactment of the preaching office, the sermon is authoritative public discourse based on a text of Scripture, centered in the death and resurrection of Christ for the forgiveness of sins for the benefit of the hearers in faith and life. Yet the text, the teaching, and the people vary during the course of the liturgical year. Through the tapestry of preaching, the sermon is able to accommodate changing texts, confess different teachings, and address various people as it continues to proclaim the unchanging Gospel of God's gracious work in Christ throughout the year. Since the sermon is such a living event, it calls for preparation in each of these four threads of discourse and for care in the use of them so that the art and the heart of preaching are maintained.

As one can see, godly concern for the proper distinction of Law and Gospel in preaching is not simply a matter of formulating one's evangelical proclamation. It is more than simply asking, "Where is the Law?" and "Where is the Gospel?" as one approaches a text for the sermon.[9] Godly concern involves recognizing that evangelical proclamation is one of four threads of discourse that constitute the sermon. Godly concern develops evangelical proclamation in conjunction with, rather than in isolation from, the other three threads of discourse. In this way, preachers properly distinguish Law and Gospel as part of a much larger process, the complex dynamics of sermon formation and proclamation. In doing so, they offer evangelical proclamation that is appropriate for the preaching occasion. They create a tapestry of preaching as God's grace is proclaimed in relationship to a specific text and specific teachings for specific people on a specific day. Such is the meaning of godly concern for the proper distinction of Law and Gospel

9 Richard Lischer identifies such an approach as a confusion of Law and Gospel. Richard Lischer, *A Theology of Preaching: The Dynamics of the Gospel* (Durham, NC: Labyrinth Press, 1992), 43.

in preaching. What about the errors of Law and Gospel negligence and Law and Gospel obsession?

Avoid Law/Gospel Negligence

Law and Gospel negligence is easy to identify. For some preachers, it arises from the influence of theory and for others from the force of habit. In regard to the influence of theory, the field of homiletics has recently expanded. With H. Grady Davis's *Design for Preaching* and Fred Craddock's *As One without Authority*, a period of growth and experimentation in homiletics was born. For half a century, new forms and methods of preaching were introduced through practice into the field of homiletics. Scholarship has clarified specific schools of homiletical thought within this broad field now known as the New Homiletic.[10] Such expansion in the homiletical field offers pastors a variety of resources from a variety of preaching traditions to use in refining their skills. Pastors today have a wide selection of "methods" from which to choose.

Law and Gospel negligence occurs when pastors use these methods without serious consideration of whether or not the resulting sermon properly distinguishes Law and Gospel. New homiletical forms and strange homiletical content are offered to the people in the name of a sermon, and, lest anyone should doubt that this is Lutheran, at some point the preacher will declare that the people are saved by grace through faith on account of Christ. Here, Law and Gospel content are relied upon to save the sermon, not the people. Rather than open the text of Scripture, the teachings of the faith, or the lives of the people to God's gracious working through the proper distinction of Law and Gospel, the preacher simply embeds Law and Gospel proclamation in the midst of other material. He satisfies some rule learned long ago about what makes a sermon Lutheran: the proclamation of Law and Gospel. Such negligence is not faithful preaching and certainly not what is meant by properly distinguishing Law and Gospel in the sermon. It turns the Word of God, His life-giving message of judgment and salvation, into some Lutheran mantra that when spoken will redeem any excuse for a sermon *ex opere operato*. Would that preaching were so easy! One form of Law and Gospel negligence, then, arises from the influence of theory and

---

10 For example, see O. Wesley Allen Jr., ed., *The Renewed Homiletic* (Minneapolis: Fortress, 2010); Charles H. Cosgrove and W. Dow Edgerton, "Preaching and Interpretation in Transition," in *In Other Words: Incarnational Translation for Preaching* (Grand Rapids: Eerdmans, 2007), 1–35; Richard Eslinger, *The Web of Preaching: New Options in Homiletic Method* (Nashville: Abingdon, 2002); Eugene Lowry, *The Sermon: Dancing the Edge of Mystery* (Nashville: Abingdon, 1997); and Paul Scott Wilson, *The Practice of Preaching* (Nashville: Abingdon, 1995), 197–262.

diminishes evangelical proclamation to a short Lutheran statement meant to save any homiletical technique.

The other form of negligence arises from the force of habit. Whereas the influence of theory can reduce evangelical proclamation to a statement, the force of habit can reduce it to a stereotype. In this case, Law and Gospel are certainly proclaimed every Sunday, but in a formulaic manner that may cause some hearers no longer to listen to what is being said. Repetition of any particular form of proclamation can cause hearers to stop listening to the actual words and instead to focus upon the act of the speaker using those words again and again. For example, a pastor once bragged to the fellow pastors in his circuit that he referred to the Lord's Supper in every sermon. As the liturgy moves from the Word to the Table, so, too, he concluded every sermon with a reference to the Lord's Supper and an invitation for the hearers to participate. Once, when the circuit meeting was hosted by that pastor's congregation, a fellow pastor had occasion to talk with a member of the altar guild. He asked her if it was true that the pastor always referred to the Lord's Supper in the sermon, and her response was as follows: "Yes, that's how we know he's almost over." In this case, while the pastor intended for his proclamation to invite hearers to God's gracious work in the Sacrament of the Altar, his formulaic and stereotypical approach invited one parishioner to look at her watch instead. For her, these words were a signal that the sermon was over, not that the feast would begin. Through repeated use of an otherwise effective structural technique, God's grace had been reduced to a transitional "in conclusion." Such stereotypical and formulaic repetition can occur with a variety of words and in a variety of ways. It is not a matter of the words that are chosen but of the continual use of those words in a highly predictable fashion. Evangelical proclamation is not the formulaic repetition of Law and Gospel vocables at certain points in the sermon, but a living proclamation of God's gracious work among His people that, like the text itself, varies in vocables from Sunday to Sunday.

Contemporary Lutheran homiletical scholarship has done well in addressing this error of Law and Gospel negligence. The proper distinction between Law and Gospel is central to Lutheran preaching and historically has been incorporated into Lutheran homiletical education through the study of Walther's *Law and Gospel* and the use of preaching paradigms such as goal-malady-means or problem-point-power. Current articles continue this tradition. While homileticians have been identifying the schools of the New Homiletic, Lutheran homileticians have responded with an increasingly focused study of Law and Gospel proclamation.[11] While homiletical

11 Simply noting the articles printed throughout more than one decade in one Lutheran journal of preaching (*Concordia Pulpit Resources*) reveals the strong emphasis on this subject: Ralph Bohlmann, "Good Preaching Is Gospel Preaching," *CPR* 1, no. 1 (1990):

theory has broadened, calling attention to the variety of content, forms, and functions of discourse in preaching, Lutheran response has appropriately narrowed, emphasizing that which is the heart of preaching, the proper distinction of Law and Gospel. In such work, Lutheran writers have rightly emphasized what continues to remain deficient in the New Homiletic: a concern for the proper distinction between Law and Gospel. Such emphasis is necessary to prevent Law and Gospel negligence when pastors incorporate the wisdom of the New Homiletic into the practice of Lutheran preaching.

In some cases, theoretical discussions in the New Homiletic have supported Lutheran concerns in the proper distinction between Law and Gospel. For example, the New Homiletic's interest in metaphor has mirrored a renewed interest among Lutherans in the metaphorical depictions of God's grace in Scripture. What Caemmerer merely outlined in an appendix to his work[12] has been expanded in the more recent work of Rossow, Kolb, and Preus.[13] Such research into the biblical language of the Gospel encourages preachers to remain faithful to the variety of ways in which God has chosen to communicate His gracious work in Scripture. Rather than use the same formulaic pronouncement Sunday after Sunday, preachers form their Gospel proclamation in response to the varied forms of proclamation present in the biblical texts. In this case, and in many more like it, current Lutheran scholarship has addressed the problem of Law and Gospel negligence in preaching. It has done so with such attention and perspicuity that there is little need to restate the wisdom here. Any preacher who errs in Law and Gospel negligence has more than enough theological and theoretical direction from contemporary Lutheran homileticians to amend this abuse.

2–3; Richard Osslund, "Doing the Law from a Free and Merry Spirit," *CPR* 1, no. 4 (1991): 7–9; Gerhard Forde, "Proclamation: The Present Tense of the Gospel," *CPR* 2, no. 3 (1992): 2–3; Richard Lischer, "How Law and Gospel Work in Preaching," *CPR* 3, no. 3 (1993): 5–7; Robert Kolb, "Preaching the Law in the '90s," *CPR* 4, no. 1 (1993): 2–4; Kolb, "Preaching the Gospel in the '90s," *CPR* 4, no. 2 (1994): 2–3; David Scaer, "Preaching Sanctification," *CPR* 4, no. 4 (1994): 2–4; Francis Rossow, "Unintentional Gospel Omissions in Our Preaching," *CPR* 5, no. 4 (1995): 2–4; Donald Deffner, "Moralism," *CPR* 5, no. 4 (1995): 14–15; Carl C. Fickenscher II, "What Does a Good Law-Gospel Sermon Look Like?" *CPR* 8, no. 4 (1998): 2–4; Gilbert Duchow, "A Seminar on Preaching: Preaching the Law-Gospel: Not in Balance," *CPR* 9, no. 3 (1999): 2–4; and Duchow, "A Seminar on Preaching: Preaching the Third Use of the Law," *CPR* 9, no. 4 (1999): 6–8.

12 Appendix III, "Biblical Modes of Depicting the Atonement," in Richard Caemmerer, *Preaching for the Church* (St. Louis: Concordia, 1959), 330–31.

13 Rossow uses categories of hearer reception to classify these metaphors in Francis Rossow, *Preaching the Creative Gospel Creatively* (St. Louis: Concordia, 1983), 32–49. Kolb and Preus use systematic categories to classify them in Robert Kolb, *Speaking the Gospel Today: A Theology for Evangelism* (St. Louis: Concordia, 1984), 123–87; and J. A. O. Preus III, "Just Words: Probing the Biblical Language of the Gospel," in *Law and Gospel in the Church and World*, Symposium Papers 5–6 (St. Louis: Concordia Seminary Publications, 1996), 105–25.

Unfortunately, this strong interest in and publication of articles about the proper distinction between Law and Gospel in preaching has caused the second error often present in Lutheran homiletics to go unnoticed: the error of *Law and Gospel obsession*. While these articles rightly emphasize that Law and Gospel is the heart of Lutheran preaching, Law and Gospel obsession mistakenly assumes that this is the whole of Lutheran preaching.

Avoid Law/Gospel Obsession

Law and Gospel obsession occurs when the preacher focuses upon the Law and Gospel dialectic in preaching with such rigor and all-consuming attention that everything that occurs in the office of preaching is reduced to an overly simplistic bad-news-then-good-news paradigm. Everything in the sermon becomes a matter of Law and Gospel. For example, consider the use of sermon structure. Since the sermon is a complex interweaving of four threads of discourse, its structure—the temporal sequencing of those threads of discourse in some orderly manner—is complex as well. Historically, the sermon structure has embraced a wide variety of forms, from verse-by-verse exegesis and application to logically structured developments of a theme to inductive struggles leading to the discovery of meaning. As preachers composed sermons, they carefully chose the sermon structure that best served the proclamation and created the tapestry of preaching appropriate for that occasion.

Law and Gospel obsession, however, reduces the freedom of form in sermon structure to a simplistic problem-solution structure or what can be called the "Law-then-Gospel" paradigm.[14] The godly concern for the role of evangelical proclamation in the sermon becomes for some an obsession that dictates the sermon's form. Caemmerer's paradigm for discerning the persuasive force of the sermon, the goal-malady-means triad, which in his own day he bemoaned that "seminarians distort into sermon outlines,"[15] ends up being distorted by pastors as well. This is what is meant by the error of Law and Gospel obsession: a godly concern becomes an obsession that limits God's gift of the dynamic art of preaching and diminishes the fullness of Lutheran homiletics. Law and Gospel obsession can affect much more than

14 For a fuller discussion of this topic see David Schmitt, "Freedom of Form: Law/Gospel and Sermon Structure in Contemporary Lutheran Proclamation," *Concordia Journal* 25, no. 1 (January 1999): 42–55; and Schmitt, "Richard Caemmerer's Goal, Malady, Means: A Retrospective Glance," *Concordia Theological Quarterly* 74, nos. 1–2 (January/April 2010): 23–38.

15 Richard Caemmerer, "Stance and Distance," in *The Lively Function of the Gospel*, ed. Robert Bertram (St. Louis: Concordia, 1966), 4.

sermon form, however. It can hinder the individual types of discourse that constitute the sermon as well.[16]

Consider the error of Law and Gospel obsession in relation to the discourse of textual exposition. As noted earlier, in a Lutheran hermeneutic, Christocentricity and textual integrity are complementary principles, not contradictory ones. While the texts from Scripture testify to Christ, they do not do so by a negation of what they mean in their own historical context. Law and Gospel obsession occurs when the principle of Christocentricity overrides the principle of textual integrity and the preacher uses a text to lead to Christ but does so by ignoring or distorting what the text actually means in its context. Often this happens by means of an atomization of the text. The preacher locates a word or phrase within the text that can be used to perform Law and Gospel application among his hearers. He then isolates that word or phrase from the rest of the text and uses it in a rhetorical design that accuses his hearers of sin and proclaims salvation to his hearers. Suppose the word is "prayer" (choose any text where the word occurs). The preacher isolates that word from the text and proclaims how his hearers do not pray as they ought. Indeed, they cannot pray as God desires because of their sin, but Jesus prays for them, saying, "Father, forgive them for they know not what they do." Because Jesus alone is righteous and offers His life as a sacrifice for sin, His prayer is heard, and now heaven is opened, and they are able to pray. . . . Almost any word or phrase can be used this way. Such a use of a vocable from the text of Scripture may lead to a Christocentric proclamation, but it does so by ignoring the text and not observing the principle of textual integrity. An obsession with evangelical proclamation causes the preacher to ignore textual exposition in the sermon.

Sometimes, instead of ignoring the text, preachers actually misinterpret it either in terms of its content or in terms of its function. For example, consider a sermon on the theme of "Blameless Hearts" based on 1 Thess. 3:9–13 (Advent 1, Series C).[17] In verses 12–13, Paul prays that the Lord would cause the Thessalonian Christians to increase and overflow in love toward one another and toward all people so that their hearts might be established blameless in holiness in the presence of God on the Last Day. The syntax communicates that Paul prays for their hearts to be established blameless by God's purposeful action, by God causing them to increase and overflow in love. Paul defines this relationship by using the articular infinitive with the preposition *eis* to express purpose. The preacher, however, seizes upon the word "blameless" and uses this word to lead to a Christocentric proclama-

16 For the sake of brevity, only textual exposition and theological confession will be considered here.

17 Charles Mueller, "Wanted: Blameless Hearts," in *Concordia Pulpit for 1980* (St. Louis: Concordia, 1979), 3–6.

tion. The Thessalonians, like the preacher's contemporary hearers, in and of themselves are not blameless but full of sin and blameworthy before God. In Christ, however, they have been forgiven of that sin and, because of Him, will stand blameless before God on the Last Day . . . . What the preacher says is true, but is it textual? Notice how Christocentric interpretation has overshadowed textual integrity. The text expressly defines the cause of such blamelessness: Paul prays that God, by causing the Thessalonian Christians to increase and overflow in love, would establish their hearts blameless in holiness before God on the Last Day. Rather than offer textual exposition (wherein God's work in causing the Thessalonians to overflow in love makes them blameless), the preacher has offered textual atomization (wherein God's work in Christ on the cross makes the Thessalonians blameless). Law and Gospel obsession has caused the preacher to isolate a word from the text and use that word, apart from its meaning in context, to offer Christocentric proclamation. In this case, Law and Gospel obsession has led to more than the neglect of the text; it has led to the misinterpretation of the content of the text.

It can also lead to error in interpreting the function of a text. Imagine a pastor visiting an elderly parishioner in the hospital. In addition to the physical ailment that brought her there, this parishioner is also losing her sight. She is unable to read even a card that her sister in Florida sent her. The pastor, in an act of Christian service, reads the card and her sister's note to her. The sister communicates her concern and affirms her certainty of God's grace even in the face of her sister's weakness. She cites Romans 8 and draws the attention of her ailing sister to God's almighty power and good purposes despite the ravages of sin. She reminds her sister that God in Christ has taken all of her cares upon Himself and then closes by encouraging her to remain strong in the faith and trust in the Lord, for He cares for her. The pastor sets down the card. He adjusts his glasses. Then he proceeds to comment on the note. He reiterates the words "remain strong in the faith" and "trust in the Lord" and reminds his parishioner that in no way can she do these things. She cannot remain strong in the faith and trust in the Lord because she is sinful, unable to fulfill even these most simple of words from her sister. With such proclamation, the pastor has isolated a phrase from the sister's note and, certainly much to the sister's displeasure, misinterpreted its function as an encouraging word. He has spoken as if her sister meant to accuse an ailing relative and drive her to sorrow by these words. What he has said about sin and the human inability to be strong and trust in the Lord is certainly true, but it is not what the words intended to communicate.

This imaginary situation in the hospital is unfortunately a frequent occurrence in the pulpit when Law and Gospel obsession influences the proclamation of paraenetic texts from Scripture.[18] The lectionary often severs paraenetic texts from their literary context and presents them in an isolated fashion to contemporary hearers. What Paul intends to be a closing exhortation in his letter, following an earlier evangelical proclamation, occurs in the service isolated from this context. The earlier evangelical proclamation is absent from the selected reading for the contemporary hearers. Rather than offer the hearers textual exposition that clarifies the literary context and involves evangelical proclamation, the preacher seeks to do it all from the selected text itself. He isolates these words of the text from their literary context and, in contrast to their paraenetic intention, uses them to accuse. Rather than hear how God through the apostle Paul once encouraged His people to rejoice always or to pray unceasingly (textual exposition), the hearers experience these vocables as direct accusation both of the early Christians and of God's people today (textual atomization): they do not rejoice and they do not pray. Comfort, however, is near as the preacher proclaims how God in Christ forgives such sin. The Christological principle of interpretation is preserved, but the principle of textual integrity is lost. What the pastor has said is true, but it is not what the text was saying. Law and Gospel obsession has led to the neglect of textual exposition in the sermon. In this case, the intent of the text is either ignored or misinterpreted, all for the sake of evangelical proclamation. Managing the principles of Christocentricity and textual integrity in the body of the sermon is much more complicated than simply making words from the text accuse and then offering a proclamation that saves. Instead, the preacher uses textual exposition to communicate the intended meaning of the text in its historical context. Through evangelical proclamation, he opens that text to Christocentric interpretation and opens the lives of the hearers to a present relationship with that God.

As Law and Gospel obsession can hinder textual exposition in a sermon, it can hinder theological confession as well. In his second thesis, Walther teaches that preachers can present all the teachings of the faith in their sermons and yet, by not properly distinguishing between Law and Gospel, err in the proclamation.[19] In this case, Walther makes a distinction between doctrinal content and the proper distinction between Law and Gospel in the communication of that content to the hearers. Using the analogy of con-

18 For a definition of biblical paraenesis in its classical setting, consult David Aune, *The New Testament in Its Literary Environment*, ed. Wayne Meeks, Library of Early Christianity 8 (Philadelphia: Westminster Press, 1987), 158–25; and Abraham Malherbe, *Moral Exhortation, A Greco-Roman Sourcebook*, ed. Wayne Meeks, Library of Early Christianity 4 (Philadelphia: Westminster Press, 1986), 121–34.

19 Walther, *Proper Distinction Between Law and Gospel*, 30–32. Cf. Walther, *Law and Gospel*, 35–48.

structing a building, Walther contrasts two builders. One builder uses the right materials (doctrinal content) but orders them in such a way (improper distinction between Law and Gospel) that they fail to build a house (the total effect of the sermon). The other builder uses the right materials (doctrinal content) and orders them in such a way (proper distinction between Law and Gospel) that they compose a house (the total effect of the sermon). This analogy works well to articulate the relationship between theological confession and evangelical proclamation in the sermon. While theological confession communicates the teachings of the faith in the sermon (doctrinal content), evangelical proclamation opens up those teachings (proper distinction between Law and Gospel) so that they are heard in relationship to God's gracious work in Christ (the total effect of the sermon). The principle of textual coherence, in which a text may be read in relationship with other texts so that it reveals a teaching of the faith, works in a complementary relationship with the principle of Christocentricity. As the doctrine is confessed, God's gracious work in Christ is proclaimed and not obscured.

For example, through theological confession, a preacher might teach divine omnipotence in the sermon. The preacher takes time to establish what it means to believe in God the Father Almighty. Through evangelical proclamation the preacher enables the hearers to receive this teaching as a word of comfort. For those secure in sin there is terror: there is absolutely nothing that can defend them from the wrath of an all-powerful God. For those insecure, however, there is comfort: Christ Jesus died for sinners and now nothing can separate them from the love of an all-powerful God in Christ Jesus. In this case, as the doctrine is treated, evangelical proclamation is offered, and the hearers receive this teaching of faith as a blessing rather than a burden. Walther describes this interplay of theological confession and evangelical proclamation as the preacher giving "to each of his hearers his due: he must see to it that secure, care-free, and willful sinners hear the thunderings of the Law, contrite sinners, however, the sweet voice of the Savior's grace."[20] Such thundering Law and sweet Gospel occur in relationship to the teaching of a doctrine, the theological confession of the sermon. The sermon offers the full development of the doctrine as well as the complementary Law and Gospel proclamation so that the doctrine is established, as Walther would say, as "a habitable and pleasant abode."[21]

In his second thesis, then, Walther establishes the relationship between theological confession and evangelical proclamation in the sermon. In this thesis, however, Walther addresses the problem of Law and Gospel negligence, not Law and Gospel obsession. In his day, preachers were composing

20 Walther, *Proper Distinction Between Law and Gospel*, 33. Cf. Walther, *Law and Gospel*, 38.

21 Walther, *Proper Distinction Between Law and Gospel*, 32. Cf. Walther, *Law and Gospel*, 37.

sermons that offered the fullness of theological confession without proper evangelical proclamation. They would present the articles of faith in accordance with Scripture but not properly distinguish between Law and Gospel as they did so. As Walther writes, though one "could truthfully say, 'There was no false teaching in my sermon,' still his entire sermon may have been wrong."[22] While this error, as noted above, continues today, the answer is not found on the opposite end of the spectrum in Law and Gospel obsession. In Law and Gospel obsession, the deficiency that Walther describes is simply reversed. Instead of sermons offering the fullness of theological confession but no evangelical proclamation, sermons offer the fullness of evangelical proclamation but little theological confession. The preachers fail to teach the articles of the faith. While their sermons are strong in proclaiming God's gracious work in Christ, they are weak in confessing all of the teachings of Scripture. This is unfortunate in liturgical preaching, for the lectionary itself encourages preachers to proclaim the whole counsel of God.

As noted above, in the liturgy, portions of texts are selected and read with other texts diachronically in seasons and synchronically in propers. Through such matrices, the liturgy operates upon the principle of textual coherence, using it to highlight the various teachings of the faith. For example, temporally considered, it seems inappropriate to have the diachronic arrangement of John the Baptizer, grown and preaching in the desert (Advent 2 and 3), before Jesus is ever born (Christmas). After all, John and Jesus were closer in age than that. Theologically, however, this diachronic order of readings highlights repentance and what it means for John to be the voice in the wilderness preparing the way for the coming of the Lord. Synchronically, the lectionary places the account of Abraham's intercession before God on the plains outside of Sodom (Old Testament, Proper 12, Series C) in relationship to Jesus' teaching His disciples to pray (Holy Gospel, Proper 12, Series C). This liturgical matrix invites the preacher to include in the sermon theological confession of the nature of prayer. These cases illustrate that the theological confession of the sermon may arise from the principle of textual coherence enacted by the liturgy. The preacher, however, does not need to limit the sermon's theological confession to the matrices of the lectionary. It may arise from a discernment by the preacher of a particular need for instruction among the hearers (for example, in a series of catechetical sermons). Recognizing such a need among the hearers and such a teaching within a text, the preacher creates the tapestry of the sermon appropriate to that preaching occasion by offering theological confession of that teaching in the sermon. This is done in conjunction with appropriate textual exposition, evangelical proclamation, and hearer depiction. Here, these four threads of

---

22 Walther, *Proper Distinction Between Law and Gospel*, 31. Cf. Walther, *Law and Gospel*, 37.

discourse work together in the sermon, and evangelical proclamation does not diminish theological confession.

The point here is simply that Law and Gospel obsession can cause preachers to overlook or to diminish the discourse of theological confession. Even though teachings such as divine providence, natural revelation, election, incarnation, and others are encouraged in preaching by the variety of lectionary readings and the matrices in which they appear, they rarely occur in the sermon. The preacher rightly proclaims God's gracious work in Christ but leaves the theological confession of the whole counsel of God undeveloped. Because of Law and Gospel obsession, the preacher devotes less time to theological confession. It is not a situation of having either evangelical proclamation or theological confession in the sermon but of having both evangelical proclamation and theological confession in a complementary relationship. The preacher joins these together in the sermon in the artful weaving of the tapestry of the sermon.

Godly concern for the proper distinction of Law and Gospel in preaching means that preachers are able to weave the tapestry of the sermon from four threads of discourse in preaching. They can offer fuller textual exposition and theological confession in the sermon and yet avoid the errors of overlooking evangelical proclamation (Law and Gospel negligence) or of focusing so much on it (Law and Gospel obsession) that the text and the teaching and the lives of the hearers are obscured.

Conclusion

In conclusion, consider the following concern of a parishioner about Lutheran preaching: "It seems that all my pastor ever preaches is Law and Gospel. I know that I am a sinner and that my salvation comes only through God's gracious work in Christ, and I truly rejoice in the life of daily repentance. It's just that when the pastor preaches, this is all he ever talks about. I don't want him to stop, but I wonder if there's more. Isn't there more for me to consider as a Christian than the confession of my sin and the proclamation of my salvation in Christ?" Faithfully answering this parishioner's concern can reveal the difference between godly concern for the proper distinction of Law and Gospel in preaching and the errors of Law and Gospel negligence, on the one hand, and Law and Gospel obsession, on the other.

Some, in answering this concern, fall into the error of Law and Gospel negligence in their preaching. They argue that, since those who have gathered are Christian and know the fundamentals of the Christian faith, there is no need to proclaim the Gospel to them all over again. For them, evangelical proclamation can all but disappear from the sermon. Parishioners may be offered topical sermons and Bible studies in place of preaching with little or no concern for the proper distinction of Law and Gospel in such proclamation. If evangelical proclamation occurs, it occurs in a simple statement meant to save the sermon from being accused of not being Lutheran rather than to save the people through the proclamation of the forgiveness of sins. Such an error fails to recognize that God instituted the office of preaching to create and sustain faith through the preaching of repentance and the forgiveness of sins and that the nature of the Christian life is daily contrition and repentance. In this case, to those who would answer the parishioner's concern by the error of Law and Gospel negligence, one stresses that pastors are called to preach Christ and Him crucified. When one has Jesus, who could want anything more?

Others, in answering this concern, fall into the opposite error of Law and Gospel obsession in their preaching. Referencing God's institution of the office of preaching and the nature of Christian life as daily contrition and repentance, they rightly explain to the parishioner that sermons are to offer evangelical proclamation (something the parishioner never denied). The problem is that they overemphasize these matters in preaching to the point of neglecting the other forms of discourse that constitute the complex dynamics of the sermon (something the parishioner desires). Textual exposition, theological confession, and hearer depiction are neglected or distorted for the sake of evangelical proclamation. Evangelical proclamation ends up working in conflict with, rather than in concert with, the other types of discourse in the sermon. In terms of what has been called the Lutheran hermeneutic, the principle of Christocentricity is practiced in a way that contradicts rather than complements the principles of textual integrity and textual coherence. The sermon offers evangelical proclamation but little else, and unfortunately this type of preaching (Law and Gospel obsession) is mistakenly claimed to be distinctively Lutheran. A quick glance at history reveals that Lutheran preaching has not always been so.

Consider the fullness of preaching among the reformers at the time of the Reformation, when this hermeneutic was articulated. In the Apology of the Augsburg Confession, Melanchthon writes that

> in our churches all the sermons are filled with such topics as these: repentance; the fear of God; faith in Christ, the righteousness of faith, the comfort of consciences by faith; the exercises of faith; prayer, what its nature should be, and that we should be fully confident that it is powerful, that it is heard; the cross; the authority of officials and all civil ordinances; the distinction between the kingdom of Christ, or the spiritual kingdom, and political affairs; marriage; the education and instruction of children; chastity; all the offices of love.[23]

23 Ap XV (VIII) 43 (*Concordia*, 193).

From such a depiction of preaching, one recognizes the heighth and depth and breadth possible in sermons that proclaim repentance and the forgiveness of sins. Evangelical proclamation opens up the other forms of discourse for public proclamation rather than shuts them down. To those who would answer the parishioner's concern by the error of Law and Gospel obsession, one affirms that pastors are called to preach Christ and Him crucified. Such proclamation, however, opens up for God's people the fullness of Scripture. When one has Jesus, one wants nothing more precisely because, in having Jesus, one has received from God all things.

The godly concern for the proper distinction of Law and Gospel in preaching enables one faithfully to answer the parishioner's concern. Is there more to consider than the confession of sin and the proclamation of salvation in preaching? Certainly, there is! This is not because one moves beyond preaching Christ, however. It is because the sermon reflects the proper function of evangelical proclamation in the complex dynamics of preaching: Christ is proclaimed and, in Christ, God graciously gives to His people all things. Rather than neglect evangelical proclamation for the sake of other types of discourse (Law and Gospel negligence) and rather than overemphasize it to the point that other forms of discourse are silenced (Law and Gospel obsession), the preacher maintains a godly concern for the proper distinction between Law and Gospel. He uses evangelical proclamation to open all things to God's gracious working in Christ. The text, the teachings of the faith, and the lives of the hearers are all heard in relationship to God's work of salvation.

Evangelical proclamation, then, is not the only thing that parishioners hear in the sermon. In addition, they hear textual exposition, communicating the intended meaning of the text in its historical context and making them witnesses now of God's saving work then. They hear theological confession, teaching the articles of the faith in a way that does not obscure but rather confesses the centrality of Christ. They also get hearer depiction, naming their contemporary life experience as a place of the working of God. Such things are spoken precisely because of what the sermon is: God's lively intervention into the lives of His people through the means of grace. In liturgical preaching, preachers rightly handle the means of grace: they interpret the Scriptures as literary texts inspired by the Holy Spirit pointing to Christ. In doing so, they weave a tapestry of four threads of discourse in the sermon. Through such proclamation, God continues to come and work graciously among His people. Into the rush and routine of daily living, God intervenes. He opens daily life to divine redemption and the world to divine action as people hear His Word, through the office of preaching, and are sent forth into the world, awakened by grace.

Balanced Preaching: Maintaining a Theological Center of Gravity

David J. Peter

During the presidential campaign of 1996, Senator Bob Dole made a campaign speech. When the oration was over, the Republican candidate attempted to correct his image of being cold, impersonal, and disconnected from the people by making physical contact with the audience. He moved to the edge of the platform on which he had been speaking, leaned over the railing, and reached out his hand to the crowd below. In an effort to connect with his audience, he stretched horizontally and extended himself beyond the guard rail. But as he reached out, the rail gave way, and Senator Dole came tumbling down into the crowd and onto the ground. Neither he nor those under him were seriously hurt by this incident, though a few minor bruises were sustained.[1]

Senator Dole's intentions were good. He sought to reach out and connect with the people. He endeavored to make contact with his audience. He intended to repudiate his reputation of being cold and aloof by extending himself out to the people. But the resulting accident didn't benefit him or those on whom he fell.

Many preachers have a similar good intention. They make a heartfelt effort to reach out in their sermons to people and their needs. They go to great lengths to connect with their hearers. They attempt to relate to their hearers and impress upon them the relevance of the sermon.

This desire is laudable. Preaching that does not connect with the audience is not effective preaching. Regrettably, much preaching does not reach out to the people. It remains aloof, austere, impractical, impersonal, irrelevant, and overly transcendent. Such preaching is *disconnected* from the people for whom it is delivered. In contrast, the preacher who loves and cares for his flock will seek to present sermons that touch the lives and the personal needs of people.

1 A video of this incident may be viewed at www.youtube.com/watch?v=hWib8GrIlA.

Sometimes the preacher's passion to connect with those who are listening to him, however, may lead to an extreme. It may cause the preacher to lose his balance, so to speak. He overextends horizontally. This is not in a physical sense, as in leaning too far out of the pulpit so that he falls! Instead, the loss of balance is in the content of the sermon. He overextends the human focus or horizontal reach so that the vertical dimension of the sermon is eclipsed. When this happens the sermon becomes more anthropocentric than theocentric. Thus the preacher hurts both his own ministry and the spiritual lives of those for whom he is called to care. And that is indeed a tragedy far worse than any physical misstep such as Bob Dole experienced.

The Horizontal and Vertical Dimensions of Preaching

The essays of this volume focus on the *context* of worship in which preaching takes place. One manner in which the context of preaching may be visualized is by use of a spatial matrix involving vertical and horizontal axes. Every sermon should have a vertical aspect and a horizontal aspect.[2] Furthermore, these dimensions should be in balance in the homily.

The *vertical dimension* refers to the *theocentric* focus of the sermon. Thus it is heavily theological. In the vertical dimension, attention is given to *God's work* of creation, salvation, and sanctification. It focuses on *who* God is and on *what* He has done and continues to do for us. It presents for us the relationship *God* has established with His people. In this sense it is *vertical*, in that it communicates the relationship of God with humanity, especially of God coming to us in Jesus Christ to redeem us from sin and to reconcile us to Himself.

This vertical dimension to preaching is evident in all faithful Law and Gospel preaching. The vertical emphasis is especially distinctive of the Reformation and of the preachers who are heirs of this tradition. It is preaching that centers on the Gospel message of justification by grace alone through faith alone in Christ alone. This vertical dimension is unabashedly theological, theocentric, Christocentric, and doctrinal.

However, the vertical dimension does not *exclude* concern for human beings. On the contrary, this concern is inherent to the vertical axis of theology. The Gospel does not transcend the realm of human creatures but transforms it. In the incarnation God invades into the human realm, and

---

2 These designations of the vertical and horizontal aspects have been employed by a number of commentators on preaching. Two recent examples are Michael Horton, *A Better Way: Rediscovering the Drama of God-Centered Worship* (Grand Rapids: Baker, 2002), 74, 216; and Timothy Saleska, "The Two Kinds of Righteousness! What's a Preacher to Do?" *Concordia Journal* 33, no. 2 (April 2007): 136–45.

through Baptism the Holy Spirit indwells God's creatures. Humanity stands at the bottom of the vertical axis, for the vertical relationship is one between God *and* human creatures. Thus we should not think of the vertical dimension as relating only to God to the exclusion of humans, since at its very heart it is the message of God relating to human beings.

The *horizontal dimension* of preaching is more human-oriented, more anthropological in nature. This dimension concerns itself with relationships among human beings. It addresses their interpersonal relationships. Attention is given to people's conditions and needs. The horizontal dimension focuses on *who* we are as humans and on *how* we relate to one another—our behavior toward one another. It is *horizontal* because it deals with relationships between human people who are created beings.

There is a very salutary use of the horizontal dimension in preaching. Indeed, it is a *necessary* aspect of preaching. There is a proper place in the sermon for addressing horizontal relationships *coram mundo*. As was stated earlier, every sermon should have a vertical aspect and a horizontal aspect that are in balance in the homily. A more Lutheran way of putting this is to say that there is a proper and necessary place for the two kinds of righteousness in preaching. The distinction between the two kinds of righteousness is a distinction well articulated in the Lutheran Confessions.[3] This distinction can be explained using the spatial imagery of a perpendicular matrix (of vertical and horizontal axes).[4]

The vertical dimension involves the relationship between God and human beings, one's life *coram deo*. This vertical relationship is established solely by a righteousness that sinful people receive by grace through faith in Jesus Christ. Accordingly, it is a passive righteousness. The second dimension, the horizontal, involves the life in which human creatures relate to one another in the world. This is a righteousness that is *coram mundo* in that it is achieved by our efforts to serve others and care for God's creation, primarily within human relationships. As such, it is an active righteousness. However, the two kinds of righteousness must be distinguished or the result will be deadly theological error. If righteousness achieved in the horizontal dimension becomes one's claim to be right with God, then works-righteousness is the result. If righteousness received in the vertical dimension by

3 Charles Arand, "Two Kinds of Righteousness as a Framework for Law and Gospel in the Apology," *Lutheran Quarterly* 15, no. 4 (Winter 2001): 417–39. See also Charles Arand and Joel Biermann, "Why the Two Kinds of Righteousness?" *Concordia Journal* 33, no. 2 (April 2007): 116–35.

4 This spatial depiction is aptly developed in the article by Charles Arand, "A Two-Dimensional Understanding of the Church for the Twenty-First Century," *Concordia Journal* 33, no. 2 (April 2007): 146–65.

grace becomes the reason one neglects his responsibilities in the horizontal dimension, then he renounces the vocations that God entrusts to him.

This understanding of the vertical and horizontal kinds of righteousness can be applied specifically to the preaching task. The application is appropriate because the distinction between horizontal righteousness and vertical righteousness interplays with the purpose of preaching. That purpose is to address hearers about their relationship with God and their responsibilities to other people. Both dimensions are needed in faithful preaching. The problem that will now be demonstrated, however, is that one dimension increasingly is eclipsing the other in contemporary preaching. The horizontal dimension has become magisterial while the vertical has been marginalized. The result is that the theological center of gravity is forfeited and the preacher loses his theological balance.

Losing Our Balance: Overextending into the Horizontal Dimension

The concern of this essay is the trend in preaching toward that which is predominantly or exclusively horizontal. It has been said that heterodoxy and even heresy arises when truth is taken to an extreme.[5] In this case, the truth of the need for a horizontal dimension in preaching is taken to an extreme when sermons neglect the vertical dimension. Assuredly, there is the need for the horizontal aspect of communicating to human beings. Pastors who love their flocks will not disregard hearers' personal, psychological, and social needs, as they perceive them to be. Pastors will seek to speak in a way that is relevant to people's life situations and personal relationships. But they will not want to do that *only*. Indeed, that will not even be their *primary* objective in preaching.

The contemporary landscape of preaching displays a trend toward overextending into the horizontal dimension. The danger arises when the preacher, in an effort to make sermons relevant and meaningful to the people, reaches out horizontally to the neglect of the vertical dimension. This temptation to flatten out the message oftentimes derives from the salutary intention to connect with the people and their needs. But the result is that the sermon's content is virtually all human and little divine, much anthropocentric and little theocentric, mostly secular and scarcely sacred. Using imagery reminiscent of Robert Dole's tumble, William Willimon

5 In describing heretics, Robert Kolb echoes the imagery used in this essay of one who bends over so far that he falls into error. The heretic, Kolb observes, is often a good-intentioned churchman who in the effort to bend toward cultural accommodation loses his balance and falls into heresy. Robert Kolb, *Speaking the Gospel Today*, rev. ed. (St. Louis: Concordia, 1995), 17.

opines that many Christian preachers have leaned too far into the priorities of the contemporary world so that they have fallen into worldly preaching.[6]

Keen observers of the homiletic scene have made similar assessment. For example, Paul Scott Wilson describes the pervasive and discouraging phenomenon of sermons that emphasize human resources over faith in the Divine.[7] We even have documentation of the preponderance of anthropological over theological content on a broad scale. For example, David Wells, in his book *No Place for Truth*, highlights this trend in his analysis of 200 "model" sermons taken from leading journals on homiletics during the latter part of the twentieth century.[8] Wells reports that only about one quarter (24.5 percent) of the sermons reflect both content and organization based upon the biblical passage used as the sermon's text. Some sermons, he maintains, are not even discernibly Christian. Less than 20 percent of the sermons centered on the person and work of God; more than 80 percent were anthropocentric.[9] In other words, in the vast majority of these "model" sermons, the horizontal dimension predominated over the vertical.

About the same time that Wells undertook his research, Marsha Witten conducted a study of forty-seven sermons on the parable of the prodigal son (Luke 15:11–31). These sermons were delivered by pastors from the Presbyterian Church (U.S.A.) and the Southern Baptist Convention. Witten's observations are presented in her book *All Is Forgiven: The Secular Message in American Protestantism*. The title reveals the findings of her study. Simply put, Witten reports a tendency to shape preaching not to what the text says about redemption—a theological and vertical message that is clearly the intent of Jesus' parable. Instead, the sermons reflect a secularizing and socializing of the message—a "horizontalizing" of it—that is quite distant from the intended meaning of the text.[10]

Other observers have noted the movement in contemporary preaching away from sermons with predominantly theological content (vertical dimension) toward those with predominantly anthropological content (horizontal dimension). Richard Thulin studied published sermons from a variety of denominational traditions and found the proclamation of the

---

6 William Willimon, "This Culture Is Overrated," *Leadership Journal* (Winter 1997): 29.

7 Paul Scott Wilson, *The Four Pages of the Sermon: A Guide to Biblical Preaching* (Nashville: Abingdon, 1999), 12.

8 David Wells, *No Place for Truth: Or Whatever Happened to Evangelical Theology?* (Grand Rapids: Eerdmans, 1993), 251–52. One hundred of these sermons came from *Pulpit Digest* and one hundred came from the journal *Preaching* dated from 1981 to 1991.

9 Wells, *No Place for Truth*, 251–52.

10 Marsha Witten, *All Is Forgiven: The Secular Message in American Protestantism* (Princeton: Princeton University Press, 1993).

triune God conspicuously missing.[11] Leander Keck argues that anthropology has usurped theology not only among many modern theologians but also among many contemporary preachers.[12] In his historical analysis of religion in the United States, James Turner speaks of the contribution that *preachers* have made to the culture of unbelief in America by accommodating the world's values rather than God's in their sermons.[13]

Marva Dawn credits the decline of God-centered preaching on post-Christian American culture that has influenced the church. In previous eras, when what was done in mainline churches was dictated by the heritage of the denominations and the culture was more foundationally Christian, there was less possibility of moving away from preaching that was centered in God. In our times of famous celebrities in the media, less structured worship, and less support for the identity of Christianity in the culture, such a move is far more likely. As a result, too much of what is happening these days in worship pulls us away from centering on God—or does not have enough substance to hint at the infinity of God's splendor.[14]

Finally, David Larsen, in his massive historical survey of Christian preachers, laments the pervasive horizontal focus of preaching today. In his reflections on the history of Christian preaching, Larsen identifies the greatest threat to faithful preaching in our day with this trend.[15]

Each of these observers of contemporary preaching recognizes a significant trend toward the marginalization of theology (and thus of God) in sermons. This, in turn, reflects an overextension of the horizontal aspect of preaching at the expense of the vertical.

As I reflect on this trend, I distinguish three streams in which the phenomenon has manifested itself: (1) sermons that adopt a relativistic epistemology ("hearer-based" preaching), (2) consumer sermons ("felt-needs based" preaching), and (3) self-help sermons ("solution-based" preaching). Each of these trends is worthy of examination.

---

11 Richard Thulin, "The Missing Church," *Homiletic* 25, no. 2 (Winter 2000): 9.

12 Leander Keck, *The Church Confident* (Nashville: Abingdon, 1993), 47–48.

13 James Turner, *Without God, Without Creed: The Origins of Unbelief in America* (Baltimore: The Johns Hopkins University Press, 1985), 245.

14 Marva J. Dawn, *A Royal "Waste" of Time: The Splendor of Worshiping God and Being Church for the World* (Grand Rapids: Eerdmans, 1999), 155.

15 David Larsen, *The Company of the Preachers: A History of Biblical Preaching from the Old Testament to the Modern Era* (Grand Rapids: Kregel, 1998), 11. Larsen relates a parallel concern in an op-ed piece in a periodical for preachers, see "The Decline of the Text," *Preaching* (March-April 2003): 27.

Sermons That Adopt a Hearer-based Epistemology

An epistemology of relativism and tolerance pervades American culture. At the center of this relativistic epistemology is the *self*. In other words, one determines what is true, what is real, what is authoritative for oneself. The typical American acknowledges little absolute truth independent of what he ascertains is true for himself. The result of this epistemological relativism is a practical tolerance: "If it's true for you, that's okay, even if it isn't true for me."

When this anthropocentric epistemology emerges in preaching, the focus is on the *hearer*—what he hears determines the meaning. Thus the listener does not hear *the* truth from the text of Scripture or the message of the sermon. Rather, he hears *his* truth. It is not so much what the sermon *means*, but what it means to *him*. Truth is understood to be relative, subjective, and personal. Such an epistemology influences not only the *hearing* of a sermon (i.e., by the audience) but also the *composition and proclamation* of a sermon (i.e., by the preacher). In each case the main referent point is the *self*. Obviously, this referent point of self dominates on the horizontal plane. Since the vertical plane is the domain of speech about God and for God, vertical preaching is not conducive to hearer-centered epistemology. But horizontal preaching certainly is!

Admittedly there are some insights accented by hearer-based epistemology (oftentimes associated with the postmodern mind-set) that are congenial to both hermeneutics and homiletics.[16] Who one is and what he or she has experienced determines to some extent how the message is heard. The hearer brings biases and filters through which he or she interprets a message and defines its meaning. The Christian preacher must be aware of these realities and seek to maximize listener involvement and understanding.

However, the faithful preacher will also recognize that it is God's Spirit working through His active Word who ultimately creates meaning by delivering the Truth. As He does so He effects the transformation from death to life in those who listen to a sermon. The Gospel—the good news that God was in Christ reconciling the world to Himself (2 Cor. 5:19)—is clearly located on the vertical dimension. It is the Gospel that is the power of God unto salvation (Rom. 1:16), not the interpretive filter of the parishioner. Glenn Nielsen warns that preaching that conforms to a hearer-based ethos is essentially an abdication of the authority of God's Word to the listener.[17]

---

16 An examination of this in the realm of hermeneutics is found in James Voelz, *What Does This Mean?* (St. Louis: Concordia, 1997), 208–16. An analysis of it in the arena of homiletics is provided in Glenn Nielsen, "Preaching Doctrine in a Postmodern Age," *Concordia Journal* 27, no. 1 (January 2001): 17–29.

17 Glenn Nielsen, "No Longer Dinosaurs: Relating Lutheran Homiletics and Communication Practice," *Concordia Journal* 25, no. 1 (January 1999): 17.

Taken to its extreme, a hearer-based epistemology is a dead-end street. David Wells writes:

> Is it not the case that the radical individualism that inhabits most churches and which, in its therapeutic form, collapses all reality into the self, is also an expression of the collapse of any functioning, overarching meaning in life? Meaning, in the absence of such purpose, simply becomes privatized and internalized. Is it therefore surprising that the overwhelming majority of the American public do not believe that there are truths which are absolute? The disposition, as we have seen, is now reverberating around the churches. So is it surprising if preaching begins to cater to this disposition and reduces the meaning of Christian faith simply to what is "practical," to techniques for surviving in a baffling and painful world?[18]

Wells's rhetorical questions trace the pathway that a relativistic epistemology leads to when adopted by the preaching church. Its destination is a horizontal reductionism that leaves preaching devoid of timeless truth, life devoid of ultimate meaning, and people devoid of lasting hope.

The danger in adopting a hearer-based epistemology in preaching is that the locus, the center of gravity in the sermon, is with the *hearer*, not with the Gospel. This hearer-based locus clearly falls within the horizontal dimension. Such preaching becomes existentialist, experiential, personalized, and privatized. Although there may be some "God talk" in this kind of preaching that superficially appears theological and vertical, the engine that drives it is human-centered and thus horizontal. One's image of God—one's understanding of God—is created by one's own intuitions, which are by sinful nature flawed and in fact opposed to God. Taken to its extreme, in this epistemology one determines for himself in a delusional manner who God is and how God relates to him, instead of the Holy Spirit enlightening through the Word to reveal the God who is otherwise hidden. When God appears in such hearer-based preaching, essentially He is created in the image of man, the hearer.[19]

The bottom line in preaching that conforms to relativistic thinking is that the hearer dictates the understanding of God. The human determines the divine. Anthropology forms theology. The horizontal dimension drives the vertical dimension.

---

18 David F. Wells, *Above All Earthly Pow'rs: Christ in a Postmodern World* (Grand Rapids: Eerdmans, 2005), 304.

19 Robert Kolb cites Helmut Thielicke in directing us to a helpful distinction between actualization of God's Word (applying it to contemporary circumstances) and accommodation of it (submitting the Word to personal and cultural norms). Kolb, *Speaking the Gospel Today*, 17.

Consumer Satisfying Sermons

Another phenomenon current in our contemporary (especially American) culture is a pervasive consumer mentality. This mind-set has influenced the life of the church to the degree that much of the church's activity has become a market commodity. This market mentality has contributed significantly to the trend toward sermons that are predominantly or even exclusively horizontal.

American Christians live in a consumer culture. The church must engage even this aspect of culture, rather than totally eschewing it. Congregational programming is frequently guided by what will best meet the "felt needs" of the members or potential members of the church. Attention to people's felt needs, whether through the congregation's programs or in its preaching, is salutary when this plays a ministerial role to direct the people's attention ultimately to their greatest need, which is forgiveness, life, and salvation in Jesus Christ. The church responds to people's perceived needs as an entry point to move them to recognize their supreme need for Christ. In these sermons the message of Christ predominates, and the horizontal dimension serves the vertical dimension. Such an approach to preaching is desirable.[20]

The danger arises when attention to felt needs becomes unbalanced and eclipses the message "that God was in Christ reconciling the world to Himself" (2 Cor. 5:19). This unhealthy influence of the consumer mentality upon the church has affected worship design and sermon content.[21]

Consumer satisfying sermons are recognizable in that they are based on the audience's needs. In these sermons, the engine that drives the subject, content, and direction of the message is the "felt needs" of the people (and, indirectly, of the popular culture). Marva Dawn observes that many preachers who have adopted this approach believe that the goal of the sermon is to satisfy these transient needs rather than meet people's genuine needs, which only the Word of God can do.[22]

This kind of needs-based preaching is on the ascendancy. David Larsen cites evidence in contemporary preaching of a shift from sermons that are based on a biblical text to those driven by the market of consumer wants.[23] Note the turn here. The change is in the prepositions. Historically, Christian preachers have preached *from*—from the text of Scripture. Today, however,

20 It must also be affirmed that Christians (including those involved in the formal programmatic efforts of a congregation) address the needs of others because God calls them to serve others. Thus a Christian cares for another human being regardless of whether or not the Christian will deliver the Gospel message. Yet a most caring activity is in fact to share the message of the forgiving love of Christ.

21 This is a major focus of Marsha Witten's book. See especially *All Is Forgiven*, 133.

22 Dawn, *Royal "Waste" of Time*, 222.

23 Larsen, *Company of the Preachers*, 16.

increasing numbers of preachers are preaching *to*—to the felt needs of the people. Lutherans highlight another preposition: *of*. Lutheran preaching should be a proclamation *of* the Gospel (objective genitive). This contemporary repositioning of the starting point for sermons means that the sermon's theme derives from the horizontal dimension of consumer needs, psychology, and sociology, instead of from the vertical dimension of theology and, more specifically, the Gospel.

In her study of forty-seven Protestant sermons, Marsha Witten documents the trend toward secularization and horizontal emphases in these sermons. She attributes much of this trend to the church's attempt to accommodate the "felt needs" of the hearers. One result is that the message of the Law is softened to avoid causing offense to the audience, the "consuming public" that might not return after hearing a discomforting message.[24] This message, essential to true evangelical preaching, is being jettisoned in many sermons because it doesn't resonate with the consuming audience. Similarly, the call to costly discipleship and sacrifice that is inherent to sanctified living is unspoken because it is an unpopular message. The comfortable message that replaces it is more palatable to consumers.

Another result of the consumer-driven sermon is that it promotes a privatizing of religion. Religion exists to satisfy the personal desires and needs of the individual self. Witten maintains that this needs-driven preaching "accepts the exile of religion into the region of private life, in its concerns largely for the psychology and affect of the individual. The solutions that are posed here to consumer 'needs' are *privatized* counterbalances to modern life, minor irruptions in the overall secularity of the social world."[25]

The concern here is *not* that sermons should be inattentive to the human condition and need, even if those needs are "felt." The problem is with unbalanced preaching that addresses the human need with satisfactions that derive solely from the horizontal dimension. If the solutions offered in a sermon are primarily psychological, sociological, anthropological, or simply utilitarian, then the sermon has neglected the vertical and theological heart of Christian proclamation.

Ultimately, this reality poses the greatest danger, which results from sermons that seek to satisfy an audience's felt needs. Such needs-driven sermons can lead in the wrong direction, away from the theological. The preacher overextends horizontally in an effort to reach out to people and their needs, and the vertical dimension of the sermon collapses.[26]

24 Witten, *All Is Forgiven*, 133.

25 Witten, *All Is Forgiven*, 134.

26 In 1982 John Stott warned preachers of becoming ministers of fashion rather than ministers of God. He acknowledges the need in preaching to build a bridge between Scripture and the contemporary culture. But this bridge must be determined more by the Word of

The solution is to be found in balance—by balancing the vertical and horizontal aspects of preaching. Yet the vertical aspect—the biblical, theocentric, and evangelical message—must be foremost established so that there is a sound center of gravity in the sermon.

"Self-help" Sermons

The third force in contemporary culture that greatly contributes to the predominance of the horizontal dimension in preaching is the trend toward "self-help" sermons. These sermons have as their themes subjects such as "how to overcome stress" and "how to be a good spouse or parent." If the relativistic sermon is hearer based, and the consumer sermon is felt-needs based, then the self-help sermon is solution based.

Once again, as with the other two forces, the issue is extremism. Nothing is inherently wrong with a solution-based message. Indeed, every sermon should present the solution to humanity's sinful condition, a solution that is found in the Gospel of Jesus Christ. This solution-based message is clearly in the vertical dimension. Moreover, there is also a salutary place for explicating horizontal righteousness in sound theological preaching. As the Holy Spirit works sanctification in the lives of His saints, those saints will benefit from the preaching of God's Word to guide them to "live a life worthy of their calling," which they have received by virtue of their identity in Christ (Eph. 4:1). Some "how to" sermons will assist them to do so, while remaining theologically sound.[27]

But the problem with many "how to" messages is that they become predominantly horizontal. In this case the preacher bases the solution to people's predicament in the human dimension instead of in the vertical and theological dimension. He finds the locus for solving the problems of the hearers *in the hearers*, instead of in God. That is why they are "self-help" sermons—they prescribe to listeners how they can solve the problems in their life by their own actions and efforts.[28]

God than by cultural ethos. John Stott, *Between Two Worlds: The Art of Preaching in the Twentieth Century* (Grand Rapids: Eerdmans, 1982), 139–40.

27 Henry Simon, "How to Preach a Lutheran 'How To' Sermon," *Concordia Pulpit Resources* 10, no. 4 (October 1–November 26, 2000). If the intended meaning of a text is to show how to behave, function, or live, then that meaning should be presented in the sermon, but always with the Gospel (the vertical!) predominating and empowering the life of sanctification.

28 Self-help sermons are attractive because they fit the sinful nature's quest to be in control, essentially to be God, see Horton, *Better Way*, 70. Yet "practical preaching" is desirable, even necessary. When the Gospel (in the vertical dimension) dominates in a sermon, then it is appropriate that the preacher also provide guidance for sanctified living that involves a didactic use of the Law and that falls within the horizontal dimension.

Oftentimes these self-help sermons imitate the self-help manuals that are so popular (and lucrative) in the book selling and digital recording market.[29] There is no doubt that the influence here derives from the secular culture, and not from the heritage of the Church, nor certainly from any biblical ethos.[30]

Marsha Witten argues that this mentality, which pervades the culture of popular books (including those of a religious nature), has now affected popular preaching, manifesting itself in the "how to" emphasis of many contemporary preachers. She states:

> In these texts, behavioral precepts are organized in a series of steps, or items on a list, which call for the reader's systematic compliance; one's progress toward spirituality is thus measured on an ascending scale. In addition, the form of this talk mirrors its popular, secular counterpart, the "how to" book. The talk may be framed as a series of self-referring, self-justifying, rules, "steps," or "principles," adherence to which induces personal growth and fulfillment. Taken to the extreme, this talk constitutes a "do-it-yourself" guide for personal satisfaction, with a few mentions of God or faith or prayer tossed in to mark itself as "religious."[31]

The result is that the sermon becomes essentially a "do-it-yourself" guide that is potently horizontal (i.e., anthropocentric) in nature and noticeably lacking in the vertical (i.e., theocentric) dimension.

The danger associated with this kind of sermon is that solutions in the horizontal dimension are then transferred to the vertical dimension. In such a case the solution to the deepest human problem, the problem of sin that alienates one from God in the vertical relationship, is identified as existing *intra nos* (inside the person) instead of *extra nos* (in God, who is other than the person). Self-help is by its very definition self-dependent and not contingent on God's rescue. Thus the "how to" format may be conducive to a horizontally designed sermon that attributes the empowerment for improvement to the self, but then also extends that self-engendered power to improving one's standing before God.[32]

---

29 It must be acknowledged that there is a salutary use of some resources, even "self-help manuals," which guide people to order their lives so that they become more productive, healthy, and even—properly understood—autonomous. But these are appropriate only in the horizontal dimension of active righteousness. When they substitute for the passive righteousness of faith, they are spiritually toxic.

30 Dawn, *Royal "Waste" of Time*, 209.

31 Witten, *All Is Forgiven*, 24.

32 This emphasis on self-actualization is evident even in some "how to" sermons that explicitly address one's relationship with God. Technically speaking, these are not horizontally oriented sermons but those in which the vertical dimension predominates. But it is in this vertical dimension that the error becomes most acute. Many of these types of sermons provide prescriptions and step-by-step methodologies for improving one's spirituality and

Preachers should encourage hearers to produce good works in service to others as the fruit of faith in the sanctified life of the Christian. Such activity of caring for others in the love of Christ is located in the horizontal dimension since it involves relationships between people. Yet its source is in the vertical relationship with God, resulting from one's identity established in the Gospel and empowered by the indwelling of the Holy Spirit. The *help* for living according to the will of God comes not from the self but from God. Thus even when preaching "the sanctified life," the Gospel message must provide the dominant dynamic. Preaching self-help solutions to the challenges of the Christian life of faith leads to futility or Pharisaism because it is devoid of the vertical power from God.

The eventual end of self-help preaching is that the horizontal dimension is promoted at the expense of the vertical. The transforming power of God through the Holy Spirit is minimized (if mentioned at all), and the self-improving ability of man is maximized. This approach may appear eminently practical and helpful, but it is in actuality devastating to the spiritual condition. The objective work of Christ, the sole source of salvation, is negated. The sanctifying work of the Spirit, the sole source of transformation, is eclipsed. Marva Dawn provides this piercing critique of the self-help message:

> Sermons cannot form the character of believers when sin is treated merely as an addiction and redemption is only therapy. The believer's new life in Christ must be based on Christ's objective work of redemption, not on our experience of it, nor on a process of self-improvement or self-actualization.[33]

Summary

There exists a demonstrable trend in contemporary preaching toward flattening out a sermon so that the human aspect dominates and the divine aspect is diminished. More and more preaching is characterized by a horizontal, anthropocentric focus, rather than a vertical, theocentric one. Three contemporary forces contribute significantly to this trend: sermons that conform to a relativistic epistemology (hearer based), sermons that conform to a consumer ethos (felt needs based), and self-help sermons that present stepped directions for self-improvement (solution based).

---

relatedness to the divine. But the initiative that establishes and the effort that maintains the human-divine relationship rests supremely with the creature, not with the Creator. This is the grossest form of theological error.

33 Dawn, *Royal "Waste" of Time*, 210.

The Dangers of Overextending into the Horizontal Dimension

The dangers of overextending into the horizontal aspects are significant. Many of those dangers have already been presented. But the threat that this horizontal phenomenon in contemporary preaching places upon the life of the Church can be summarized in the following five points.

Predominance in the Horizontal Dimension Leads to God-less Preaching

Overextending the human dimension of the sermon minimizes the role of God as the subject of the sermon. God is marginalized to such a point that the Deity becomes for all practical purposes irrelevant to the message.[34] Richard Lischer observes that many contemporary preachers have reduced God's role to mere backlighting on the set of the sermon.[35] This reduction of the divine transforms the sermon into psychological, sociological, or purely utilitarian insights devoid of God-centered content. The secularization of preaching becomes a *fait accompli,* and sermons become functionally God-less. Such preaching, Thomas Long observes, is ultimately pragmatic atheism.[36]

One result of this is that preachers have unwittingly contributed to the prevailing culture of unbelief in our society.[37] As sermons have become more a-theological (and thus more atheistic) they have become less nourishing to the spirit. Indeed, a-theological sermons (if they can even be called sermons) are deadly in the fullest sense of the term.[38]

---

34 Paul Scott Wilson observes that God-less preaching frequently develops in preachers who have neglected to nurture their own faith in God. Wilson, *Four Pages of the Sermon*, 20.

35 Lischer, "Cross and Craft: Two Elements of a Lutheran Homiletic," *Concordia Journal* 25, no. 1 (January 1999): 10.

36 Thomas Long, "Imagine There's No Heaven: The Loss of Eschatology in American Preaching," *Journal for Preachers* 30, no. 1 (Advent 2006): 26.

37 Turner, *Without God, Without Creed*, 301. Craig Gay labels this phenomenon the "grave-digger dilemma," in which Christian preachers ultimately (albeit unintentionally) bring about the demise of Christianity through their God-less preaching. Craig M. Gay, *The Way of the (Modern) World: Or, Why It's Tempting to Live as if God Doesn't Exist* (Grand Rapids: Eerdmans, 1998), 256.

38 Michael Horton compares a preacher who neglects theology to a physician who neglects his understanding of anatomy. Both bring about the demise of those under their care. See Horton, *Better Way*, 38.

Overextension in the Horizontal Dimension Leads to Idolatrous Preaching

By concentrating on the self, whether that be the self's role in determining meaning (as in relativistic epistemology), the self's insistence that "felt needs" be met (as in the consumer-satisfying emphasis), or the self's improvement through "how to" techniques (as in the solution-based sermon model), the self is elevated to an idolatrous position. The emphasis on self-help replaces the *dunamis* of the Gospel. God's power is displaced with self-actualization. As a result, the self forms a god to its liking. James Turner maintains that much contemporary preaching has created God in the image of man.[39] In his Large Catechism Martin Luther defines one's god as that upon which one relies and depends.[40] Predominantly horizontal preaching directs its hearers to rely and depend upon their own understanding (relativistic epistemology), their own choices (consumer ethos), and their own solutions (self-help). Ultimately, this kind of preaching elevates the self to godhood.

Simply put, one's God is that which has first place—priority—in one's life. Similarly, one could say that what is truly God in the sermon is that which has priority in the message. Richard Lischer observes that much contemporary preaching displaces the priority of the sermon from the Word of God to the listener.[41] As preachers undertake to serve the hearers more than to serve God, they also fear and love the hearers more than God and so make the hearer into an idol.[42]

In predominantly horizontal preaching the focus is on the human and not the divine, except that (ironically) the human is elevated to the divine. This is why over-extension in the horizontal dimension makes for idolatrous preaching. The need in the Church is to dethrone the self in preaching and to confess that God is God. David Wells states: "What distinguishes the Church from this [consumer satisfaction] industry is truth. It is truth about God and about ourselves that displaces the consumer from his or her current perch of sovereignty in the Church and places God in the place where he should be."[43]

---

39 Turner, *Without God, Without Creed*, 113.

40 LC I 3 (*Concordia*, 359).

41 Lischer, "Cross and Craft," 9.

42 Edward Grimenstein locates the cause for much idolatrous preaching in the fact that the preacher fears, loves, and trusts his audience more than God. Edward O. Grimenstein, "Secularism, Idolatry, and Preaching," *Logia* 12, no. 3 (2001): 25.

43 Wells, *Above All Earthly Pow'rs*, 303.

Predominantly Horizontal Preaching Is Law-oriented Preaching

Preaching that is predominantly utilitarian is essentially legalistic. It is deficient if not devoid of the Gospel. It focuses on what *we do*, not on what *God does* through the Gospel. It is at best synergistic (i.e., humans cooperating with God to achieve righteousness). At times it is even monergistic on the wrong side of the theological equation (i.e., humans achieving their own righteousness exclusive of God). Sermons that espouse purely psychological, social, or practical principles may indeed possess an appearance of being religious, since they espouse morality. But morality does not equate with the Gospel. Kurt Hamsum, a Nobel Prize winner from Norway, commented on sermons he heard in his visit to America. He observed that they were predominantly moralistic rather than genuinely theological.[44] Such a verdict could be made of a growing number of sermons today. They do not contain much theology that delivers the Gospel but only morality that delivers the Law. Thus they are Law-oriented.

Exclusively Horizontal Preaching Is Hopeless Preaching

This consequence derives from the three previously described consequences of horizontal preaching. For if such preaching is God-less, then it is also devoid of the ultimate hope that God alone provides. If the message is idolatrous, it fails to deliver eternal hope, since it directs the listener to gods—such as the god of self—that are incapable of delivering from sin. If the horizontal preaching is Law-oriented, it offers no hope for reconciliation with God (humanity's greatest need), since the only means for delivering that hope, the Gospel, is absent.

Martin Luther recognized that eternal hope derives from the vertical aspect of preaching, not from the horizontal. United with the voice of Scripture, he maintained that such hope rests not on human merit or on self-advancement, but rather on God's mercy.[45] Luther argues that this kind of hope *never* has any other object or matter or foundation than God's mercy. Yet horizontal preaching has as its object and matter and foundation the needs, experiences, and solutions of man. Consequently, horizontal preaching is hopeless preaching in regard to humanity's greatest need, the forgiveness of sins. For only in the Gospel—that vertical message of what God has done for us in Christ to redeem us from our sin—is there hope to deliver us from our destiny in damnation.

---

44 Larsen, *Company of the Preachers*, 851.

45 See *What Luther Says: A Practical In-Home Anthology for the Active Christian*, ed. Ewald Plass (St. Louis: Concordia, 1959), 668–69.

Principally Horizontal Preaching Leads to Irrelevant Preaching

At first glance it appears contradictory to claim that preaching which dominates in the horizontal dimension is irrelevant. What is meant by this is that it may appear immediately relevant, but it will not be ultimately and eternally relevant.

To be relevant means to relate to something. Preachers who seek to be relevant endeavor to relate the Word of God to the real life experiences of their listeners. They attempt to address the contextual issues of the day. This is desirable and even necessary for effective preaching to take place. Relevance is essential to communication, and communication is integral to preaching. The apostle Paul sought to contextualize his message to engage various audiences with the goal of converting them: "I have become all things to all men so that by all possible means I might save some" (1 Cor. 9:22; see also vv. 19–21). This he did "for the sake of the Gospel," that is, in service to it (1 Cor. 9:23).

Translating the Gospel (which by its very nature resides in the vertical dimension) into words and images that contemporary people can understand and to which they can relate is an important part of good preaching. Practical application of biblical truth is also desired. Foremost of all, the evangelical preacher seeks to proclaim the Evangel in order to deliver God's absolution to sinners. The herald announces God's forgiveness to the repentant. Essentially he declares that God's grace is "for you"—personally and tangibly. He *relates* Christ's work to the sinner and his or her need for forgiveness. This vertical preaching is the highest form of relevance.

But preaching that dominates in the horizontal sphere misses that mark. Preachers who do so sell their birthright for a pot of porridge. A steady diet of such sermons may appear immediately relevant—touching upon immediate needs and concerns of people, such as the friends with whom they associate, the ways they interact with family members, even the manner in which they serve others. But since it neglects the sinner's greatest need for the righteousness of Christ, this pattern of horizontal preaching is ultimately and eternally irrelevant.

Preaching that corresponds to a relativistic epistemology is ultimately irrelevant because it denies absolute truth, which in reality is the standard for what is and is not relevant. Of course, the highest form of truth is theological truth—truth about God and from God who is the Truth (John 14:6). This truth is proclaimed in the vertical dimension. Thus to diminish or completely miss the vertical axis in preaching is to deliver a supremely irrelevant sermon.

Similarly, consumer-satisfying preaching is ultimately irrelevant because it fails to dispatch to the hearer that which is most needed, righteousness *propter Christum*. The one who is complacent in his or her sin will not want to hear the message of the Law. The one who is self-sufficient will not care to hear the message of the Gospel. But that doesn't mean that these messages are irrelevant. Indeed, these messages are *eminently* relevant! There is nothing the complacent or self-sufficient individual needs to hear more! So to neglect proclaiming this vertical message because it is not satisfying to the consumer is to omit that which is of the highest relevance. It is to commit oneself to preaching that is not relevant for eternity.

Indeed, there is the need for the preacher to connect with the real-life conditions and concerns of people, such as raising children, engaging in vocation, living ethically, etc. This kind of relevant preaching that relates to and reflects hearers' experiences in the here and now is not to be neglected. Frequently the biblical text addresses these everyday creaturely activities and circumstances, and so should the preacher who expounds that text! But it is those matters that are relevant for eternity which are supremely relevant. Most sermons in which the horizontal dimension is dominant focus on subjects and topics that are temporal and transitory. They have little lasting value and certainly are devoid of value that endures into eternity. Os Guinness observes that the most relevant issues revolve around eternal matters.[46]

The preacher who says things that are eternal will be speaking in the vertical dimension and so will be always relevant. Conversely, words from a preacher who speaks only in the horizontal dimension may seem relevant for the moment, but eventually—and eternally—they will be irrelevant. Truly relevant preaching addresses eternal matters about the eternal One and speaks words from the eternal One.

Maintaining Balance

The answer to the problem here described is not to expunge preaching of all horizontal elements. It is to maintain balance. There is a need to properly balance the vertical and horizontal aspects of preaching. We would err to insist upon sermons that are exclusively vertical, proclaiming a transcendent God without guiding people to live out the call of God in their interactions with others. We would be truly unfaithful to promote predominantly horizontal sermons that are psychological, sociological, or merely utilitarian in

46 Os Guinness, "Sounding Out the Idols of Church Growth," in *No God But* God, ed. Os Guinness and John Seel (Chicago: Moody, 1992), 169. Guinness provides a thoroughly expanded treatment of this subject in another book, *Prophetic Untimeliness: A Challenge to the Idol of Relevance* (Grand Rapids: Baker, 2003).

content but lacking in theological substance. It is not a matter of "either/or"—the false dichotomy of "either vertical or horizontal" preaching. It is instead a matter of "both/and"—proclaiming *both* the vertical relationship between God and man *and* addressing how this vertical relationship impacts the horizontal dimension of interpersonal relationships and needs.

When both the vertical and the horizontal aspects are present in a sermon—and balanced appropriately—then the design of the sermon is, in one sense, cruciform.[47] The image of the cross is formed by the balanced intersection of a vertical post and a horizontal beam. Likewise, a theologically sound sermon that connects with the hearers is formed by the balanced interaction of vertical and horizontal aspects.

Although both the vertical and horizontal dimensions are to be present and balanced in preaching, the vertical is always to have priority. In ancient times the vertical beam of the cross was secured in the ground before the horizontal beam was attached. Likewise in preaching the theological foundation is to be grounded so that the human interpersonal application may be properly connected. Marva Dawn argues that first and foremost God is to be the subject and object of preaching.[48] Faithful Christian preachers first proclaim a right relationship with God made possible through Christ's salvific work (the vertical), and then they guide hearers to relate to other people based on this right relationship with God (the horizontal).

This is the approach that Paul and other apostles used in the writing of their Epistles. For example, in the Letter to the Ephesians Paul spends the first three chapters addressing the vertical relationship God has established with us by His grace. The last three chapters then describe how we are to "live the life worthy of the calling" we have received in our horizontal relationships with each other (Eph. 4:1). This same kind of vertical and then horizontal movement is also evident in the Epistles to the Romans, Galatians, Colossians, and in 1 Peter.

One way of maintaining this vertical-horizontal balance is to make sure, as D. Stewart Briscoe puts it, that one's sermon is God-centered and people-related, not people-centered and God-related.[49] Preaching that displays a balance of the vertical and horizontal dimensions remains theocentric and Christocentric while also addressing the condition, needs, and interpersonal relationships of the hearers. Indeed, it focuses on God's grand purpose in Christ to provide for our greatest need—the forgiveness of sins. That same

47 Robert Kolb describes the cruciform life that is evoked by this design of a sermon, see "Luther on Two Kinds of Righteousness: Reflections on His Two Dimensional Definition of Humanity at the Heart of His Theology," *Lutheran Quarterly* 13 (1999): 455–56.

48 Dawn, *Royal "Waste" of Time*, 206.

49 D. Stuart Briscoe, *Fresh Air in the Pulpit: Challenges and Encouragement from a Seasoned Preacher* (Grand Rapids: Baker, 1994), 124–25.

divine forgiveness empowers us to live in reconciliation and harmony with one another. The right vertical relationship with God (based on the righteousness of Christ given freely by His grace) enables the right horizontal relationships to exist among us (as Christ's life is lived in and through us to others by the presence and power of His Spirit). It is one's identity grounded in the vertical dimension that moves him or her to live according to God's will in the horizontal dimension.

The Worship Context: Resources for Maintaining Balance

Fortunately, God has provided to His Church resources that will aid in maintaining this balance in preaching. These resources are inherent to the context in which preaching occurs—the context of *worship*. The foremost resource is none other than God's own Spirit, which more accurately is identified as the *source* for faithful preaching than as a resource for it.[50] There are other resources, which will briefly be considered here, including the liturgical order, the biblical text, and the Reformation hermeneutic of properly distinguishing between Law and Gospel. Obviously these resources are not innovations. They are treasures that have been used by faithful preachers throughout the history of the Church. The problem now is that these are increasingly neglected. It is not coincidental that a movement away from these resources has accompanied a movement away from preaching in the vertical dimension. But a return to these resources will bring renewed equilibrium and balance to the content of preaching. Thus we conclude this chapter with a review of homiletical resources deriving from the context of worship: resources from the liturgical context, resources from the lectionary context, and resources from the Reformation hermeneutical context. Attention to each of these will contribute to a restoration of balance in preaching.

Resources from the Liturgical Context

While on vacation one summer, my family and I attended a worship service as visitors. In very many ways the sermon was a disappointment. The Bible was not in evidence, and Jesus was the most missed of missing persons

50 Preachers who rely on the Holy Spirit for inspiration and power for preaching most likely will be in tune to the vertical dimension, and it will show in their preaching. A reliance on the Holy Spirit through devoted reception of the means of grace in personal Bible reading and reflection, in careful exegetical study, and in regular reception of the Lord's Supper will support preaching that properly balances the vertical and horizontal dimensions. Persistent prayer that petitions the Holy Spirit to enlighten one's proclamation (both in its preparation and presentation) will also guide the preacher into all truth and bring glory to Christ (John 16:13–15).

in the content of the message. Essentially the sermon reflected the classical tact of what is commonly referred to as the "Social Gospel." The hearers were exhorted to advocate for the hurting and seek justice for the oppressed. It was exclusively a horizontal-oriented sermon.

Yet the vertical dimension was not absent from the worship service. Blessedly, it was retained in the liturgy. I heard the scriptural revelation quoted in virtually every element of the *ordo*. The Holy Trinity was blessed, and the divine blessing from the triune God was bestowed upon the worshipers. In the confession of sin I was reminded of my abject spiritual poverty *coram deo*. In the absolution I heard the word of forgiveness of sin. Almost every element of the liturgy (despite the sermon) directed me to focus on the Divine One and receive from Him forgiveness, life, and salvation.

It was in this liturgical context that the God-less, Christ-less, Gospel-less sermon appeared especially out of place. Each of the other elements of the liturgy focused my attention on the triune God as well as on my responsibilities to my neighbors. A sermon that did the same would have aligned perfectly with its liturgical context. My family and I left the service wishing for much more in the sermon, but we were grateful for what we had received through the liturgy.

A sermon that appropriately balances the vertical and horizontal dimensions coheres well with the message of the historic liturgy in which it is set. A sermon that does not do so seems out of place within such a context. Accordingly, preachers can draw upon the resources of the liturgy to find balance in their preaching simply by aligning their sermons to the balance that is found in the liturgy.

Several of the chapters in this volume aid the reader in a better comprehension of and appreciation for the liturgical context of the sermon. However, at this point I will speak briefly about how the liturgy forms a balanced framework of being God-centered (vertical dimension) as well as people-related (horizontal dimension). The pastor who is familiar with this balance in the liturgy will seek to align the sermon to that balance.

The vertical dimension dominates the liturgy. The Invocation leads worshipers to call upon the name and presence of the triune God. The Confession and Absolution cause those present to turn their focus to a God who condemns their sin but also delivers the forgiveness of sin for the sake of Jesus Christ. The Kyrie directs one to the peace that only the Lord can bestow. The Hymn of Praise guides worshipers to glorify Father, Son, and Holy Spirit. The readings of Scripture open the people's ears to hear the prophetic and apostolic Word of God. The Creed gives form to the worshipers' confession of who the divine persons of the Trinity are and what they have done (and continue to do) to benefit the world. The Sanctus and Agnus Dei help those present to recognize and prepare for the immanent incarnational presence of Christ, which is delivered in the Sacrament of the Altar. Lastly, the words of the Benediction bestow the Lord's ongoing blessing upon those preparing to depart. Interspersed within these liturgical elements are prayers—the Collect of the Day, the Prayer of the Church, the Lord's Prayer, the Prayer of Thanksgiving, and the Post-Communion Collect—which direct the worshipers' thoughts and words heavenward. These components of the liturgy establish a solid vertical orientation to the worship service. No wonder it is called the *Divine* Service!

Yet there is also a consistent horizontal dimension evident in the liturgical order. Frequently throughout the service first person *plural* pronouns are employed: "*We* confess that *we* are by nature sinful an unclean . . . In peace let *us* pray to the Lord . . . *We* worship You, *we* give You thanks . . . *We* lift them to the Lord . . . *Our* Father who art in heaven . . . Have mercy upon *us* . . . Grant *us* peace . . ." Most of the second person pronouns that the pastor speaks are intended as *plural* pronouns: ". . . I therefore forgive *you* all *your* sins . . . The Lord be with *you* . . . The body and blood of our Lord Jesus Christ strengthen and preserve *you* . . . The Lord bless *you* and keep *you* . . ." Each of these plural pronouns reminds us human beings not only that we worship together as a community of faith but that we live our lives in relationship with one another and with others in the world.

Furthermore, the liturgy specifically addresses our relationships both with God and with one another as an *integrated* reality. In the Confession we state that not only have we failed to love God with our whole heart, but "we have not loved our neighbors as ourselves." In the Kyrie we not only pray *to* the Lord, but we pray *for* others—"For the peace of the whole world, for the well-being of the Church of God, and for the unity of all let us pray to the Lord." In the Creed we confess that we are part of a larger community—"the holy Christian Church, the communion of saints," which is the creation of the Holy Spirit. During the Prayer of the Church petitions are offered to God for people in need. The Peace of the Lord (Pax Domini) is extended to fellow worshipers. In the Post-Communion Collect the celebrant implores God that through the gift of the Sacrament of the Altar He would strengthen us "in faith toward You and in fervent love toward one another." This proper integration of one's relationship with God (vertical) and relationships with other humans (horizontal) in the liturgy presents to worshipers a vision of life that is in cruciform balance.

The preacher who is in sync with such integrated balance in the liturgy will not suffer homiletic vertigo. The liturgical context of the sermon will orient the preacher so that a balanced center of gravity is maintained in preaching. The pastor who is at home with the cruciform ethos of the worship service will align his preaching accordingly, delivering sermons that are focused on the Divine One while addressing human interaction.

Resources from the Lectionary Context

A second resource for maintaining balance in the preaching task is the corpus of Scripture on which the sermons are to be based. Preachers who carefully exposit the written Word of God—the biblical text—will more likely make God the subject and object of preaching because God is the subject and object of the Bible. Preachers who expound the whole of a biblical passage, not just using the passage as a springboard to explore personal issues and insights, will by virtue of the guidance of Scripture remain balanced in the two dimensions. There is no more vertically oriented book than the Bible. By remaining a servant to the Bible, the expositor will be strengthened to resist horizontalizing influences brought to bear by popular culture.

The key here is for the preacher to be a servant of the Word foremost, even before being a servant of the people (in the sense of following their dictates or addressing their felt needs). William Willimon writes:

> Too often the term "servant leader" is code for servility to the congregation. We can't be faithful servants of our congregations, as *Christian* congregations, without being (in Luther's favorite designation for pastors) *ministeri verbi divini*, "servants of the Word." One reason the preaching office is primary is that it is a primary means of forming us preachers into the sort of people who take God more seriously than ourselves or our congregations. To be a preacher is to be trained and formed by the weekly disciplines of bending our interests to the countercultural concerns of the Word. I'm concerned that too many recent books on preaching are mostly about our listeners, analyzing the limits and the interests of our congregations and their ability to hear, when they ought to be most interested in what the Trinity is able to speak.[51]

Preachers who endeavor to be faithful "servants of the Word" will maintain a solid theological center of gravity in their sermons.

In this regard a valuable aid is the lectionary. This resource guides the pastor to preach on texts that the broader Church in its wisdom has recognized as balancing the vertical and horizontal dimensions. Instead of letting the hearers or felt needs or popular culture dictate the subject of the sermon, the pericopal system allows God to speak to the issues that are really relevant and significant. These issues are primarily in the vertical dimension—issues such as the forgiveness of sins, justification by divine grace, and the renewing work of the Holy Spirit.

---

51 William Willimon, "Pastors Who Won't Be Preachers: A Polemic Against Homiletical Accommodation to the Culture of Contentment," *Journal for Preachers* 29, no. 4 (2006): 40.

This is not a call to slavish adherence to the lectionary. Periodic usage of free texts for individual sermons and for sermon series can be beneficial. Certainly homilies based on free texts can appropriately balance the vertical and horizontal dimensions. But over the long haul preachers who generously use the appointed readings recognize that the lectionary can be a sturdy guard rail that prevents them from falling into anthropocentric preaching. The chapter in this book entitled "'Working' the Lectionary" provides a more thorough reflection upon this valuable resource.

Resources from the Reformation Hermeneutical Context

Finally, the Lutheran tradition has emphasized a resource that truly balances the vertical and horizontal aspects of preaching and keeps them in proper relationship. This is the hermeneutic of the proper distinction between the uses of Law and Gospel. Once again, a more comprehensive treatment of this subject is delivered in the chapter in this volume by David Schmitt, "Law and Gospel in Sermon and Service." But here is offered a more specific application of this hermeneutical key to the task of balancing the vertical and horizontal dimensions.

The distinction between Law and Gospel recognizes that people's greatest need is for the forgiveness of sins. As sinners, they must come to recognize this need. However, this is not a self-evident "felt need." It will not ordinarily be perceived through hearer-based hermeneutics. It is best revealed by the message of the Law addressed to sinners' fallen condition. Likewise, the Gospel is the only solution to this ultimate need, delivering the righteousness of Christ that is *extra nos* to sinful human beings. Thus the best "solution-based" sermon is not a "how to" message that directs the hearer inward to self-improvement. Instead, it is that message which directs the hearer outside of the self to the Savior, Jesus Christ, for the forgiveness of sins. Maintaining this emphasis assures the primacy of the vertical dimension in the sermon.

But the dialectic of the Law and Gospel distinction also plays itself out in the horizontal dimension. The Law serves various functions, frequently categorized into three—the first, second, and third uses of the Law.[52] The second use is described in the previous paragraph: that which reveals sinners' guilt before God and their need for forgiveness. In this regard it is vertical as it points the sinner to a broken relationship with God. Yet this use does not exclude the horizontal dimension, since much of the guilt revealed by the Law regards how one has sinned against one's neighbors.

---

52 The Epitome of the Formula of Concord aptly summarizes these uses. See FC EP VI 1 (*Concordia*, 486).

The other two uses of the Law are typically more horizontal in their orientation. According to its first use, the Law directs the behavior of people as they live together in society and protects them from the violence of others (as well as deters them from directing undue violence toward others). This function of the Law should not be a primary goal of Lutheran preaching, but it may still have effect. The third use of the Law flows from the proclamation of the Gospel. It guides Christians in the Spirit-wrought new identity in Christ and in renewed will toward service in the world and for the benefit of others. This channeling is precisely into the horizontal dimension of human interaction.

Frequently the biblical text that is being exposited has as its intended goal the love of neighbors and thus the fulfilling of the Second Table of the Decalogue.[53] So also the sermon, in faithfulness to the text, exhorts and encourages the hearers to love and serve their neighbors (horizontal aspect) because they are new creations in Christ (vertical aspect). This new identity derives from the Gospel, and the indwelling Holy Spirit works these fruits of faith that align with God's Law. This is where the proper distinction between the uses of Law and Gospel is so critical. It is only the Gospel that empowers and motivates the new obedience to God's will, especially His will to serve other people. But the Law instructs the Christian, who is saint and sinner at the same time, regarding what the will of God is for us in our human relationships.

Thus the proclamation of the Gospel must predominate in a sermon; the vertical dimension cannot be neglected. Yet the horizontal dimension may manifest itself in the preacher's employment of the second (condemning) and third (guiding) uses of the Law.[54] The Law-Gospel dialectic enables the preacher to achieve supremely balanced vertical-horizontal preaching.

Conclusion

On the campaign trail in 1996, Bob Dole would not have fallen from the elevated stage and suffered the mishap he did if he had maintained physical balance. If he had sustained a reasonable vertical center of gravity, he could have safely reached out to shake hands with the people attending his speech. No harm would have been done to anyone. If Dole had maintained a balance of both his vertical and horizontal posture, he would have reached out to the people without losing his equilibrium.

---

53 Paul R. Raabe, "The Law and Christian Sanctification: A Look at Romans," *Concordia Journal* 22, no. 2 (April 1996): 178–85.

54 Tim Saleska describes how the Gospel and both uses of the Law are employed by the preacher to produce *tsaddikim*, righteous people. See "Two Kinds of Righteousness!" 136–45.

This image is relevant to the preaching minister as well. While reaching out to the people via the horizontal dimension of preaching, the pastor seeks to maintain a center of gravity in the vertical dimension of the Gospel. Indeed, the vertical dimension is the ground and foundation of the horizontal, but without neglecting the horizontal concerns of people's needs and affects. In every case, however, the sermon must be firmly grounded in Gospel-centered theology or it will collapse into horizontal manifestations of moralism and utilitarianism. William Willimon reminds preachers of their calling:

> We are to be "God people," those who "interject Jesus into the conversation" in a world that would rather think in exclusively anthropological categories. To be a preacher is to be trained to talk about what God wants to talk about and to talk in the way that God talks (i.e., *Scripture*).[55]

The argument of this essay is not for a polarity of vertical preaching *versus* horizontal preaching. It does not promote a false dichotomy of "either/or." Instead, a "both/and" approach is advocated—both vertical and horizontal. Sermons are to be vertical in that they are theological, a word (*logos*) about and from God (*theos*). Yet such sermons also will demonstrate a horizontal orientation (which is also theological) by connecting the messages of Law and Gospel to the everyday lives of people, especially as they interact with others in their various vocations and relationships. Faithful pastors will seek to balance the horizontal dimension of preaching by maintaining a theological center of gravity. In this way they will reach out to hearers without losing balance.

55 Willimon, "Pastors Who Won't Be Preachers," 38–39.

Sacramental Preaching: Holy Baptism

Robert C. Preece

Crossing the Trinity River at Dallas, where a humble stream is named after God, made the pastor think of another crossing—the baptismal crossing both upon the forehead and upon the heart. There on the I–35 bridge on the way to church a pastor's own Baptism resurfaced and baptismal sermon illustrations began crossing his mind—not unlike a recent summer Sunday morning . . .

The bright sun fell like water through the stained-glass windows, splashing lightly upon the pews, the people, and the old stone font carved by a sainted parishioner in the early twentieth century. A sermon example was on its way to the preacher, who now sat waiting for the last stanza of the Hymn of the Day. Could it be? This late? Could a baptismal example make its appearance at the eleventh pre-pulpit hour? Yes! Thanks be to God! Yes!

So up to the pulpit he went with outline, notes, Scripture, Law, Gospel in head, heart, and hand. "Grace, mercy, and peace be unto you from God our Father, and our Lord and Savior, Jesus Christ." The congregation replied, "Amen."

> But he, desiring to justify himself, said to Jesus, "And who is my neighbor?" Jesus replied, "A man was going down from Jerusalem to Jericho, and he fell among robbers, who stripped him and beat him and departed, leaving him half dead. Now by chance a priest was going down that road, and when he saw him he passed by on the other side. So likewise a Levite, when he came to the place and saw him, passed by on the other side. But a Samaritan, as he journeyed, came to where he was, and when he saw him, he had compassion. He went to him and bound up his wounds, pouring on oil and wine. Then he set him on his own animal and brought him to an inn and took care of him. And the next day he took out two denarii and gave them to the innkeeper, saying, 'Take care of him, and whatever more you spend, I will repay you when I come back.' Which of these three, do you think, proved to be a neighbor to the man who fell among the robbers?" He said, "The

> one who showed him mercy." And Jesus said to him, "You go, and do likewise." (Luke 10:29–37)

"Here ends the text," said the preacher, and then he began the linkage of light and Baptism, life and liturgy, text and sermon. The preacher's anticipated and prepared introduction shifted to one that was extemporaneous. The opening lines now proclaimed:

> Do you see the sunlight pouring in upon us, light from the Creator's hand through the spangled glass, falling upon the pew and upon you and the font? My dear parishioners, God the Holy Trinity has come to us sinners who've been beaten up along life's way. Some bruising is of our own making; some at the hands and emotions of others. He comes and pours out His light and love upon us in Christ. He forgives and restores. He gives us life and salvation, healing and wholeness, like the Samaritan who poured oil and wine in the poor man's open wounds. Here, now, God pours His Word for the cleansing, healing, and wholeness of our souls. The Father's light falls there upon the font, a sign of His Son's redeeming love. At that fountain or another, He poured out His grace upon each of us. Does not the cascading light provide a sign of the water flowing like a river? It comes together with the Word, the only Word that matters: "Fear not, for I have redeemed you; I have called you by name, you are Mine. When you pass through the waters, I will be with you" (Isa. 43:1b–2a). Light for darkness; water for cleansing; worship for praising. Not the Good Samaritan but the only Son of Man and Son of God, Jesus Christ, our Lord, once touched us with baptismal Word and water. Forgiven and healed, raised and strengthened, we set out intentionally to find those fallen neighbors at the side of the road in need. Let me tell you today about the Good Samaritan and the one Christ.

The preacher then returned to his outlined text. But Baptism, with the metaphor of light pouring like washing water, had influenced the homily in the liturgy of an ordinary Sunday morning. The memory of sacramental act and symbol, a sign of baptismal washing, had naturally emerged. Was there a direct baptismal reference in the Good Samaritan text? No. But a connection? Yes! For such lively scriptural connections in sacramental preaching, preachers must pay close attention to life, church, and personal experience. If attention is given to all that goes on round about the preacher, obvious examples and opportunities emerge. The Word connects!

Baptism, the initial life-giving Sacrament, when remembered in preaching, bolsters the believer in faith for Christian life, love, and service. In four parts, this essay will review Baptism in connection with the preaching of the Gospel:

1. Baptism remembered in biblical preaching begs repentance.

2. Baptism remembered in biblical preaching initiates renewal.
3. Baptism remembered in biblical preaching links liturgical worship to life.
4. Baptism remembered bears sermonic repetition and may seek the support of Christian hymnody.

Baptism Remembered in Biblical Preaching Begs Repentance

Peter the preacher said, "Repent and be baptized every one of you in the name of Jesus Christ for the forgiveness of your sins" (Acts 2:38). The confirmands on the annual retreat had been baptized in infancy. The Petrine command was, in this circumstance, understandably reversed: Since you are baptized, repent, every one of you, in the name of Jesus for the forgiveness of your sins. Baptism and repentance, repentance and Baptism constitute dual links in a short but saving two-link chain.

The confirmation retreat continued by the lake. It was going well—fun and games, trail trips and boat rides, food and song, Bible study, "trust walks," and "trust falls." At last the scheduled time for devotions arrived. Here was an old collect of the church. The petition contained the potential water-related word, "cleanse," a first subtle, holy hint pointing toward Baptism. That and one other word in the prayer would be heard clearly by at least one catechumen. "O God, before whom all hearts are open, all desires known, and from whom no secrets are hid, cleanse the thoughts of our hearts by the inspiration of thy Holy Spirit that we may perfectly love thee and worthily magnify thy holy name."[1] The pastor/preacher, with an eye open for Baptism-related sermon illustrations, prayed quietly, and the confirmands even more quietly said, "Amen." It was then, after the devotion, that she approached the pastor.

"The word 'magnify'—it's so beautiful."

"Magnify," he said, paying attention with questioning inflection.

"Yes," she responded, "in the prayer 'that we may worthily *magnify* thy holy name.'"

"Really," resumed the pastor, pleased that the eighth-grade adolescent had been listening and praying, not just waiting for the devotion's benediction. "Why does that word, that phrase, catch your attention?"

"Oh, it's so beautiful that God would cleanse our hearts and we get to *magnify* His holy name."

---

1 *Prayer Book and Hymnal* (New York: Church Publishing, 1986), 323.

Blessed humility and repentance were obviously at hand, and a homiletical example had surfaced from a young Christian growing by theological leaps and poetic bounds. A baptismal connection for preaching was also coming into view. God's name and Baptism deserve to be magnified; cleansing from sin contemplated; repentance linked to Word, water, and the ideal way of Christian life—perfectly loving and worthily magnifying the God who is named Father, Son, and Holy Spirit.

The pastor on the retreat was soon to leave the gathering and return to the Sunday parish pulpit. What if the Gospel appointed were Luke 18:9–17 for Proper 25, Series C? Could the confirmand's encounter with the words "cleanse" and "magnify" be amplified and used in preaching examples one day later? Could they be used, for example, to bind Baptism and repentance to Jesus' well-known parable about the Pharisee and the tax collector recorded in the Gospel?

That parable begs true repentance. The two men did not engage each other. However, they did encounter God—one for merciful goodness, the other for clear and frank judgment. From the pulpit the usual major interpretive points might be made about the arrogance of the one, the repentant spirit of the other; the unjustified religionist versus the justified penitent; the tax collector's corrupt desires contrasted with his confession of sorrow and contrition. But the parable also reveals mercy and the penitent cleansing of a tax collector's heart.

Could Baptism and its cleansing/washing viably connect with this parable? Might penitent people, like the tax collector, head home from worship justified? For the Christian penitent, God washes away sin, death, and hell. He grants forgiveness, life, and salvation. He did so first through His means of baptismal grace. Repenting parishioners could for themselves magnify and celebrate their justification like that of the tax collector, having received a righteousness from God initially at the font. Again the Word and Sacrament connect!

Luther asks, "What does such baptizing with water indicate?" He answers: "It indicates that the Old Adam in us should by daily contrition and repentance be drowned and die with all sins and evil desires, and that a new man should daily emerge and arise to live before God in righteousness and purity forever."[2] Post-font sins, already forgiven, are confessed in corporate worship. Baptism emphasized and remembered regularly in preaching would surely lead to the repeated contrition and rehearsal of repentance sought by Luther.

Eugene Brand writes: "One sees the Christian life as God's ever renewed gift, having as its paradigm baptismal death and resurrection. So long as

2 *Luther's Small Catechism*, 25.

people live between the times and their lives are a struggle between the old and new Adams, those lives have a baptismal shape renewed by daily repentance and forgiveness."[3] When the word for preaching tips toward repentance and soul cleansing, then Baptism examples are legitimately sounded from the pulpit. Preaching about the parable of the Pharisee and the tax collector, the proclaimer may point listeners to their Baptism. In their daily death and resurrection struggle against evil, Christ the Victor remains triumphant.

Luther went on to explain that Baptism, both by its power and by its significance, includes what is sometimes referred to as the "third Sacrament," formerly called penance. He asserted that penance was really nothing more than Baptism. In his view, if one lives in repentance, one walks in Baptism.[4] Preachers can help people walk in the Word and in their Baptism. When sermons summon repentance, Baptism calls for attention, exhorting the faithful to live and act upon the Word and the Sacrament they received from God.

A parable about repentance may become a homiletical touchstone for the Sacrament, the Word, and the Gospel to be presented and recalled in metaphors and illustration. The teenage "theologian" listened closely, and then gave her pastor words for a baptismal preaching point. The Church still pleads: "Cleanse the thoughts of our hearts by the inspiration of thy Holy Spirit that we may perfectly love thee and magnify thy holy name." The Collect suggests that Baptism and consequent lifelong repentance be remembered in preaching. The example had emerged as attention was paid both to the young Christian's response of faith and to the scriptural parable itself. The connection is appropriately made with ease.

Baptism Remembered in Biblical Preaching Initiates Renewal

First and foremost, any remembering or preaching that leads to renewal asserts that renewal itself is a gift from God. Renewal is the work of God within the believer's heart. Baptismal reference made from the pulpit to the already baptized does not merely urge, "Try harder, just try harder, and be renewed," but rather motivates the faithful by the same Gospel of Christ's love that effected Baptism in the first place. The grace that led to repentance extends to renewal.

The Latin word for renewal, *renovatio*, produces the English cognate *renovation*. The preacher's work and prayer for the people implores the Holy

---

3 Eugene L. Brand, *Baptism: A Pastoral Perspective* (Minneapolis: Augsburg, 1975), 66–67.

4 Brand, *Baptism*, 66–67.

Spirit through the Word to rebuild, reshape, re-energize—to renovate the heart. Preaching about Baptism and the recollection of the love and grace of God poured out at the font presses penitent believers toward the remodeling of their ethical, behavioral, and moral lives. Renewal is but another word for sanctification, a work of the Spirit. Luther wrote: "I believe that I cannot by my own reason or strength believe in Jesus Christ, my Lord, or come to Him; but the Holy Spirit has called me by the Gospel, enlightened me with His gifts, sanctified and kept me in the true faith."[5]

In his despair and depression Luther remembered, "But I am baptized."[6] Likewise, in sanctified contemplation of thinking, saying, and doing the right, the good, the true, and the noble, the Christian may recall, "I am baptized." In the Small Catechism Luther points to Titus 3:5–6: "[H]e saved us, not because of works done by us in righteousness, but according to his own mercy, by the washing of regeneration and renewal of the Holy Spirit, whom he poured out on us richly through Jesus Christ our Savior."

Renewal is the work of the Third Person of the Holy Trinity operating through Word and Sacrament, received and remembered. In a critical review of a quotation from the seventeenth-century dogmatician Johannes Quenstedt, Werner Elert discusses renewal and its God-based initiative. Quenstedt delineated rebirth, justification, and renewal by indicating that the first has the "bringing forth of faith as its object; the second, the imputable righteousness; the third, the inherent righteousness . . . [and] that only rebirth and justification are acts of God."[7] For "in renewal the person reborn cooperates with God, 'not,' it is true, 'by means of his own strength but by means of strength given by God.' "[8]

But Elert cautions: "No reference to the fact that the strength employed by man in this connection is 'strength given by God' could do away with the fatal recollection of the medieval doctrine of 'cooperating grace' [*gratia cooperans*] . . . Yes, the Apology stated plainly, 'good works . . . are evidences of righteousness, [and] Scripture wants the righteousness of the heart to be surrounded by fruits.' "[9]

But the Holy Spirit working through the means of grace effects renewal as well as rebirth and justification. Thus, from Elert's view, any homiletical comment on a Christian's renewal must always be made totally and completely reliant upon the God of the Word and the water for truly good results.

---

5 *Luther's Small Catechism*, 15.

6 D. T. Strelan, *God for Us* (Adelaide, South Australia, 1988), 26.

7 Werner Elert, *The Structure of Lutheranism* (St. Louis: Concordia, 1962), 149–50.

8 Elert, *Structure of Lutheranism*, 150.

9 Elert, *Structure of Lutheranism*, 150.

Otherwise a synergistic outcome is inevitable, leading only to unsanctified arrogance or sinking despair on the part of the Christian hearer.

With that dogmatic understanding in place, baptismal theology may rightly and effectively raise the categories of reform, reconstruction, and renovation. Pericopes for the days in the three-year series, particularly the Epistles, anticipate renewal, often freighted with instruction for Christian behavior. For example, the Epistle for Proper 16, Series A, is Rom. 11:33–12:8. As the preacher reads and reflects on the lesson, baptismal interpolations and connections appear.

> I appeal to you therefore, brothers, by the mercies of God, to present your bodies as a living sacrifice, holy and acceptable to God, which is your spiritual worship. Do not be conformed to this world, but be transformed by the renewal of your mind, that by testing you may discern what is the will of God, what is good and acceptable and perfect. (Rom. 12:1–2)

The remaining verses of Romans 12 are nothing less than the call to renewal first sounded and expected at the font. "Depart, you unclean spirit, and make room for the Holy Spirit," in the words of Luther's baptismal rite.[10] And the words of St. Paul to the Roman Christians go on explicitly to tell what that renewal—begun at Baptism, lived in the Spirit, powered by the Spirit—looks like.

Renewal means the following: "Love one another with brotherly affection. Outdo one another in showing honor. Do not be slothful in zeal, be fervent in spirit, serve the Lord. Rejoice in hope, be patient in tribulation, be constant in prayer. Contribute to the needs of the saints and seek to show hospitality" (Rom. 12:10–13).

The Holy Gospel connected with the remainder of Romans 12 in the lectionary (Matt. 16:21–28) records the Messiah's invitation to self-denial, with a cross lifted, for faithful following. Was not the self denied at the font, the cross embraced and borne, and the first steps taken to follow Christ? Preachers may proclaim Baptism by making references to it regularly, frequently, cogently. Recall it. Encourage renewal, which arises from many texts appointed for the Day of the Lord, the *dies Domini*, the day the Church remembers His death and resurrection, often eucharistically, always scripturally. Why not "baptismally"? In the setting of the worshiping congregation, liturgical act and symbol declare that Jesus' death is reversed and His life renewed in His resurrection. He imparts that life and breath to His people. The believer's baptismal drowning is reversed for good, and that same believer comes up to "walk in newness of life" (Rom. 6:4)—forever.

10 Frank C. Senn, *Christian Liturgy* (Minneapolis: Augsburg Fortress, 1997), 290–91.

Preachers standing in the pulpits of the Lord and His Church may point confidently to the font as object, to splashed water as sign, to the birth waters of life as illustration calling for the incredible novelty of holiness in a fallen world. Referencing written scriptural expectations and Christian ethics, a preacher may say with certainty, Here is what renewal looks like in its results, all made possible by the God of our salvation, Father, Son, and Holy Spirit, in whose name the baptized move, live, and have their very being.

In his fresh translation of Valentin Thilo's hymn "O People, Rise and Labor" (*LW* 25), F. Samuel Janzow suggests renewal by catching the Advent preparation spirit. The hymn text is surely suitable for the baptismal refashioning of life. The Gospel appointed for the Third Sunday in Advent, Series B, John 1:6–8, 19–28, would bear pulpit expansion as John the Baptist and his preaching are clearly heard across the centuries. The people's desire for the rebuilding of Christian life is undergirded by the hymn text given below (see italicized words). John the Baptist himself and baptismal recollection encourage renewal when the assembly sings,

O people, rise and labor
To *renovate* the heart
That mankind's mighty Savior,
Whom God's love set apart
To *free* you all from sin,
May do the promised wonder
And with his life and splendor,
Victorious, *enter* in.

Prepare with earnest rigor
The way for your great guest.
Make straight his path with vigor,
Rebuild your lives with zest.
The sunken valleys fill,
Restore eroded places,
Where sinbursts leave their traces,
Cut down the prideful hill.

A heart that humbly serves him
Stands highest in his sight.
The haughty heart, the proud whim
Go down in anguished night.
But those who love God's Word
And go where he is pointing
Are fit by his *anointing*
To *host* their gracious Lord.

Dear Lord, in high compassion
Bend down with Advent grace.

My heart, I pray, *refashion*
With mercy from your face.
Come from the thankless inn
To make my heart your manger
That I, no more a stranger,
Eternal praise *begin*.

The baptized who hear the preacher quote this text and who sing it are directed toward and empowered for renewal in body, soul, and spirit.

Baptism Remembered in Biblical Preaching Links Liturgical Worship to Life

Worship offered to God in liturgy and in a church building designed with font, table, and pulpit as triple foci possesses inherently and architecturally the power of "relating." That is to say, in the church building Baptism coupled with the Word may be related to the next touch point in life. For example, every Divine Service begins with the trinitarian invocation; baptized life began with the same words. Making the sign of the cross and saying the words on Monday morning after Sunday worship link liturgy, sacred space, and practice to sacrament and life. In *Jerusalem*, Karen Armstrong demonstrates the interconnectedness between sacred space, sacred act, and ordinary life. She speaks of holy place and hints at such sacramental transactions accompanied by faith. Far beyond the concept of *ex opere operato* (the mere work working mechanically), a personal faith is assumed and held. She writes:

> Like the Sacred Mountain, the Temple was a symbol of the reality that sustains the life of the cosmos. Like Jacob's ladder, it represented a bridge to the source of being, without which the fragile mundane world could not subsist. Because it was built in a place where the sacred had revealed itself in the past, worshippers could hope to make contact with that divine power. When they entered the holy precincts, they had stepped into another dimension which, they believed, existed contemporaneously with the mundane world and kept it in being. Mount Zion had become radically different from the surrounding territory, therefore: in Hebrew the word for "holy" (*kaddosh*) means "other," "set apart." The very plan of the building, with its three-tiered gradations of sanctity culminating in the Devir (the Holy of Holies), symbolized the transcendence of the sacred. Entry to the Devir was prohibited to all except the priests; it remained silent, void, and inaccessible. Yet since it enshrined the Ark and the Presence, it tacitly bore witness to the fact that the sacred could enter the world of men and women: it was at once immanent and transcendent.[11]

11 Karen Armstrong, *Jerusalem* (New York: Ballantine, 1996), 50–51.

One can transfer Armstrong's thoughts about the Jerusalem temple with its transcendence and immanence to Baptism observed, noted, preached near fonts, churches, chapels, or baptistries—all bearing witness that the sacred can and does enter and re-enter the world of humankind sacramentally. The transcendence of baptismal promise for life eternal with the one, true, and eternal God reaches and impacts everyday places and spaces. Proclaimers relate the sacred act of Baptism to the ordinary, the transcendent to the immanent, when they raise and answer questions such as these: "How shall I live? What will I say? What would the Christ have me do according to His Word because I am baptized?"

As another resource, the preacher could refer to the liturgical appointments for illustrations of Baptism linked to life. For example, the chrism cloth or garment put on at Baptism symbolizes that the faithful are robed in the righteousness of Christ. "Jesus, Thy blood and righteousness My beauty are, my glorious dress; Midst flaming worlds, in these arrayed, With joy shall I lift up my head."[12] As the little robe is placed on a child immediately after Baptism as a sign that a sinner is clothed in Christ's holiness, there is a prophetic hint of a confirmation robe and a funeral pall yet to come—being born, living, confessing, or dying, the baptized are robed in Christ for celebration and service. That will preach! The robe bestowed, put on in sacred space, ties the transcendent grace of God to the immanent order of mortality; life is bound to Life, the One who is the resurrection and the life. Ephesians 4:24 (part of the Epistle for Proper 14, Series B) states: "[P]ut on the new self, created after the likeness of God in true righteousness and holiness." "Put on" could be translated "wear." Wear the new self, the righteousness and holiness of Christ. A sermon example connected to such a text is literally held in hand in the form of the baptismal garment about to be put on, used, worn.

Other possible homiletical references to the baptismal liturgy abound in the pericopes; they are many in quantity and wide in scope. Beyond the water and washing/cleansing motif and the robing that invites the wearing of Christ, the christening or anointing with oil upon the head and heart works well with the election concept designating the one baptized as child of God. The sponsors' promises link well to the daily Christian commitments people have to one another, especially in the closest relationships. The baptismal confessing of the Apostles' Creed suggests the Christian stance of faith to be taken publicly. All of these may link easily with the ample variety of appointed readings, presenting a veritable mine of preaching illustrations. Such homiletical ore needs only to be dug out without dross near the font and the pulpit—only the purity of the fine sermonic gold remaining for the

12 *LSB* 563:1.

preacher's crafting. Baptism remembered in corporate worship settings links liturgy to life.

Baptism Remembered Bears Sermonic Repetition and May Seek the Support of Christian Hymnody

Why sermonic repetition? Because each reemphasis predisposes the listener to biblical repentance, true contrition, forgiveness, and genuine amendment of sinful life. Because when the sacrament is devoutly remembered, the soul and body are renewed by the power of the Holy Spirit like a plant, being well-watered to bear fruit: love, joy, peace, patience, kindness, goodness, faith, meekness, and self-control. Because as Baptism is remembered in the liturgical practice of the people, the step is more easily made toward daily life application, where the deeper meanings and concepts of the sacrament are explored in light of the events and circumstances of one's experience. The impact of Baptism remembered carries over into ordinary issues and activities as the believer is challenged to ask: What should I believe, how should I act because I am baptized in Christ? Sinful reactions give way to holy responses.

Furthermore, baptismal theology repeated from the pulpit with links to the readings of the day may also look for reference to the hymnal in the pew. A sermon theme from the Holy Gospel tethered to Baptism and illustrated by the Old Testament or Epistle may be supported by hymn selection. For example, Heb. 5:5 (part of the second reading for Lent 5, Series B) says, "You are My Son, today I have begotten You." Our Lord's own Baptism reappears in the hearer's mind, with a little pulpit prodding. Listening to these and similar words of the Father's voice at Jesus' Baptism in the Jordan, the hearer's own Baptism may be remembered. For in that sacred and eternal moment the baptized was reborn a child, a son or daughter of God, flesh giving birth to flesh, Spirit giving birth to spirit (John 3:6). The Holy Gospel for the day, Mark 10:46–52, speaks of blind Bartimaeus receiving his sight and following Jesus in the way. Similarly, sinners blind to sin receive their sight at Baptism and see the world differently; they understand they are to be in the world but not of the world. So a sermon might be crafted around Bartimaeus receiving his sight through faith at the hand of Jesus just as sinners, blind and dead in trespasses and sin, receive the visionary faith in Baptism to see the world differently—an order to be redeemed, suffering of body and soul to be relieved, salvation to be proclaimed in Jesus' name by the children of God. Add a hymn or two to highlight the issue: "Amazing grace—how sweet the sound—That saved a wretch like me! I once was lost but now am found, Was blind but now I see!"[13] The baptized walk alongside sainted Bartimaeus, along the way of Christ, sons and daughters of God, born to eternal life at the font. Or yet another hymn: "All who believe and are baptized Shall see the Lord's salvation."[14] The baptized participate in the death and resurrection of Christ; they are a new creation, washed, adopted, sighted for faith and service and evangelism that others may see, repent, believe, and know the Lord's salvation. Baptism, the Holy Sacrament, when water is poured in the name of the Holy Trinity, bears frequent pulpit repetition and linking to pericopes and hymns.

Conclusion

High on a hill in southwestern Israel a Nabatean trading post remains after centuries. The floor plan of a seventh-century church is outlined in the stone pavement at the top of the hill, clearly marking nave, aisles, and altar area. To the epistle, or southern, side of the altar is a dry three-foot-deep hole faced with tiles; it is in the shape of a cross, having four equal cross arms, each two feet wide.

"What is this?" the tourists ask over and over again. Guides explain that the cross-shaped hole in the floor is a baptismal pool into which the candidates would step and kneel to be baptized according to ancient practice. Reader, please take note: Each one washed there was baptized only once, but that Baptism has been remembered literally thousands of times and more. Each time the story is told to tourists of Christian faith, they are reminded: "I, too, am baptized, washed with faithful folk from long ago, who now stand on the other side of the heavenly Jordan." Their own washing may be brought to mind again as they walk around, reflect, even climb down into the now dusty and dry font that soaks the hallowed memory with positive, Scripture-based recollection: "I am a forgiven child of God destined forever to be with God in Christ. I am baptized. Pastors proclaim it from the pulpit, font, and table. I am baptized and with all the saints I sing, 'O happy day, when Jesus washed my sins away, O happy day!'" With faith in Christ, crucified yet risen, we remember the Baptism in our past, its impact in our present, its promise for our future. The preacher has reason to say so again and again.

---

13 *LSB* 744:1.

14 *LSB* 601:1.

Sacramental Preaching: The Lord's Supper

Kenneth W. Wieting

The Risen Christ Comes

Jesus comes! Always one with the Father and the Holy Spirit, He comes! As God's "yes" to every promise (2 Cor. 1:20), fulfiller of Moses and the Psalms and the Prophets (Luke 24), He comes. Righteous and having salvation (Zech. 9:9), with rest and refreshment for burdened souls (Matt. 11:28–30), He comes. Praised by His holy angels and the saints in glory (the Preface and Sanctus), He comes. In Word and Meal, both Giver and Gift, the risen Christ comes.

The reason His Church gathers together in worship each week is because Jesus comes. In the days between the first Easter and our Lord's ascension, the Church enjoyed the awesome privilege of communing with Jesus Christ, victor over the grave. She heard her risen Lord teach of His death and resurrection from the Scriptures. She recognized Him in the breaking of the bread (Luke 24). The presence of the risen Christ overshadowed all else. The wondrous truth is that it still does.

In the midst of two or three gathered in His name, He promises to be present yet today (Matt. 18:20). Because Jesus is the same yesterday, today, and forever (Heb. 13:8), He comes not to be served but to serve (Matt. 20:28). What He began to do and teach before He was taken up into heaven (Acts 1:2), He continues to do and teach. That is why He comes to His Bride, the Church. Jesus is still preaching good news to the poor in spirit. Jesus is still inviting sinners to come to Him for the rest and refreshment of His forgiveness.

We cannot go back to the cross. The forgiveness of sins was achieved on the cross, but it is not given out on the cross. What Jesus won on the cross, He now comes to distribute in the Sacrament, as also in the Gospel where it is preached. As Luther states:

> If now I seek the forgiveness of sins, I do not run to the cross, for I will not find it there. Nor must I hold to the suffering of Christ as Dr. Karlstadt trifles, in knowledge or remembrance, for I will not find it there either. But I will find in the sacrament or gospel the word which distributes, presents, offers, and gives to me that forgiveness which was won on the cross.[1]

That is why the Word made flesh comes to His Church! He comes to offer, present, and distribute all that He won for her on the cross. Through His chosen means, the risen Christ comes to bring life into a dying world. There can be no greater misunderstanding of the Divine Service than to deny or downplay the reality of Christ's presence and the purpose for which He is present.

A grave omission in the teaching and life of the Church in our time concerns an understanding of the presence of Christ. By this I do not mean His omnipresence, His presence everywhere. Rather, this omission concerns His saving presence, His presence in specific, concrete, forgiving ways that He has promised. This is not Jesus in our hearts whom we control with our feelings. Rather, this is Jesus who comes to us from the outside to crush our hearts with His Law and also to heal them with His grace.

This is why the risen Christ comes in the flesh to His gathered people. What happens in the Divine Service is a matter of life and death because the Lord brings life to us dying sinners. The new life He bestowed in Holy Baptism He now comes to feed and nourish. This foundational reality is why not only the liturgy but also the sermon must clearly confess and faithfully proclaim the presence of the risen Christ and the precious gifts He comes to bestow.

Regarding the article on justification, the Apology of the Augsburg Confession states quite clearly:

> So the worship and divine service of the Gospel is to receive gifts from God. On the contrary, the worship of the Law is to offer and present our gifts to God. . . . This passage, too, brings the greatest comfort, as the chief worship of the Gospel is to desire to receive the forgiveness of sins, grace, and righteousness.[2]

These treasures are received only from the risen Christ who delivers them to His people in the humble means He has chosen.

1 Martin Luther, *Against the Heavenly Prophets* (1525), AE 40:214.

2 Ap V (III) 189 [310] (*Concordia*, 130).

The Sermon Proclaims Christ Who Is Now Present

The sermon will therefore encourage and invite the hearers to receive right now what Jesus is present to bestow. That is, not only will the sermon trumpet our Lord's completed work at the cross and open tomb and not only will it trumpet the truth that this blessed release from sin is "for you" (the hearers), but the sermon will also trumpet the presence of the risen Christ to bestow His healing forgiveness in that very service through His appointed means. The sermon will proclaim how the gap between the cross and us sinners is right now, today, bridged in the water of Baptism, in the Sacrament of Christ's body and blood, in Holy Absolution, and in the proclamation of the Gospel. The sermon will not merely talk about Christ but speak the very word of Christ through which the Word made flesh is present.

The center of human history is Christ's service to us on the cross. The center of our present lives is Christ's ongoing bestowal of the fruits of His cross in Word and Sacrament. That is why nothing in all the world even comes close to the importance of gathering each week in the presence of the risen Christ to receive His gifts. The faithful do not simply hear about Christ; rather, Christ is present in His Word for their salvation (Rom. 10:17). In the audible Word He is the one who is present to teach. In His visible Word He is the one who is present to feed.[3]

In other words, the Gospel is not just history; it is history in action. It is the beautiful, gracious history of God's undeserved love in Christ poured out at the cross. But it is also the Christ of this hour because He lives. Victor over death and the grave, He lives bodily to bestow upon His Church the fruits of His cross. He lives to release us from bondage and to heal us with His gifts of forgiveness, life, and salvation. That is why He comes among us in the flesh.

The Sermon Proclaims the Problem and the Cure

Such healing is received only by the "poor in spirit," the "weary and heavy laden," the "contrite in heart." Such beggarly and burdened hearts are those who repeatedly have the mirror of God's Law held before them. The heart that can evade seeing how it really looks in the eyes of God will have no great concern for the presence of the risen Christ or receiving His gifts. That is why the Law is to be preached with total severity, from each text. Specific Law, anchored in each week's pericopes, must be carefully proclaimed. The

3 Ap XIII (VII) 5 (*Concordia*, 184).

sin of each heart is always death deep (Rom. 6:23). Our missing of God's mark of perfection is always a total miss (James 2:10). If God kept a record of sins, not one of us could stand (Ps. 130:3). Our need for God's forgiveness is constant (1 John 1:8–9).

Yet our hearts are by nature dull and apathetic concerning our desperate need as poor, miserable sinners. In the Smalcald Articles, Luther writes: "This hereditary sin is such a deep corruption of nature that no reason can understand it. Rather, it must be believed from the revelation of Scripture."[4] In love for Christ's sheep, the sermon must include a clear statement of the Law from each text. This is unpleasant work. Since the Law always accuses, this will hurt and condemn and kill those who hear it rightly.

That is why a clear and concrete proclamation of the Gospel anchored squarely in that day's texts must predominate. Only the Gospel can heal the hurt, comfort the condemned, and raise to life the one struck down by the Law. Again, this proclamation should normally flow directly from the Gospel for the day or perhaps from one of the other propers.

Important here is a plea for preaching the full, literal Gospel. That is, even as we see men mistreating Jesus on Calvary, we should not fail to see God forsaking His Son there. We should proclaim not only the blood but also the anguish.[5] The full, literal Gospel includes the profound truth that on the cross Jesus suffered under the full wrath of God as our substitute. This is the wonder of wonders. He who told His apostles to fear the one who could destroy both body and soul in hell (Matt. 10:28) Himself suffered this ultimate punishment of body and soul for us. When Jesus cried out, "It is finished," He proclaimed that all the punishment for all of our sin was paid in full.

It is this Jesus—the one who became sin for us (2 Cor. 5:21–22), the one who suffered for us (Matt. 27:46), the one whom death could not possibly hold (Acts 2:24), the one recognized in the breaking of the bread (Luke 24:35)—it is this Jesus who comes to serve us with forgiveness, life, and salvation. Risen from the grave, He comes to teach us and have Table fellowship with us, no less than He did with the Emmaus disciples (Luke 24). That is why the Lord's Supper is central to regular weekly worship and not an appendage or an occasional extra. That is also why the sermon is properly used to set the table, inviting those guests prepared to commune to receive the heavenly food Jesus comes to serve.

This preparation, of course, is not isolated from one's instruction in and confession of the faith. Ever since New Testament times, church fellowship

---

4 SA III I 3 (*Concordia*, 270).

5 Francis C. Rossow, *Preaching the Creative Gospel Creatively* (St. Louis: Concordia, 1983), 27. See all of chapter 1, pages 21–31, for an excellent discussion of the full, literal Gospel.

has been altar fellowship. The weekly preaching of and invitation to receive Christ's forgiveness in Communion goes hand in hand with faithful administration of the loving practice of close(d) Communion.

The Sermon Sets the Table

In the Large Catechism Martin Luther writes: In this sacrament Christ "offers to us the entire treasure that He has brought for us from heaven. With the greatest kindness He invites us . . . like when He says in Matthew 11:28, 'Come to Me, all who labor and are heavy laden, and I will give you rest.'" And again: "We must never think of the Sacrament as something harmful from which we had better flee, but as a pure, wholesome, comforting remedy that grants salvation and comfort. It will cure you and give you life both in soul and body."[6]

This is why our forefathers celebrated the Lord's Supper every Sunday and on other festivals when the Sacrament was offered to those who desired it after they had been examined and absolved.[7] If the risen Christ comes to us in the Sacrament with all the treasure He brought from heaven for us, then surely the sermon most properly sets the table by proclaiming this treasure. If the risen Christ brings healing medicine for body and soul in the Sacrament, then surely the sermon most lovingly sets the table by inviting sin-sick hearts to receive the medicine. The sentences of the offertory such as "Create in me a clean heart, O God" (Ps. 51:10), second this invitation. The offertory is not primarily a response to the sermon; rather, it invites us to look forward to the celebration and reception of the Sacrament,[8] where Jesus' medicine so heals our hearts. Indeed, the *sursum corda* ("Lift up your hearts") tells us that our hearts are now with the Lord who comes to us in His body and blood.

The order followed by the risen Christ is first to teach and second to feed. His Christ-centered proclamation of the Scriptures on Easter eve set the table for revealing Himself in the breaking of the bread (Luke 24). In the Emmaus account, it is not the teaching but the breaking of bread (Luke 24:30) that is the moment of revelation. For the first time a disciple of Jesus recognizes by faith that Jesus is the suffering and rising Messiah prophesied in the Old Testament.[9] The disciples emphatically restate this humble means of recognizing Jesus as they explain to others what the risen Christ gave them (Luke 24:35).

---

6 LC V 66, 68 (*Concordia*, 438).

7 AC XXV 1 (*Concordia*, 50).

8 Luther D. Reed, *The Lutheran Liturgy* (Philadelphia: Fortress, 1947), 308.

9 Arthur A. Just Jr., *Luke*, 2 vols. (St. Louis: Concordia, 1996), 2:1006–7.

At Emmaus, the disciples invited Jesus to be their guest, but the roles were instantly reversed as Jesus assumed the position of host.[10] This alone, along with the meal's solemnity as a reclining banquet, suggests that the breaking of the bread at Emmaus must be viewed as the eucharistic meal, one taken at the table of the Lord.[11] Since it was the risen Christ who personally set their hearts burning by opening the Old Testament Scriptures to them, and since He was present with them and teaching them for some time, it was clearly according to His will that the recognition did not come until the breaking of the bread. Shouldn't our preaching likewise set our people's hearts on fire prior to the Holy Meal?

This is astounding testimony to the central place of this gift. God in the flesh, fresh from the grave, victor over sin, death, and Satan, with authority over all things, chooses to reveal Himself in the breaking of the bread. There is teaching followed by eating, eating at which Jesus is the host. His disappearance after being recognized conveyed the nature of His ongoing sacramental presence in the breaking of the bread. He is still there with His Church, in the flesh yet unseen.

This is why the order of the liturgy has been first Word and then Meal down through the centuries. It is no accident that as the risen Christ comes among His people today, He still comes first preaching Himself and then giving Himself to be recognized and received in the breaking of the bread. His Word sets the table for His Supper. The proclamation of Christ is followed by food for the journey, that is, by the provision of His very body and very blood for the forgiveness of sins.

This is exactly how the Holy Spirit led the early church persistently to hold fast to Christ after Pentecost. The church in Jerusalem continually devoted herself to the teaching of the apostles, to the common participation in the Eucharist wherein the risen Christ was recognized, and to "the prayers," which framed the service of these gifts to the baptized and flowed from the service of these gifts to the baptized (Acts 2:42). While our confessions object to using the phrase "the breaking of the bread" to refer to receiving only one kind in the Sacrament (i.e., the body of Christ), they do not object to seeing it as the Lord's Supper.[12]

In the deepest of mysteries, the risen Lord continued to come to His Church to teach her and then to feed her in the breaking of the bread. He was received with devotion, with steadfast perseverance, where He had promised to be present. The ascension of Jesus Christ had not left His Church

---

10 Eugene LaVerdiere, *Dining in the Kingdom of God* (Chicago: Liturgy Training Publications, 1994), 169.

11 LaVerdiere, *Dining in the Kingdom of God*, 170.

12 Ap XXII 7 (*Concordia*, 209).

with leftovers and sentimental tokens. He was present with them at table in a way that was no longer physically visible but that now included the heavenly food of His holy body and His holy blood. What He began to do and teach before He was taken up He now continued to do and teach in this new way.

Later, when it became impossible to meet together daily, the breaking of bread was celebrated on the first day of the week (Acts 20:7). This weekly devotion to the presence of Jesus by His gathered church continued down through the centuries. There were abuses and misunderstanding—there always are. But the reality is "until the sixteenth century, we have no evidence of a significant Christian community that did not celebrate the Eucharist on the Lord's Day."[13] In this regard,

> the mightiest weapon which the Reformation employed against Rome was not Rome's errors, but Rome's truths. It professed to make no discoveries, to find no un-heard of interpretations; but taking the Scriptures in that very sense to which the greatest of her writers assented, uncovering the Law and the Gospel of God she retained . . . the Reformation took into its heart the life-stream of sixteen centuries.[14]

This included sixteen centuries of receiving the twin peaks of the Divine Service, first the word of Christ, then the meal of Christ. That is why the Lutheran Confessions trumpet so clearly that same devotion to the breaking of the bread found in Acts 2:42. They state:

> We do not abolish the Mass, but religiously keep and defend it. Masses are celebrated among us every Lord's Day and on other festivals. The Sacrament is offered to those who wish to use it, after they have been examined and absolved. And the usual public ceremonies are observed, the series of lessons, of prayers, vestments, and other such things.[15]

Sasse expresses it rightly when he writes: "No Christian of the Reformation, apart from the followers of the Reformation at Zurich and Geneva, could conceive of a Sunday divine service without the Lord's Supper, just as already in the church of the New Testament there was no Lord's Day without the Lord's Supper."[16] Elsewhere Sasse states that the Lord's Supper

---

13 Paul Marshall, "The Little Easter and the Great Sunday," *Liturgy* 1, no. 2 (1980): 28; quoted in *LWHP*, 34.

14 Charles Porterfield Krauth, *The Conservative Reformation and Its Theology* (repr., St. Louis: Concordia, 2007), 203.

15 Ap XXIV (XII) 1 (*Concordia*, 220).

16 Hermann Sasse, *We Confess the Sacraments*, trans. Norman Nagel (St. Louis: Concordia, 1985), 99.

stands at the center of the Divine Service; in fact, it is the real Divine Service. It is out of the Lord's Supper that the liturgy grew.[17]

Where the Supper Is Absent

As one preaches and teaches about the gift of the Lord's Supper in the Divine Service, is it proper to preach on the Sacrament when it is not offered at that service? In the Preface to the Small Catechism, Luther responds, "Preach in such a way that by their own will, without our law, they will urge themselves and, as it were, compel us pastors to administer the Sacrament."[18]

To this end, an encouraging restoration is taking place within the congregations of the LCMS in recent years. In the spring of 1999, all pastors of the LCMS were surveyed concerning the opportunity to receive the Lord's Supper. More than 45 percent (2,494) of active LCMS parish pastors responded to the survey, with geographic distribution proportionate to Synod membership. Of the pastors responding, 495, or 19.8 percent, indicated that the opportunity to receive the Lord's Supper was made available at each Sunday service and other regular weekly services. Nearly half of these pastors (241) had recovered this opportunity within the last five years. In addition, another 512 (20 percent) indicated that they were at that time studying the Sacrament of Holy Communion with their congregations to lead them in the recovery of the Lord's Supper in each weekly Divine Service.[19] These statistics describe a very significant restoration in providing the opportunity for God's people to commune when they come for regular weekly worship, in making available the Sacrament as the risen Lord comes to bestow His gifts in the Divine Service.

Textual Handles for Setting the Table

Many images and events in the Scriptures provide an entrée to proclaiming the benefits of the Lord's Supper. Moses and Aaron and the elders eating and drinking in the presence of God (Exod. 24:9–11), the wedding banquets, the changing of water into wine (John 2), Jesus eating with Zacchaeus and other sinners (Luke 19:5–9) and with His disciples before His crucifixion and after His resurrection, all suggest the heavenly feast that Christ the Bridegroom provides. The multiplying of a few loaves to feed 5,000 (John 6) and the provision of manna in the wilderness (Exod. 16:3–4) suggest heavenly food for pilgrims on a journey.

17 Hermann Sasse, *Scripture and the Church: Selected Essays of Herman Sasse*, ed. Jeffrey J. Kloha and Ronald R. Feuerhahn (St. Louis: Concordia Seminary, 1995), 11.

18 SC Preface 22 (*Concordia*, 315).

19 *Supplement to the Reporter—Prepared by the Commission on Worship* 4, no. 4 (Fall 1999): 3.

Since the reception of the Sacrament is a common proclamation of the Lord's death until He returns (1 Cor. 11:26), texts that speak of proclaiming Christ ("But who do you say that I am?" [Matt. 16:15]) or of His death (John 12:20–33) or of His second coming readily suggest the proclamation of the Sacrament. The eschatological emphasis in Advent and at the end of the church year is intimately related to the heavenly food with which Jesus feeds His Church.

Setting the table is also possible by means of the liturgy (the Salutation, Sursum Corda, Sanctus, Agnus Dei, etc.) and the propers of the day. The preaching of and invitation to the Sacrament should not merely be repeated each week with mantra-like phrases such as "Word and Sacrament." Rather, it should flow from the concrete words and thoughts of the appointed readings. The following are suggestions for proclaiming the Lord's Supper connected to particular statements of Law and Gospel from four texts. (See the appendix for brief paragraphs highlighting the proclamation of the Lord's Supper from additional texts.)

Proper 22 (October 2–8), Series A

Matt. 21:33–46; Phil. 3:4b–14; Isa. 5:1–7

"We Have an Extraordinary Landlord"

Specific Law—God had difficulty with His people. They were not content with His care. They treated holy things as if they were common. They grumbled and griped and grabbed after other gods. They consistently rejected the prophets God sent them. The tenants acted like owners and refused to give God His due. God still has difficulty with His renters today. The new Israel, Christ's Church, is still inclined to grumble and gripe and grab after other gods. We also are inclined to see ourselves as the owners. We also are inclined to take God off His throne and put ourselves on.

Helpful Context—It was Tuesday of Holy Week! In about forty-eight hours, the Jewish leaders would do to Jesus what He described the renters doing to the son of the landlord.

Specific Gospel—God sent His Son, not because He was foolish but because He was forgiving. While the renters were scheming to kill the son and illegitimately claim his inheritance, God was planning to sacrifice His Son and give them the inheritance. The Son came not to cast the former tenants out of the vineyard, but to include others in the vineyard. The Landlord's long-suffering, forgiving love was so extraordinary that He put His own Son on the cross to give us the vineyard. Instead of bringing us to a wretched end, God brought Christ to our wretched end and now gives us His wondrous inheritance through faith. We have an extraordinary Landlord.

Setting the Table—When God comes looking for good grapes in you, He finds only good grapes. Why? Because from the winepress of His wrath against Christ, God has pressed a new vintage of sweet wine that heals your wounds and makes your heart new. By the grace of God, the final sending of His Son still goes on today. The crucified and risen Christ has come into our midst again this day to give us His body to eat and His blood to drink for our forgiveness. He comes with the full approval of our extraordinary Landlord, and He gives only good fruit.

Lent 3, Series B

John 2:13–22 (23–25); 1 Cor. 1:18–31; Exod. 20:1–17
"The Cleansing of the Temple"

Specific Law—When Jesus cleansed the temple, He expressed displeasure with a convenient user-friendly system that seemed to please everyone else. What raised His loving, sinless anger was His intense concern for pure worship of God the Father. When God meets man, nothing is to rob the church of the purpose for which God comes among His people. Our sin is the same, a tendency to substitute other things for true worship.

Helpful Context—The disciples fear trouble and speak of Jesus what was written of the Messiah in Psalm 69:9: "For zeal for Your house has consumed me . . ." Jesus spoke of the destruction of the temple and raising it again in three days—meaning the temple of His body. Three years later, during Holy Week, Jesus cleansed the temple again.

Specific Gospel—On Friday of Holy Week, the sign Jesus had spoken of was in full view. The destruction of the temple of His body was in progress. He who swung a whip in the temple received the sting of the whip on the temple of His body. He who poured out the money in our text poured out His blood on the cross. On that day the only coins flying about the temple were the thirty pieces of silver Judas flung into the sanctuary. He who drove out the lambs in our text was Himself sacrificed as the Lamb of God on Good Friday.

Setting the Table—He who turned over the tables in our text, set the table with the new covenant of His own body and His own blood on Maundy Thursday. He did raise the temple of His body on the third day, and the risen Christ is still in God's house today. He has come into our midst with all of the zeal He had in the Jerusalem temple. His intense concern for the right worship of God has not lessened. His every thought is on us and on our need. He comes to us not with whip in hand, but with heavenly food in hand! He comes to overturn all of Satan's accusations and give us peace by giving us Himself.

Easter 4, Series C

John 10:22–30; Rev. 7:9–17; Acts 20:17–35; Psalm 23
"Good Shepherd Sunday"

Specific Law—By nature we listen to the wrong voices, including our own. By nature we think that Christianity is primarily a religion of doing or morality or feelings, not of hearing the voice of the Good Shepherd. By nature we accuse Jesus of being unclear in what He says, just as the Jews in the temple accused Him. We complicate what God has made crystal clear. We keep on asking questions He has already answered. Our ears itch to hear that it is our doing or our decision or our desire that makes the blood of Jesus work for us.

Specific Gospel—Thank God this is not what the voice of the Good Shepherd says to us. Instead of talking about our hold on God, He lovingly bears witness to God's hold on us through His Word. "[My sheep] listen to My voice," Jesus said. "No one will snatch them out of My hand. No one is able to snatch them out of the Father's hand. I and the Father are one" (John 10:16, 28–30). What pure and pointed Gospel! The Son who is one with the Father took on human hands for us. The hands of the God-man were spiked to the cross on Pilate's watch. When they had done all that was written about Him, they took Him down from the tree and laid Him in a tomb (Acts 13:28–30). But God raised Him from the dead. Those scarred hands moved with life again. It is His hands that hold you and will not let you go.

Setting the Table—It is He who leads you in the paths of righteousness. It is He who will comfort you in the valley of death's dark shadow land. This very day it is He who prepares a table before you in the presence of your enemies. On His table He places His very body and His very blood under the bread and wine for your forgiveness. Your enemies—Satan, the world, and your sinful nature—are right here too. But they cannot stop Him from restoring your soul. Surely goodness and mercy will follow you all the days of your life, and you will dwell in the house of the Lord forever.

Proper 4 (May 29–June 4), Series C

Luke 7:1–10; Gal. 1:1–12; 1 Kings 8:22–24, 27–29, 41–43

"Are You Worthy of the Lord's Help?"

Specific Law—The Jewish elders thought love for the nation and building the synagogue made the centurion worthy of Jesus' help. Such thinking is very destructive to the Christian faith, and it is still with us today. It reasons that someone is worthy of God's help who is kind and charitable toward the church or community, someone who is honest and does his best. Thoughts of personal worthiness for God's help negatively affect our prayers, our hunger for forgiveness, our contentment in suffering, and so much more. The thinking that God should change things because we deserve it is no small matter. It is idolatry.

Helpful Context—The Gospel records a startling difference in perspective concerning personal worthiness for the assistance of Jesus. Contrary to the Jewish elders, the centurion voiced a far different attitude: "Lord . . . I am not worthy to have You come under my roof" (Luke 7:6).

Specific Gospel—Jesus delights in the faith of this man! He is amazed by the faith of a heart that recognizes its unworthiness and yet expects healing from the authority of His Word. In our text, Jewish elders say nice things of the centurion. On a different day, Jewish elders will say evil things about Jesus. Rather than saying He built us our synagogue, they accused Jesus of threatening to tear down the temple. Rather than saying He loves our nation, they said He is disturbing our nation. It is better that one man die for the sake of the people.

And die He did, having been made sin for us. He died as one so evil that He wasn't worthy to go under the Father's roof. The Father cast Him out as He bore our sin. As our substitute, Jesus suffered the wrath of God. He gave Himself for all sinners who needed rescue.

Setting the Table—Are you worthy of Jesus' help today? Martin Luther considered that question concerning the gift that the risen Christ comes to serve us today, the Lord's Supper. He answered: "That person is truly worthy and well prepared who has faith in these words, 'Given and shed for you for the forgiveness of sins.' "[20] Are you here today as one who knows you have it bad with sin and yet who trusts Jesus to give you life by the authority of His Word? Are you here as one who believes that you are unworthy to have Jesus come under the roof of your mouth with His very body and very blood? Do you nonetheless trust the authority of His Word to give you forgiveness in this way as He has promised? Then by Jesus' own evaluation, you have great faith, faith that receives the greatest healing of all.

Appendix: Additional Suggestions for Setting the Table

Mark 15:1–6; Zech. 9:9 (Sunday of the Passion, Series B)—In this text the Lord's Supper can be proclaimed by way of the Sanctus. On Palm Sunday Jesus came humbly in the flesh. He came to give a kingly ransom for us sinners on the cross. He still is King of kings, and He still comes humbly in the flesh today to forgive us. That's why we greet Him with our glad hosannas in Holy Communion each Lord's Day. "Rejoice greatly, O daughter of Zion! . . . Behold, your King is coming to you; righteous and having salvation is He" (Zech. 9:9).

Luke 9:28–36 (The Transfiguration of Our Lord, Series C)—While God has not let us see Jesus with our eyes, He has opened our ears to receive His Word in faith and our mouths to receive His body and His blood for

20 *Luther's Small Catechism*, 31.

forgiveness. The risen Christ who is present with us today will take you to be with Him forever. That is why He comes among us with the fruits of His death. That is why He designed the proclamation of His death from our very eating of this bread and drinking of this cup (1 Cor. 11:26). What Moses and Elijah and Jesus spoke of on the holy mountain, we continue to receive and proclaim today.

Luke 10:25–37 (Proper 10 [July 10–16], Series C—The Good Samaritan)—In this text the Lord's Supper can be proclaimed by way of the Samaritan's compassion, a word used only of God in the New Testament, and by way of the provision at the inn until the Samaritan returns. Our compassionate Savior has found us broken, dying sinners, washed us in Baptism, and bound us up, pouring in the oil and wine of His forgiveness. He has taken us into His Church and there provided all of the strengthening food and healing medicine we need until He returns.

Luke 1:26–38 (Advent 4, Series B, and The Annunciation of Our Lord)—In this text, the Lord's Supper can be proclaimed by way of verse 37, "nothing [literally, no word] will be impossible with God." The word that caused Mary to conceive the Christ Child in her womb was not impossible with God. What God said, He did in the virgin's womb! The risen Christ comes in the flesh today, placing His body and His blood under the bread and wine for our forgiveness. What God says, He does! No word is impossible with God!

John 1:29–42a (Epiphany 2, Series A)—The Lord's Supper can be proclaimed in this text by way of the Agnus Dei. "Where are You staying?" the two disciples asked Him. Jesus said, "Come and you will see" (John 1:38–39). "Where are You now?" we ask. "Come and eat. Come and drink," Jesus responds. The liturgy gives us that very answer as it leads us to sing to the risen Christ as we come to receive the Sacrament, "Lamb of God, You take away the sin of the world; have mercy on us . . . grant us peace."

Preaching through the Seasons of the Church Year

Charles A. Gieschen

Already in the act of creation recorded in Genesis 1, God established an order for the passage of time. He created the patterns of days, weeks, and years as He set our galaxy in place. This patterned order of time has been observed with various rituals among humans over the centuries. Some of these rituals are daily (e.g., meals, labor, prayers, rest), some are weekly (e.g., public worship, day of rest), and others are annual (e.g., birthdays, anniversaries, festivals, holidays, holy days). It is clear from Holy Scripture that God desires that His people observe the passage of our limited time within the broader context of His deeds throughout time. Ancient Israel was given a pattern for observing daily temple worship, weekly Sabbaths, and annual festivals.[1] Observances such as the weekly Sabbath and the annual festival of the Passover helped the faithful of Israel to understand their daily lives in light of the mighty creative and redemptive acts of God that have eternal significance.[2] This reflection on the gracious work of God throughout time sustained faith, empowered love, and inspired hope during the moment-by-moment struggles of sinners living in a fallen world.

Most of the Christian Church, influenced in part by ancient Israel, follows an annual pattern for the observance of time that helps us to view our daily life continually in light of God's mightiest redemptive act: the incarnation, life, death, resurrection, and return of Jesus Christ.[3] This annual pattern, called the church year, is constructed around the commemoration of the resurrection of Christ each Sunday and each year.[4] George M. Bass,

1 Such guidance is found in Exodus 20–40 and Leviticus; see also Roland de Vaux, *Ancient Israel* (New York: McGraw, 1961).

2 See Patrick D. Miller, "The Human Sabbath: A Study in Deuteronomic Theology," *The Princeton Seminary Bulletin* 6 (1985): 81–97.

3 A review of the origins of the Christian year will not be addressed here; see especially Thomas J. Talley, *The Origins of the Liturgical Year* (New York: Pueblo, 1986).

4 For a general description of the church year as observed in many LCMS congregations, see James L. Brauer, "The Church Year," in *LWHP*, 146–74. The discussion below will follow

a strong advocate for the interrelationship of the church year and preaching, pointedly states: "Easter is the source of the Christian year, the most important festival and the reality from which all the other festivals, seasons, and liturgical details derive their meaning."[5] In addition to the observance of the Resurrection of Our Lord that commences the "Great 50 Days of Easter," other major events from the life of Jesus form the basis for the remaining seasons of the church year: Advent, Christmas, Epiphany, Lent, and Pentecost. Furthermore, many denominations observe various other sacred days that commemorate particular saints (e.g., St. Peter and St. Paul, Apostles) or special events (e.g., the Reformation). As the seasons of nature progress from death to life to growth to harvest, so the church year mirrors these patterns as it focuses on Christ in its seasons. Secular time becomes sacred.[6]

Certain portions of the liturgy—the propers—change with the days and seasons of the church year to reflect these specific events from the life of Christ (e.g., Introit, Collect of the Day, hymns, and lections). Because of the relationship between the liturgy and the sermon, there is a close relationship between preaching and the church year. Lectionary readings, especially the Holy Gospel, are selected to coincide with the observance of the church year. Therefore, pastors who turn to a lectionary for their sermon texts will be preaching on some theme that is linked with the church year.[7] Sometimes, however, pastors are more sensitive to the church year in selecting the hymns than in preaching on one of the readings for the day. Furthermore, alternative patterns for worship, be they "contemporary worship," sermon series, or programmatic emphases, may lead pastors to weaken or abandon the church year structure. This study will demonstrate that sensitivity to the themes and cadence of the church year assists the pastor in proclaiming sermons that are Christocentric and consistent with the proclamation of the rest of the service.

---

the structure, nomenclature, and lectionary of the church year found in *LSB*. The content of this chapter, however, is also applicable to those who use other variations of the church year. For a discussion of the centrality of Sunday for Christian worship as the "Lord's Day" and its relationship to the resurrection, see Jean Danielou, *The Bible and the Liturgy* (Notre Dame, IN: University of Notre Dame Press, 1956), 242–61.

5 George M. Bass, *The Renewal of Liturgical Preaching* (Minneapolis: Augsburg, 1967), 30. This volume arises out of the liturgical renewal movement within Lutheran circles during the middle part of the twentieth century. Although dated and somewhat polemical in tone, it contains many valuable insights on preaching within the context of the church year.

6 See the helpful discussion by Arthur A. Just Jr., "Liturgical Renewal in the Parish," in *LWHP*, 32.

7 For a compilation of the historic one-year lectionary and other older lectionaries, see Paul Nesper, *Biblical Texts*, 2nd ed. (Minneapolis: Augsburg, 1961), 207–442.

First, sensitivity to the church year will assist the pastor in proclaiming Christocentric sermons that integrate the past and future work of Christ with His present sacramental life in the midst of the church. As stated above, the focus of the church year is nothing less than the life of Christ. The Christ who lived, died, rose, and is coming again is the object of faith from the moment of our rebirth to our death: "Let us . . . [look] to Jesus, the founder and perfecter of our faith, who for the joy that was set before Him endured the cross, despising the shame, and is seated at the right hand of the throne of God" (Heb. 12:1–2). The church year spotlights the life and words of Christ so that the catechetical core of Christianity is repeatedly set forth before the faithful on an annual basis. Each year Christ's return, incarnation, birth, Baptism, miracles, teaching, death, resurrection, and ascension are trumpeted out for those who have ears to hear and eyes to see. Nothing is more important for the life of the church than the life of Christ.

This focus on Christ's life during the church year, however, is no mere historical exercise. We cannot go back in time to these events that are the heart of the Gospel. Christ's historical life, therefore, is the annual drama that unfolds anew during the church year in order that the Holy Spirit founds and forms the church in this Christ who continues to be present with forgiveness, life, and salvation. The church year continually testifies that these *one-time* historical events of Christ's life are *timeless* by weekly proclaiming them as the events that define the Christ who is present *in our time*, washing away sin in Holy Baptism, absolving transgressions through the proclamation of the Gospel, and feeding the faithful with the forgiveness found in His flesh and blood. Gustaf Wingren affirms that Christ's *past* salvific actions are mediated to our *present*:

> But we are present in that series of [Christ's] actions *now*, for they did not just take place in the past, but are now taking place since the Word comes to us and brings everything with it. Christ is in the Word, and approaches us in preaching with his work, just in that regular preaching that treats one "part" [of Christ's life during the church year] after another.[8]

This Christocentric focus not only occurs during the first half of the church year but also continues through the second half. Typical descriptions of the Sundays after Pentecost depict it as a shift from the life of *Christ* to the life of *the Church*.[9] It is preferable, however, to see this season as the continuation of the life of Christ in His Body, the Church. Christ's life and presence

---

8 Gustaf Wingren, *The Living Word: A Theological Study of Preaching and the Church* (Philadelphia: Muhlenberg, 1960), 198.

9 Following the lead of *LW*, Brauer and others call the Sundays after Pentecost "The Time of the Church"; see *LWHP*, 149.

on earth continues after the ascension and Pentecost. The life of Christ and that of the Church should not be divided or separated; Christ is our life. Those who have been united with Christ in Holy Baptism have been crucified with Him and now share in His cruciform life and resurrection victory (Rom. 6:1–11). Patrick Cowley acknowledges this unity of the life of Christ depicted in the church year with the life of Christ lived out in the church of each age in these poignant words:

> The Church is ever reliving its Lord's life. It is always experiencing his sufferings, crucifixion, resurrection, and glorification. The whole cycle of Christ's life is daily, hourly, being reproduced in the Church's life, because there is a very real sense in which the Church relives its Lord's incarnate life.[10]

Therefore, sermons sensitive to this Christocentric pattern of the entire church year will proclaim annually "the essential fullness of the Christian faith in the person of Jesus Christ."[11]

Second, sensitivity to the church year will assist the pastor in proclaiming sermons that are consistent with the proclamation of the rest of the service. Some pastors may fear that sensitivity to the church year in preaching will control the sermon content more than the biblical text, or it will not serve the spiritual needs of the congregation. Such fears are unfounded. The content of a biblical text and a church year theme are not in conflict; church year themes are drawn and proclaimed from the realities revealed by central biblical texts, especially from the four Gospels. Sensitivity to the themes and cadence of the church year does not mean that the preacher sets the biblical text aside to develop a church year theme, but that he faithfully proclaims truths from a specific biblical text that are harmonious with the proclamation of the rest of the service (e.g., hymns, lectionary, and propers). To use a musical analogy: though the sermon is a solo, the song that it sings should blend with the concert sung before and after it. Furthermore, sensitivity to the church year helps shape preaching so that congregations are not held captive by the idiosyncratic concerns of particular pastors, but have a faithful and balanced proclamation of Christian doctrine and life.

This sensitivity to the church year will be cultivated in the pages that follow by reviewing the basic themes of each of the major seasons as drawn from the lectionary readings and expressed in the worship of the church.[12]

---

10 Patrick Cowley, *Advent: Its Liturgical Significance* (London: Faith Press, 1960), 13.

11 Bass, *Renewal of Liturgical Preaching*, 26.

12 Harry F. Baughman advocates carefully studying all the propers for the day, summarizing their content, and using such thematic summaries in the sermon; see *Preaching from the Propers* (Philadelphia: Board of Publication of The United Lutheran Church in America, 1949), 17. Resources that assist in this task include Luther D. Reed, *The Lutheran Liturgy*

This discussion of the seasons will proceed chronologically from Advent through Pentecost. Some concrete examples of how these themes can be proclaimed from the readings will be offered. Most of these examples will use the Holy Gospel lection because of its dominant liturgical and homiletical role in expressing the church year themes. In addition to examining these primary seasons with their festivals, the relationship of various other sacred days in the church year to preaching will also be addressed.

Advent

It is very typical to hear discussion of the "three advents" of Christ during this season: His first coming as the Babe of Bethlehem, His second coming as the returning King, and His continual coming in Word and Sacrament. Often it is the first coming that receives emphasis during this season, even though Christ's birth is not a prominent focus of this season until the Fourth Sunday of Advent. Bass states that the common understanding that Advent is primarily a season to prepare for Christmas is "one of the most widespread liturgical misconceptions in the church."[13] Such an understanding is influenced in part by the fact that the consumer-oriented media of our world begins bombarding us unabashedly with the "Christmas holiday" six to eight weeks before its arrival. The view that Advent is primarily a preparation for Christmas instead of Christ's return sometimes leads pastors to view the season as one of imitating ancient Israel waiting for the Messiah as we wait to celebrate Jesus' birthday. Cowley offers this corrective:

> Advent is not a season of Christian make-believe during which Church people pretend that they are back in the Before Christ centuries, and hopefully awaiting and powerfully pleading for the Messiah to come as Deliverer and Savior as once Israel waited and prayed. Instead during Advent, and gladly remembering that he has come and conquered, Church people look to the end of all earthly time, and pray for the complete accomplishment of his redemptive act when he shall be indeed King of kings, Lord of lords, and Master of all.[14]

Thus, despite the fact that Advent begins the church year and leads into Christmas, it also has strong thematic ties to the last three Sundays of the church year that focus on the end times and Christ's return.

Christ's second coming is the focus of the memorable collects of this season that are built around the dynamic ancient prayer, "Stir up":

(Philadelphia: Muhlenberg, 1947), and Barry L. Bobb and Hans Boehringer, *Proclaim: A Guide for Planning Liturgy and Music*, 2nd ed. (St. Louis: Concordia, 1994). Reed's *Lutheran Liturgy* is particularly helpful for the propers and lectionary used in *TLH*, while the *Proclaim* volumes are meant to be used with the three-year lectionary of *LW*.

13 Bass, *Renewal of Liturgical Preaching*, 37.

14 Cowley, *Advent*, 27.

> Stir up Your power, O Lord, and come . . .
>
> Stir up our hearts, O Lord, to make ready the way of Your only-begotten Son . . .
>
> Stir up your power, O Lord, and come and help us by Your might . . .[15]

These prayers are founded upon some of the pleas in the Psalms: "Stir up Yourself, and awake to my vindication, to my cause, my God and my Lord" (35:23 NKJV) and "Stir up Your strength, and come and save us!" (80:2 NKJV). In the context of Advent, these prayers are not pitiful pleas of desperation. We confidently pray, sing, and preach about Christ's coming again in light of His victorious resurrection and ascension.

As Advent focuses on the second coming of Christ, it gives attention to the importance of *readiness* for this coming by faithfully receiving the Christ who is present and coming to us now. Note especially the emphasis on God helping our readiness for the coming of His Son in the collect for the Second Sunday in Advent: "Stir up our hearts, O Lord, to make ready the way of Your only-begotten Son." This readiness and how it is accomplished is visible also in these lectionary readings from Advent:

> Therefore, stay awake, for you do not know on what day your Lord is coming. . . . Therefore you also must be ready, for the Son of Man is coming at an hour you do not expect. (Matt. 24:42, 44; Advent 1, Series A)
>
> May the Lord make you increase and abound in love . . . so that He may establish your hearts blameless in holiness before our God and Father, at the coming of our Lord Jesus with all His saints. (1 Thess. 3:12–13; Advent 1, Series C)
>
> May the God of peace Himself sanctify you completely, and may your whole spirit and soul and body be kept blameless at the coming of our Lord Jesus Christ. He who calls you is faithful; He will surely do it. (1 Thess. 5:23–24; Advent 3, Series B)

Although there are often attempts to distance the preparatory nature of Advent from that of Lent, there is value in seeing that both seasons have traditionally been penitential seasons.[16] The call to prepare through repentance

---

15 These are the opening phrases of the Collects for the First, Second, and Fourth Sundays in Advent. See *LSB: Altar Book*, 553, 555, 557.

16 One of the very visual attempts to distance these seasons, especially in Roman Catholicism after Vatican II (1962–65), has been the widespread adoption of blue as the liturgical color of Advent in place of the traditional violet, which is also the color of Lent. The continued use of violet in both of these seasons has value in that it signals their inherent unity as penitential seasons of prayerful spiritual preparation.

is sounded by John the Baptist through the Gospel reading for the Second Sunday in Advent: "Repent, for the kingdom of heaven is at hand" (Matt. 3:2; Series A). John the Baptist becomes a model for Advent preaching as he both announces the imminent coming of Christ and confronts sinners in a refreshingly direct manner so that they become ready through repentance and faith. This theme is expressed well in a hymn that often is used on the Second Sunday in Advent:

> Then cleansed be ev'ry life from sin;
> Make straight the way for God within,
> And let us all our hearts prepare
> For Christ to come and enter there.[17]

In addition to the readiness theme, a second primary theme of this season is *eager expectation* for the coming of Christ. Unlike the end of the church year when the woeful judgment theme is sounded, Advent usually speaks of Christ's coming with joyful anticipation: "Rejoice greatly, O daughter of Zion! Shout aloud, daughter of Jerusalem! Behold, your king is coming to you; righteous and having salvation is He" (Zech. 9:9; Introit, Advent 1). This heightened expectation, which has a strong element of joy, sets the services, including the preaching, of Advent in stark contrast to the end of the church year or the preparatory season of Lent. Not only did Christ come the first time, but He accomplished salvation. This leads us to wait for Christ's coming in the confident joy of Easter.[18] One of the ancient and most prominent hymns of this season sounds this theme in its refrain: "Rejoice! Rejoice! Emmanuel Shall come to thee, O Israel!"[19] This theme is especially strong during the Third Sunday in Advent, which marks a shift from the readiness themes of the first two Sundays to the joy that comes with the eager expectation of Christ's return.[20] Note how the Epistle reading reflects this focus: "Rejoice in the Lord always; again I will say, Rejoice. Let your reasonableness be known to everyone. The Lord is at hand" (Phil. 4:4–5; Advent 3, Series C).

There is a subtle shift during Advent from a strong focus on readiness and eager expectation of Christ's second coming to a focus on celebrating His first coming by receiving His coming to us now in Word and Sacrament. This shift is visible in the Fourth Sunday in Advent when the Holy Gospel focuses on prenativity narratives (Luke 1:26–38, Series B; Luke 1:39–45

---

17 Charles Coffin, "On Jordan's Bank the Baptist's Cry," *LSB* 344:2.

18 Cowley, *Advent*, 33–34.

19 "Oh, Come, Oh, Come, Emmanuel," *LSB* 357 refrain.

20 The Third Sunday in Advent and the Fourth Sunday in Lent both relax some of the traditional preparatory themes because the season is more than half over and the joy of the upcoming celebration is anticipated. Some congregations observe the ancient custom of changing the paraments from violet to rose for these two Sundays.

[46–56], Series C; and Matt. 1:18–25, Series A). The readiness and expectation mount during the weeks of Advent until one celebrates the first coming and receives Christ as He comes in the Christ Mass on the Nativity of Our Lord. It is especially on the Fourth Sunday in Advent that one's preaching turns to readiness and expectation concerning the upcoming celebration of our Lord's nativity.

Despite its brevity, one of the oldest and most profound Christian prayers is the stark plea: "Come, Lord Jesus!"[21] This heartfelt imperative encapsulates the essence of the Advent season: readiness and eager expectation for the coming of Christ, especially His *parousia* or coming in glory on the Last Day. Bass summarizes the cadence of the season in this manner:

> The Sundays in Advent are a liturgical method of annually opening the Bible to those parts which proclaim the advent of our Lord. They are the season of Maranatha, "Come, Lord Jesus," pointing to his presence and the promise of his coming again even as his first coming is remembered. They do lead the people of God to one day, the Festival of the Incarnation, and to Christ's Mass, when all three themes are celebrated. They make Advent into a protracted prayer that reaches its greatest intensity just before Christmas: "Come quickly, Lord Jesus."[22]

Christmas

Although Christmas was not observed during the first three centuries of Christianity, it has become one of the primary festivals of the church year and even rivals Easter in worldwide recognition because of its widespread observance as a holiday. It is the secular celebration of Christmas, however, that poses one of the biggest challenges for the Christian observance. There is a tendency in wider society to focus on the sentimentality of Christ's birth for one short day. Focus on the incarnation and the connection between the birth and death of Christ are almost nonexistent in such celebrations. Christmas decorations begin coming down on December 26 and the world moves on to its New Year's Eve revelry.

There are four aspects of this season that are to be proclaimed as part of its Christian observance. First, the birth of Christ is to be proclaimed within the wider context of Christ's work for the salvation of all humanity. The church year is a reminder that Christmas is not a disconnected holy day, but a day and season that draw significance from their relationship to other

21 See Rev. 22:20 and 1 Cor. 16:22. The liturgical use of this prayer in the earliest Jewish Christian congregations is supported by the fact that Paul transliterates the Aramaic form of this prayer into Greek, rather than translating it. See also Oscar Cullman, *Early Christian Worship* (Philadelphia: Westminster Press, 1953), 13–14.

22 Bass, *Renewal of Liturgical Preaching*, 49.

days and seasons, especially those observing Christ's death for our sins and His resurrection for our victory over death. So also as we proclaim from the familiar narrative of Christ's birth in the Gospel of Luke, it is important to note that this birth narrative is part of a broader story that is dominated by the Passion and resurrection narratives. This is especially important for Christmas Eve sermons, since there are often more visitors, from various religious and secular backgrounds, in this service than any other during the church year. Bass properly notes: "The full significance of the incarnation cannot be perceived, nor can the proper interpretation of Christmas be preached, when Christmas overshadows Easter. Without the cross the church would never have remembered Christ's cradle."[23] Christ's birth, therefore, should be proclaimed in the context of His death and resurrection as well as our predicament of sin and death. Paul Gerhardt certainly does this in his great Christmas hymn:

Christ, from heav'n to us descending
And in love our race befriending;
In our need His help extending,
Saved us from the wily foe.

Jacob's star in all its splendor
Beams with comfort sweet and tender,
Forcing Satan to surrender,
Breaking all the pow'rs of hell.

From the bondage that oppressed us,
From sin's fetters that possessed us,
From the grief that sore distressed us,
We, the captives, now are free.[24]

Second, the miraculous conception and incarnation of our Lord is to be given ample emphasis as one proclaims His birth. During the Christmas season, we are not marveling at the wondrous birth of a boy; we are marveling at the miracle of God becoming also man. It is noteworthy that the Nicene Creed focuses our attention on the incarnation even more than the actual birth: "And in one Lord Jesus Christ . . . who for us and for our salvation came down from heaven and was incarnate by the Holy Spirit of the virgin Mary and was made man." The preexistence of the Son and His conception by the Holy Spirit in the womb of a virgin are a vital part of the proclamation of this season and are a vital foundation for proclaiming the universal nature of Christ's saving work. This emphasis is especially prominent

23 Bass, *Renewal of Liturgical Preaching*, 54.

24 Paul Gerhardt, "Come, Your Hearts and Voices Raising," *LSB* 375:2–4.

on the Second Sunday after Christmas when the Holy Gospel is the prologue of John: "In the beginning was the Word . . . and the Word became flesh."[25]

Third, the celebration of Christ's birth should focus on His continuing presence in Word and Sacrament. We cannot travel back in time to ancient Bethlehem, but through these mysteries of God that same Christ comes to us so that we, too, can behold, worship, and adore Him. As the Christmas Gospel is proclaimed and the Sacrament is celebrated, we are beholding the long-awaited Christ, humbly wrapped in words, bread, and wine. We can truly sing with the angels: "Glory to God in the highest, and on earth peace among those with whom He is pleased" (Luke 2:14), because we, too, are in His gracious presence. The relationship between the incarnation and Baptism is expressed well in St. Paul's letter to Titus: "But when the goodness and loving kindness of God our Savior appeared, He saved us, not because of works done by us in righteousness, but according to His own mercy, by the washing of regeneration and renewal by the Holy Spirit" (Titus 3:4–5; The Nativity of Our Lord). The sermons of this season should explicitly speak forth this sacramental presence.

Fourth, the birth of Christ should be celebrated and proclaimed throughout this short season. Christmas should not be reduced to a one-day event in the church, as it is so often in society. The Eve of the Nativity of Our Lord ushers in twelve days of joyous observance in the church year. All pastors who stress the reverent observance of Advent should also cultivate a twelve-day observance of Christmas. Jubilant singing should fill our sanctuaries and homes during these holy days. This twelve-day observance can be enhanced by offering additional services that mark the holy days of this season, such as St. Stephen, First Martyr (December 26); St. John (December 27); Holy Innocents (December 28); or the Circumcision and Name of Jesus (January 1). Such observance, as Bass explains, can enhance the proclamation of Christ's birth in its wider context:

> The liturgical significance placing St. Stephen's Day, St. John's Day, and the Holy Innocents' Day immediately after Christmas is that they help keep the celebration of Christmas in its proper theological framework even while they bring the promise of the Gospel into contact with life's greatest problems. They strengthen the contrasting elements of birth and death, life and resurrection in the redeeming activity of Christ. They show the glory of Christ, especially on the anniversary of the glorious birth, from the point of view of promised deliverance from death and destruction. They point to final victory as well as to faithful suffering and martyrdom here on earth.[26]

25 John 1:1–14 is also the Holy Gospel for the Christmas Dawn service.

26 Bass, *Renewal of Liturgical Preaching*, 60.

The twelve days of Christmas can be brought to an appropriate close with the observance of Epiphany in a special service, either on the evening before or on the Epiphany of Our Lord (January 6).

Epiphany

The relative brevity of the joyous Christmastide transitions smoothly into the brightness of the Epiphany season as the Church focuses on the reality of Christ as "God in flesh made manifest" to the whole world.[27] This season, like no other in the church year, meditates on the divine nature of Christ as apparent in His life and teaching. *Who* Jesus is (Epiphany) forms the foundation for our understanding of *what* He has done (Lent and Easter). This focus on the person of Christ does not mean that the Epiphany season has little to say for the life of the church. Bass perceptively states: "As the church learns who Jesus really is, it will also become aware of its own identity, nature, and mission."[28] Four events from Christ's life that speak forth His divine nature have traditionally been at the heart of the observance of the Epiphany season: the visit of the Magi, the Baptism of Jesus, the wedding of Cana miracle, and the transfiguration. Although the first of these is identified as "the Epiphany," each is an epiphany or clear manifestation of God in Christ.

The Epiphany of Our Lord focuses our attention on the account of the visit of the Magi sometime after the birth of Jesus (Matt. 2:1–12). This account sets the tone for the whole season: "Where is He who has been born king of the Jews? For we saw His star when it rose and have come to worship Him" (Matt. 2:2). The following themes are introduced in this reading and proclaimed throughout this season: Christ's identity, the light that is in the world, and recognition of Christ followed by worship. These themes are a fulfillment to the marvelous promise in Isaiah:

> Arise, shine, for your light has come, and the glory of the Lord has risen upon you. For behold, darkness shall cover the earth, and thick darkness the peoples; but the Lord will arise upon you, and His glory will be seen upon you. And nations shall come to your light, and kings to the brightness of your rising. (Isa. 60:1–3; The Epiphany of Our Lord)

The second "epiphany," the Baptism of Jesus, is observed on the first Sunday after the Epiphany, known as the Baptism of Our Lord. The identity of Jesus is at the center of the accounts of Jesus' Baptism in Matt. 3:13–17

27 This phrase, which encapsulates the meaning of "epiphany," is from Christopher Wordsworth's hymn "Songs of Thankfulness and Praise," *LSB* 394.

28 Bass, *Renewal of Liturgical Preaching*, 69.

(Series A), Mark 1:4–11 (Series B), and Luke 3:15–22 (Series C). The testimony of the Spirit as a dove and the Father as the voice both witness to Christ as God made manifest. This event testifies to the importance of all that Jesus does and says as the visible "image of the invisible God" (Col. 1:15).

The third "epiphany," the miracle of changing water into wine at the wedding at Cana, is traditionally understood as the first of Jesus' miracles (John 2:1–11). The evangelist John makes it quite clear that this event should be understood as a "sign" that reveals the identity of Jesus: He "manifested His glory. And His disciples believed in Him" (John 2:11). Other readings from the Gospels during the Epiphany season testify to the divine nature of Christ and the presence of the kingdom of God as Jesus cast out demons and healed the afflicted.

The fourth "epiphany" is the Transfiguration of Our Lord.[29] The accounts in Matt. 17:1–9 (Series A), Mark 9:2–9 (Series B), and Luke 9:28–36 (Series C) all testify to the identity of Jesus at a very crucial time in His ministry: He was about to "set His face to go to Jerusalem" (Luke 9:51). The divine identity of this flesh-and-blood Jesus is again acclaimed by the theophanic cloud, the voice of the Father, and the witness of Moses and Elijah. This revelation was granted to the inner circle of Jesus' disciples to sustain them in the midst of the most glorious and troubling "epiphany" of God: Christ's upcoming crucifixion.

The Epiphany theme of spreading the light of Christ to the lost, especially to the Gentiles, is found already in the Magi account and continues to surface in the lections appointed for this season. A prominent example of this from the Old Testament is Jonah's preaching to Nineveh and the resulting faith of these Gentiles (Jonah 3:1-5, 10; Epiphany 3, Series B). A second example is the call of the disciples, where Jesus promises to make them "fishers of men" (Mark 1:14–20; Series B, Epiphany 3). Another example is Jesus' announcement of His ministry in the Nazareth synagogue through reading Isaiah 61:

> The Spirit of the Lord is upon Me, because He has anointed Me to proclaim good news to the poor. He has sent Me to proclaim liberty to the captives and recovering of sight to the blind, to set at liberty those who are oppressed, to proclaim the year of the Lord's favor. (Luke 4:18–19; Epiphany 3, Series C; cf. Old Testament reading, Isa. 61:1–2a)

29 It should be noted that Transfiguration was originally observed on August 6. Later, it was moved to the end of a shorter Epiphany season, followed by three pre-Lent Sundays, called Septuagesima, Sexagesima, and Quinquagesima because of their numerical position before Easter. While the *LSB* one-year lectionary has retained the observance of pre-Lent, the *LSB* three-year lectionary extends the Epiphany season and places Transfiguration immediately before Ash Wednesday.

The relationship between the historical accounts of these "epiphanies" of our Lord and how our proclamation of these events continues to make the King and His kingdom manifest for the life of the Church is expressed well in this hymn by Johann Allendorf:

> Jesus has come as the mighty Redeemer.
> See now the threatening strong one disarmed!
> Jesus breaks down all the walls of death's fortress,
> Brings forth the pris'ners triumphant, unharmed.
> Satan, you wicked one, own now your master!
> Jesus has come! He, the mighty Redeemer!
>
> Jesus has come as the King of all glory!
> Heaven and earth, O declare His great pow'r,
> Capturing hearts with the heavenly story;
> Welcome Him now in this fast-fleeting hour!
> Ponder His love! Take the crown He has for you!
> Jesus has come! He, the King of all glory![30]

Lent

> Dear brothers and sisters of our Lord Jesus Christ, on this day the Church begins a holy season of prayerful and penitential reflection. Our attention is especially directed to the holy sufferings and death of our Lord Jesus Christ.
>
> From ancient times the season of Lent has been kept as a time of special devotion, self-denial, and humble repentance born of a faithful heart that dwells confidently on His Word and draws from it life and hope.
>
> Let us pray that our dear Father in heaven, for the sake of His beloved Son and in the power of His Holy Spirit, might richly bless this Lententide for us that we may come to Easter with glad hearts and keep the feast in sincerity and truth.[31]

These words not only announce the start of the Lenten season but also signal its focus: the suffering and death of Christ for sinners as the foundation for keeping the Easter feast. This reverent reflection on the Passion of Christ takes the Church to the core of Christ's work: "While we were still sinners, Christ died for us" (Rom. 5:8; Lent 2, Series B). The historical roots of Lententide remind us that it was a time used by the church for catechetical instruction of repentant sinners preparing for the participation in Holy Baptism and Holy Communion that are central to keeping the

---

30 Johann L. C. Allendorf, "Jesus Has Come and Brings Pleasure," *LSB* 533:3–4.

31 *LSB: Altar Book*, 483.

Easter feast. George Bass highlights this sacramental goal of Lententide that is often missed in the observance of Lent: "The prayers and penitential sacrifices of Lent culminate in the font of baptism, where the faithful die with Christ and are raised up through him, and in the table where his presence is celebrated."[32] The forty days of Lent, therefore, give attention to the work of Christ, especially His passive obedience "to the point of death, even death on a cross," as the source of the forgiveness and life Christ offers to people today (Phil. 2:8; Sunday of the Passion, Series C).

There are several themes that receive attention in the proclamation of Christ's suffering and death during Lent. First, the proclamation of His Passion testifies to the serious condition of our sinfulness and the need for "humble repentance." The Law must always be proclaimed in its full severity, but few seasons give the pastor the opportunities to reflect on the doctrine of sin that Lent does. A sincere look at the judgment of sin in Christ's crucifixion not only tells us much about God but also tells us much about ourselves. The devastating reality of our sin is sounded forth especially as Lent begins on Ash Wednesday: "Hide Your face from my sins, and blot out all my iniquity" (Ps. 51:9; Introit for Ash Wednesday). The call for repentance and assurance of God's mercy is reflected in the verse preceding the Holy Gospel used throughout Lent: "Return to the Lord, your God, for He is gracious and merciful, slow to anger, and abounding in steadfast love."[33]

A second, related theme that is proclaimed from the context of the Passion is the reality of temptation in the world and the denial of our sinful self. The lectionary for the First Sunday in Lent especially contains readings that focus on this theme. The account of the fall in Gen. 3:1–21 (Series A) displays the reality of temptation and man's response that leads to the fall of the world into sin. The Gospel readings consist of the accounts of the temptation of Christ in the wilderness (Matt. 4:1–11, Series A; Mark 1:9–15, Series B; and Luke 4:1–13, Series C). Here we see the same reality of temptation and selfish desire overcome by Christ. The temptation of Christ not only points to Christ as our only source of hope in facing temptation but also spotlights the Lenten theme of forty days of self-denial. The Passion narrative, which is usually the focus of midweek services, gives significant attention to the temptations and betrayals of Peter and Judas. The purpose of this theme in Lent is not to turn our focus inward to battle evil, but to show us our poverty in facing the sinful world and self with the result that we rely anew on Christ and His work: "I count everything as loss because of the surpassing worth of knowing Christ Jesus my Lord" (Phil. 3:8; Lent 5, Series C). This perspective is also reflected in the Lenten hymn by Thomas Kingo:

32 Bass, *Renewal of Liturgical Preaching*, 81.

33 Divine Service, Settings One and Two, *LSB*, pp. 157 and 173; cf. Joel 2:13b.

On my heart imprint Your image,
Blessed Jesus, King of grace,
That life's riches, cares, and pleasures
Never may Your work erase;
Let the clear inscription be:
Jesus, crucified for me,
Is my life, my hope's foundation,
And my glory and salvation![34]

Third and certainly foremost, proclamation of the Passion focuses us on the substitutionary work of Christ for all sinners. Although the death of Christ is inherent in the proclamation of the Gospel in every sermon, it is especially during the Lenten season that pastors are given the luxury to unpack the Passion of Christ in a more detailed and in-depth manner. The Sundays in Lent, which are not considered part of the forty days of Lent, often focus on incidents that led to Jesus' Passion. For example, the Gospel readings for Series A and B contain several events from the Gospel of John that contributed to Jesus' arrest: the cleansing of the temple (Lent 3, Series B) the interaction with the Samaritan woman and resulting mission to the Samaritans (Lent 3, Series A); the healing of the blind man (Lent 4, Series A); and especially the raising of Lazarus (Lent 5, Series A). Series C Gospel readings are drawn from Luke's narrative of Jesus' journey to Jerusalem. This movement to the cross climaxes on Palm Sunday, known also as Sunday of the Passion, when an extended portion of the Passion narrative from one of the Gospels is read. This movement toward the cross during Lent does not intimate that the story ends with death; the Passion is always understood and proclaimed in light of the resurrection. The Gradual for the Lenten season illustrates such a focus on the Passion that also affirms the resurrection: "[O come, let us fix our eyes on] Jesus, the founder and perfecter of our faith, who for the joy that was set before Him endured the cross, despising the shame, and is seated at the right hand of the throne of God."[35]

The five midweek services following Ash Wednesday and services during Holy Week allow the pastor to focus more on the Passion narratives in his sermons.[36] These narratives, which are the dominant content of each of the four Gospels, point to the crucified Christ as the source of the forgiveness: "And I, when I am lifted up from the earth [on the cross], will draw all

34 Thomas Kingo, "On My Heart Imprint Your Image," *LSB* 422.

35 *LSB: Altar Book*, 379.

36 Bass has an unnecessary polemic against the Lenten focus on the cross and the reading of the Passion history; see *Renewal of Liturgical Preaching*, 83. Although we should never disconnect the cross from the resurrection in our preaching, even during Lent, a strong focus on the Passion during the forty days is very healthy as the foundation for speaking forth the resurrection during the fifty days of Easter.

people to Myself" (John 12:32; Lent 5, Series B). Our proclamation should focus much more on the *theological significance* of the suffering and death of Christ than on the physiological details of this event. Therefore, we proclaim the crucifixion as the once and for all time sacrifice for sin: "Although He was a son, He learned obedience through what He suffered. And being made perfect, He became the source of eternal salvation to all who obey Him" (Heb. 5:8–9; Lent 5, Series B). It is the significance of the death of Christ for the salvation of the world that led the apostle Paul to state unabashedly: "But we preach Christ crucified" (1 Cor. 1:23; Lent 3, Series B). Faithful pastors are passionate about proclaiming the Passion of Christ.

Lenten preaching is central to pastoral care because Christ's Passion, like no other event in history, defines the profile of the triune God we worship. God is seen for who He is in what He does. This preaching gives essential contours to the Christ who serves us each Lord's Day because it portrays the death that we participate in at the font and show forth at the Table (Rom. 6:3; 1 Cor. 11:26). Such meditation leads the faithful to praise Christ profoundly for His work of redemption:

> Here might I stay and sing,
> No story so divine!
> Never was love, dear King,
> Never was grief like Thine.
> This is my friend,
> In whose sweet praise
> I all my days
> Could gladly spend![37]

Easter

From the midst of the early morning shadows cast into an empty tomb came the wondrous news of Christ's resurrection: "I know that you seek Jesus who was crucified. He is not here, for He has risen, as He said" (Matt. 28:5–6; The Resurrection of Our Lord, Series A). The Resurrection of Our Lord, without question, has been the central festival of the Church since her birth.[38] The Paschal Lamb who was slaughtered is standing with the rest of history in His grip (cf. Rev. 5:6–7). It is not only the culmination of God's plan of redemption in Christ's life and work, but it also sets before the Church the culmination of her life in Christ: the victory over death, eternal life, resurrected flesh, and restored creation. This relationship is often implicit in the lectionary of this season but should be explicitly proclaimed in sermons, even as it is

37 Samuel Crossman, "My Song Is Love Unknown," *LSB* 430:7.

38 See Raniero Cantalamessa, *Easter in the Early Church* (Collegeville, MN: Liturgical Press, 1993).

trumpeted forth in many of the Easter hymns, such as this one by C. F. W. Walther:

> O, where is your sting, death? We fear you no more;
> Christ rose, and now open is fair Eden's door.
> For all our transgressions His blood does atone;
> Redeemed and forgiven, we now are His own.[39]

The keeping of the Easter feast calls not only for remembrance but also for participation. This participation in the death and resurrection of Christ is probably most vividly experienced in the Easter Vigil. The reading of the mighty acts of God, from the creation to the flood to the exodus, puts the resurrection in its proper context. God's salvific acts throughout history now culminate—in the Vigil—in the dying and rising of catechumens in baptismal water and in the feasting of the faithful on the body and blood of the Paschal Lamb. It was especially the exodus that had a significant impact on shaping the Jewish Christian understanding of the death and resurrection of Jesus as well as how one participates in this reality through the Sacraments.[40] They saw the obvious relationship between the Passover events of ancient Israel and those celebrated in the Christian feast. In both events the blood of the lamb causes death to pass over the faithful who then through water are brought to the promised land. Note how this hymn uses the exodus imagery to proclaim the Easter gift imparted in the Sacraments:

> Where the paschal blood is poured,
> Death's dread angel sheaths the sword;
> Israel's hosts triumphant go
> Through the wave that drowns the foe.
> Alleluia!
>
> Praise we Christ, whose blood was shed,
> Paschal victim, paschal bread;
> With sincerity and love
> Eat we manna from above.
> Alleluia![41]

As in this hymn, the proclamation of this season points not only to the empty tomb but also to the means where this resurrection victory is given.

The joyous fifty days of this season include several Sundays *of*, not *after*, Easter. Christ's resurrection appearances that followed His exit from the tomb on that glorious morn are not only the focus of the day of Easter but also dominate the Second and Third Sundays of Easter. The pastor does

---

39 C. F. W. Walther, "He's Risen, He's Risen," *LSB* 480:4.

40 Exodus 12; see also Danielou, *Bible and the Liturgy*, 162–90.

41 "At the Lamb's High Feast We Sing," *LSB* 633:3–4.

not need to dream up fantastic illustrations for these sermons: What could be better for a globe of dying people than speaking of the risen and living Christ? The Second Sunday of Easter is especially known for its focus on the doubting Thomas account in John 20:19–31. Even as much of the world stands outside in doubt of Christ's resurrection, it is the pastor's privilege to gather the church before the altar so that her doubts are replaced by peace. We have no need to thrust our fingers into Christ's hands or side. We hear His living voice, taste His resurrected flesh and blood, and declare: "My Lord and my God!" (John 20:28). As pastors speak forth this reality, we can be encouraged by the words of Jesus: "Blessed are those who have not seen and yet have believed" (John 20:29b). This focus on the resurrection is enhanced during this season by the lectionary readings from the sermons in Acts in place of readings from the Old Testament.

With the Fourth Sunday of Easter, the Easter season gradually shifts its focus to the coming physical departure of Jesus and His promises concerning the Holy Spirit. The comforting focus of the Fourth Sunday of Easter is the beloved Good Shepherd sermon in John 10. The Fifth, Sixth, and Seventh Sundays of Easter all draw their Gospel readings from the farewell narrative in John, especially those portions where Jesus promises the Holy Spirit. The sermons on these Sundays can easily blend proclamation of the resurrection with teaching about the Holy Spirit by emphasizing the Spirit's work of making the risen Christ present through the means of grace. Jesus speaks of this work of the Spirit:

> And I will ask the Father, and He will give you another Helper, to be with you forever, even the Spirit of Truth, whom the world cannot receive, because it neither sees Him nor knows Him. You know Him, for He dwells with you and will be in you. I will not leave you as orphans; I will come to you. Yet a little while and the world will see Me no more, but you will see Me. (John 14:16–19a; Easter 6, Series A)

Forty days after His resurrection, Christ ascended to heaven in triumph. Ascension Day has, unfortunately, become perhaps the least-observed major festival of the church year. Despite this, there are few days that rival its significance. This festival gives occasion to proclaim the completion of Christ's "earthly" ministry, His victorious coronation on the divine throne, His rule over all creation, our ascent with Him to the heavenly places, and His eventual "descent" as judge and deliverer. These themes all abound in the Epistle for the day:

> What is the immeasurable greatness of His power toward us who believe, according to the working of His great might that He worked in Christ when He raised Him from the dead and seated Him at His right hand in the heavenly places, far above all rule and authority and power

> and dominion, and above every name that is named, not only in this age but also in the one to come. And He put all things under His feet and gave Him as head over all things to the church, which is His body, the fullness of Him who fills all in all. (Eph. 1:19b–23)

There are two problematic perspectives that arise in the church concerning the central message of the Easter season. There are those Christians who feel that the church should spend less time reflecting on the death of Christ and more time on His resurrection. The resurrection of Christ, however, should consistently be proclaimed in concert with the reality of His death. Even as the Passion of Christ is not to be preached without a view toward the resurrection, so also the resurrection is not to be proclaimed without a look back to the Passion. Christ's resurrection victory is based upon His obedience unto death. These two events should be carefully woven together as a single reality in our preaching so that neither is ignored and both shape our life in Christ. The Proper Preface for Easter is an example of weaving these two into one fabric: "By His dying He has destroyed death, and by His rising again He has restored to us everlasting life."[42]

There are other voices in the Church that call upon pastors to move beyond the death and resurrection of Christ as the central focus of preaching to other important matters of Holy Scripture; such sermons are sometimes viewed as "milk" for infant Christians. Pastors, however, must never be ashamed of the Gospel, no matter how often or much they preach it (Rom. 1:16). Gustav Wingren addresses this problematic perspective by reaffirming the centrality of cross and resurrection preaching for the ongoing life of the Church:

> It is false intellectualism to separate those who belong to the church from the missionary *kerygma*. That is considered possible only because of the idea in the background that once anyone has heard the Gospel he ought to go on gradually to something else. In fact the message of Christ's death and resurrection has as its most prominent objective that we who hear it should die and rise again, and, since our own will refuses to submit itself to this living process, the word about Christ is always new, unexpected and fresh even to the day of our death. The early Christian *kerygma* of Christ's work in death and resurrection has demonstrated, as no other factor in human history has, that it holds the power of renewing the Sunday preaching. In analyzing the essential nature of preaching it is impossible to overlook that. The message of the cross and resurrection is the main pillar, not only of missionary preaching, but of preaching in general.[43]

42 *LSB: Altar Book*, 152.

43 Wingren, *Living Word*, 18–19.

One final point about Easter needs to be made. The resurrection of Christ is a reality that is not only celebrated and proclaimed on Easter Sunday and during the great fifty days of Easter but also each Lord's Day throughout the church year: "Every Sunday the church remembers Jesus' resurrection, thanks God for it, and bases its worship and thanksgiving upon its present reality."[44] Christ's resurrection led early Christians to view Sunday as not only the first day of the week, a day when creation was begun, but also as the eighth day, the day when creation was restored and eternity dawned.[45] This theological reality breathes new life into our worship and preaching each Sunday throughout the church year.

Pentecost

The Sundays after Pentecost begin and flow from the festival of Pentecost, the day that celebrates the pouring out of the Holy Spirit upon the Church (Acts 2:1–21; Second Reading for the Day of Pentecost). As stated earlier, Pentecost need not be viewed as the time of a distinct shift in the church year from the life of Christ to the life of the Church. Why is Pentecost so connected to the life of Christ? Luther states it well in his explanation to the Third Article of the Apostles' Creed: "I believe that I cannot by my own reason or strength believe in Jesus Christ, my Lord, or come to Him; but the Holy Spirit has called me by the Gospel, enlightened me with His gifts, sanctified and kept me in the true faith."[46] Therefore, Pentecost does not give us the opportunity to move beyond Christ in our preaching; rather, it is a time for us to proclaim how the Holy Spirit empowers our union and life with Christ. The other major festival of this season, the Holy Trinity, follows one week after Pentecost. Its placement in the church year gives the preacher the opportunity to proclaim the life of Christ and the work of the Holy Spirit in the broader context of the doctrines of the triune God and creation.

Unlike the other seasons of the church year, there is not a defined pattern to the progression of the many Sundays after Pentecost until the last three Sundays when the focus shifts distinctively to the end times. Some have asserted that there is a movement from teaching *about* Jesus to the teaching *of* Jesus.[47] This distinction, however, is an oversimplification since much of Jesus' teaching is about His own person and work. It is better to emphasize that these Sundays are often opportunities to preach about the kingdom of God, since many of the Gospel readings are from scenes in Jesus' earthly

---

44 Bass, *Renewal of Liturgical Preaching*, 96.

45 Danielou, *Bible and the Liturgy*, 222–86

46 *Luther's Small Catechism*, 17.

47 See discussion of this position in Bass, *Renewal of Liturgical Preaching*, 123.

ministry recorded by Matthew, Mark, and Luke.[48] During this season, one learns much about Christ and the church's life in Christ.

The last three Sundays of the church year are opportunities to preach about eschatology or the end times. Unlike Advent, where the proclamation emphasizes the joyful and eager anticipation of the Last Day, the focus on these weeks is readiness for judgment upon Christ's return. The Series A Gospel readings for these three Sundays, for example, are from Jesus' eschatological discourse in Matthew: the parable of the ten virgins (25:1–13), the parable of the talents (25:14–30), and the coming of the Son of Man to judge (25:31–46). This theme climaxes on the Last Sunday in the Church Year, also known as the Sunday of Fulfillment, as is evident in its Collect: "Lord God, heavenly Father, send forth Your Son, we pray, to lead home His bride, the Church, that with all the company of the redeemed we may finally enter into His eternal wedding feast."[49] Each of these final Sundays of the church year is very valuable in preparing the Christian for death since our "last day" may dawn before the Last Day. The end of the church year offers a natural opportunity to preach about life beyond death through Christ, with the result that the faithful face their last hour with a prayer such as this:

> Lord, let at last Thine angels come,
> To Abr'ham's bosom bear me home,
> That I may die unfearing;
> And in its narrow chamber keep
> My body safe in peaceful sleep
> Until Thy reappearing.
> And then from death awaken me,
> That these mine eyes with joy may see,
> O Son of God, Thy glorious face,
> My Savior and my fount of grace.
> Lord Jesus Christ, my prayer attend, my prayer attend,
> And I will praise Thee without end.[50]

Minor Festivals

Lutherans observe fewer minor festivals than some church bodies. Yet we have retained the general practice of commemorating days that recognize saints or angels (e.g., apostles, All Saints', and St. Michael and All Angels) or events in the lives of saints (e.g., Reformation Day, the Visitation, and the Conversion of St. Paul). Such observances are usually on a fixed day each

48 See the excellent discussions about the kingdom of God and parables in Voelz, *What Does This Mean?* 244–62, 310–15.

49 *LSB: Altar Book*, 941.

50 Martin Schalling, "Lord, Thee I Love with All My Heart," *LSB* 708:3.

year. Thus they sometimes fall on a Sunday and should be observed, but often are on a weekday. Although it is permissible to move such festivals to the nearest Sunday, it is not always advisable when such movement may cloud the established pattern for the Sundays in the church year. Observance of the minor festivals that occur on weekdays can be done in the context of congregations, schools, and Christian homes that observe some form of the daily office. Most of these festivals have their own propers and lections; some even have their own hymnody.

It has been stated above that the entire church year has a Christological focus. This is true even for these minor festivals. Although the titles for these days are connected with individuals, observances are not meant to glorify these individuals. Bass appropriately stresses their relationship with festivals observing events in Christ's life:

> They are celebrations of the life "in Christ," testifying that the God who acted in the saints and martyrs of the church is still at work today to redeem and empower all men to follow in the footsteps of the saints of Christ. By themselves the saints have no lasting significance; they are remembered because they were so completely Christ's men, women, and children, as their willingness to die for him demonstrates. Their festivals were Christ's festivals, then and now.[51]

Therefore, preaching done on these festivals can and should give attention to the lives of these individuals, but always and primarily point beyond them to the Christ who gave Himself for them and united Himself with them. This Christological focus is expressed well in the following hymn:

> By all Your saints in warfare,
> For all Your saints at rest,
> Your holy name, O Jesus,
> Forevermore be blest!
> For You have won the battle
> That they might wear the crown;
> And now they shine in glory
> Reflected from Your throne.[52]

Conclusion

Sensitivity to the themes and cadence of the church year assists the pastor in proclaiming sermons that are Christocentric and consistent with the proclamation of the rest of the service. The faithful observance of the church year involves use of a lectionary, praying particular collects, singing appropriate

51 Bass, *Renewal of Liturgical Preaching*, 144.

52 Horatio Bolton Nelson, "By All Your Saints in Warfare," *LSB* 517:1.

hymns; it also and especially involves a sermon where the salvation that was accomplished in the past is proclaimed as a present reality in the Christ who offers Himself now in the Divine Service. The sermon, more than any other variable portion of the liturgy, speaks forth these historical events of Christ's life as present realities in which the congregation now shares. Christ's story becomes our story as our days, weeks, and years are lived out in His presence.

Arthur Just summarizes the magnificent benefits of faithful observance of the church year:

> If the congregation is not faithfully observing the church year, it is ignoring a premier opportunity to elevate the Gospel of him who dies and rises for the life of the world into the center of its life. *Reverence* of sacred time assists the congregation to believe that it worships a presence whose mighty deeds of salvation took place in time because that presence enfleshed itself in time and space. *Fidelity* to the historical acts of Jesus' life as marked in the church year allows the congregation to see that these past acts of salvation are now made present realities, that the future benefits of salvation are now available to the congregation sacramentally. Christian time is God's time; the church year is God bringing home his Son to the congregation year after year. The daily, weekly, yearly rhythm of commemorating the saving deeds of Jesus Christ forms the congregation into a Christian community living in time sanctified by Jesus Christ. As a restored creation, the Christian lives out his restored life in restored time within the framework of the church year. Ordinary time has become sacred.[53]

53 Just, *LWHP*, 33.

"Working" the Lectionary

Carl C. Fickenscher II

> Now an angel of the Lord said to Philip, "Rise and go toward the south to the road that goes down from Jerusalem to Gaza." This is a desert place. And he rose and went. And there was an Ethiopian, a eunuch, a court official of Candace, queen of the Ethiopians, who was in charge of all her treasure. He had come to Jerusalem to worship and was returning, seated in his chariot, and he was reading the prophet Isaiah. And the Spirit said to Philip, "Go over and join this chariot." So Philip ran to him and heard him reading Isaiah the prophet and asked, "Do you understand what you are reading?" And he said, "How can I, unless someone guides me?" And he invited Philip to come up and sit with him. Now the passage of the Scripture that he was reading was this: "Like a sheep He was led to the slaughter and like a lamb before its shearer is silent, so he opens not his mouth. In his humiliation justice was denied Him. Who can describe his generation? For his life is taken away from the earth." And the eunuch said to Philip, "About whom, I ask you, does the prophet say this, about himself or about someone else?" Then Philip opened his mouth, and beginning with this Scripture he told him the good news about Jesus. (Acts 8:26–35)

What an opportunity the Holy Spirit presented that day. What a text!

Philip could never have planned it as well, even with a week to prepare. Given one opportunity to touch the heart of a stranger (and perhaps, by *his* witness, countless others in his homeland), Philip could not have found a more appropriate text in the entire existing canon than Isaiah 53. The one—and only—appointed reading for that particular day was obviously God-ordained.

No doubt every preacher wishes such a relevant text would fall to him from heaven each week. No such luck. But all luck and any immediate working of the Holy Spirit aside, the preacher does have an equivalent blessing. We call it the lectionary. Humanly devised, not divinely inspired, the readings it appoints may not always jump off the page with application so readily apparent. Nevertheless, with a bit of labor not unbecoming the called *doulos* of the Word, the lectionary does, week after week, year after year, yield the very opportunity God gave Philip. It is a matter of working the lectionary.

As we work through this essay together, we will begin by reviewing how the lectionary itself works, understanding the system and exploring the relationships among its appointed readings. Next, we will consider the value of working with the lectionary, including its facility to produce sermons that are more truly textual than otherwise likely. Finally, we will offer suggestions, with examples, for putting the lectionary to work in actual preaching.

How the Lectionary Works

A lectionary, or pericopal system, is a schedule that assigns pericopes (sections of Scripture, from the Greek *perikopto*, "to cut around") to be read on specific Sundays of the church year. Since the pre-Christian era, God's people have seen advantages in following an orderly pattern of biblical readings. The Jews followed a pericopal system.[1] So did the early church.[2] In fact, through the centuries Christians have followed a calendar of readings that bears great resemblance to those of the earliest days.

The lectionaries now in widest use in North America are based on the work initiated by the Second Vatican Council. With modest revisions by the various denominations, the *Ordo Lectionum Missae* (1969) has found acceptance in many non-Roman Catholic churches.[3] These lectionaries offer a three-year cycle, with an Old Testament reading (or, during the Easter season, a "First Reading" from the Book of Acts), a reading from one of the Epistles, and a reading from the Gospel appointed for each Sunday and festival.[4]

The anticipation is that congregations using a lectionary would read all three of the readings for the day. Hymns, responsive psalmody, collects, and other elements of the service are most often chosen to conform to the theme of the readings. Perhaps most important, the sermon text is likely to be one of the scheduled lections.

The Gospel reading for each service sets the theme. The first year of the three-year lectionary (Series A) is based on the Gospel according to St. Matthew, the second (Series B) on Mark, and the third (Series C), on the

---

1 Alfred Edersheim, *The Life and Times of Jesus the Messiah* (Grand Rapids: Eerdmans, 1950), 1:105.

2 Luther D. Reed, *The Lutheran Liturgy* (Philadelphia: Muhlenberg, 1947), 47.

3 James L. Brauer, "The Church Year," in *LWHP*, 150–51.

4 The examples that follow are all drawn from the three-year lectionary prepared for *LSB*, pp. xiv–xxiii.

Gospel according to St. Luke. Readings from John are interspersed throughout. During the festival half of the church year—Advent through Pentecost—the Gospel readings narrate whichever event in the life of Christ is being celebrated on a given Sunday. Thus, for example, in Series A, the Gospel for the Transfiguration of Our Lord, the last Sunday after Epiphany, is Matt. 17:1–9, followed the next Sunday, the First Sunday in Lent, by Matt. 4:1–11, the temptation of our Lord. Then, during the Sundays after Pentecost, the Gospels proceed in generally continuous readings of the books, omitting, of course, those passages already covered in the festival half.

Meanwhile, throughout the year, the Old Testament readings are chosen to coordinate with the Gospels of the day. Frequently they relate as prophecy-fulfillment, as when Isa. 7:10–17, the prophecy of the virgin birth, is read in conjunction with Matt. 1:18–25 (which includes the evangelist's citation of Isaiah) on the Fourth Sunday in Advent (Series A). On other occasions the relationship might be called illustrative narrative, in which either the Old Testament reading or the Gospel is a story that illustrates a teaching in the other. Thus for Proper 12 (Series C) God's willingness to hear Abraham's persistent prayer for Sodom, Gen. 18:20–33, illustrates Jesus' teaching that the Father is eager to answer our prayers, Luke 11:1–13. In numerous other cases, the Old Testament and Gospel readings are simply parallel. For instance, on Proper 5 (Series C) Elijah and Christ each raise widows' dead sons: 1 Kings 17:17–24 and Luke 7:11–17.

For specific festivals, the Epistle likewise reflects the themes set by the Gospel. The preacher can, therefore, expect to find a strong connection among all three readings for the day. The Transfiguration of Our Lord (Series B) is a prime example. The Gospel narrative (Mark 9:2–9) depicts the event itself. The Old Testament reading (2 Kings 2:1–12) helps explain why Elijah is an appropriate witness with Christ on the mountain. And the Epistle (2 Cor. 3:12–18; 4:1–6) recalls the other ancient visitor, Moses, who had also seen God's glory on an earlier mount.

For most of the seasons of Epiphany and Easter, and the Sundays after Pentecost, however, the Epistles read continuously through a selected letter, rather than being keyed to the Gospels. For example, while the Gospels from Proper 3 to 19 in Series A proceed with their ordered reading of Matthew, the Epistles follow in a *lectio continua* fashion through Romans. With continuous readings of a Gospel book and of an Epistle running simultaneously, one can clearly not anticipate a unified theme each week. Normally the Epistles will follow themes of their own.

Whatever the relationship among a Sunday's readings, the preacher does well to discover it. Not just his sermon text, but all the readings—as well as the other propers—create the context in which the congregation hears his message. Moreover, discovering the common thread among the readings can open his own understanding of the chosen text, especially when the day's unifying theme is not so obvious.

Sometimes discovering the theme of the day is work indeed. Those occasions, though, often yield surprising and most satisfying nuggets.

Consider the Third Sunday in Advent, Series C. The Old Testament reading and Epistle reflect a sense of joy and anticipation. Zeph. 3:14 and 17 exults: "Sing aloud, O daughter of Zion; shout, O Israel! Rejoice and exult with all your heart, O daughter of Jerusalem! . . . The LORD your God . . . will rejoice over you with gladness; He will quiet you by His love; He will exult over you with loud singing." In Phil. 4:4, Paul echoes: "Rejoice in the Lord always; again I will say, Rejoice."

No sooner have worshipers heard such words of delight than they rise to hear the question of John the Baptist (Luke 7:20): "Are You the one who is to come, or shall we look for another?" Their question is a mirror held before our own anticipation as we continue our journey to Jesus' nativity. Jesus' response is to heal many people and cast out evil spirits, before stating that "the one who is not offended by Me" will be blessed (Luke 7:23). Then Jesus calls the crowds to task for their expectations concerning John and indeed of the Messiah—expectations of fine clothes and luxury. But the reality is that despite John's great task as the forerunner of the Messiah, "the one who is least in the kingdom of God is greater than he" (Luke 7:28). And it is this very reality that causes the Pharisees and lawyers to reject John and his baptism as well as Jesus Himself. There doesn't appear to be much joy in this Gospel reading.

Yet the Gospel informs the joyful words of the first two readings—and vice versa. On the one hand, the joy of Zephaniah and St. Paul cannot be a warm-fuzzy, doesn't-it-feel-nice, gee-it's-almost-Christmas emotion. No, John's words remind that the coming of the Messiah is serious business. The joy and the anticipation of the Messiah are real, but they are grounded in the mighty acts of God that bring forgiveness: "The LORD has taken away the judgments against you; He has cleared away your enemies. The King of Israel, the LORD, is in your midst . . . a mighty one who will save" (Zeph. 3:15, 17). Zephaniah points to the cross on which sin, death, and Satan are defeated. Thus Paul is able to rejoice—and say it again—despite being in prison, where emotionally he perhaps felt anything but joyful. The peace of God that he had through Christ not only surpassed all understanding but also superseded the woes of his surroundings.

On the other hand, the tenor of the day, made clear by the first two readings, reminds the preacher that even his Gospel text is not Law only. Those who reject John should stand in terror before Christ on account of their sin. Yet there is also in the crowd tax collectors and others who have been baptized by John, who have witnessed Jesus' miracles, and who have received with joy His teaching and "declared God just" (Luke 7:29). They have been accepted, forgiven. The anticipated One, the object of John's ministry, is coming to gather them into His barn. Might the preacher miss seeing the joy on those faces if not cued by the other readings for the day? Perhaps. Yet, understood together, the readings for this day convey a powerful theme: True joy is humble trust in Christ's salvation.

Take another example. It is true that during nonfestival portions of the church year the Gospel and Epistle readings will often not coincide in theme. When two different books are each being read essentially straight through, they will, obviously, follow different trails. Still, the preacher should not too quickly assume that his Gospel and Epistle are unrelated.

Granted, it might appear that the readings for Proper 4 in Series A present two quite disjointed emphases. As one would expect, the connection between the Old Testament reading and Gospel is strong. Deut. 11:18–21, 26–28 promises blessings to Israel if they "obey the commandments of the LORD" and warns of curses should they disobey. Similarly, Matt. 7:15–29 endorses the man who "does the will of [the] Father who is in heaven," who "hears . . . and does" the words of Jesus, but calls "foolish" everyone who "hears these words . . . and does not do them."

For the same Sunday, the Epistle, Rom. 3:21–28, which begins a sixteen-week continuous reading of Paul's letter, certainly has significance enough in its own right: "All have sinned and fall short of the glory of God, and are justified by His grace as a gift, through the redemption that is in Christ Jesus" (Rom. 3:23–24). Nothing, however, about obeying, doing, practicing the commands or will of God. In fact, Paul maintains "that one is justified by faith apart from works of the Law" (Rom. 3:28).

Nothing about obeying, doing, practicing? Searching for a connection among the readings might just remind the preacher of other words of Jesus. Asked by the Jews, "What must we do, to be doing the works of God?" He replied, "This is the work of God, that you believe in Him whom He has sent" (John 6:28–29). Scripture, it turns out, frequently calls faith a doing of the will of God.[5]

Is that what Moses and Jesus had in mind in the day's other pericopes? Indeed. The Old Testament reading begins with the command to "lay up these words . . . in your hearts," that is, to believe (Deut. 11:18). And in the Gospel, Jesus is emphatic that "every healthy tree bears good fruit" (Matt. 7:17) and that only a good tree can do so. What is it that makes a tree good

5 Francis Pieper, *Christian Dogmatics* (St. Louis: Concordia, 1951), 2:441.

but faith? It may well be the Epistle, the one which seemed quite unrelated, that actually unlocks the other two. These are *all* texts about faith![6]

The lectionary has been carefully devised to expose meaningful unities among distant passages of Scripture. While the preacher should recognize the system's intent and limitations and not try to impose artificial connections, there are beautiful if sometimes hidden gems to be mined.

Worth the Work of Lectionary Preaching

Of course, understanding how the pericopal system works and even appreciating the unity it brings to the service are not in themselves compelling reasons to use the system in preaching. What real advantages or assists, if any, does lectionary preaching offer?

Preaching the pericopes is certainly not the only valid option available. Preachers in some Christian traditions are quite accustomed to a "free text" every Sunday. They open their Bibles, study diligently, reflect, and then select a text for the following Sunday from anywhere between Genesis and Revelation. Over a period of time, they will likely also preach various sermon series, either on chosen topics or continuously through books of the Bible. Either way, their text selections are free of any historic or structured outside influence.

Such an approach has much to commend it. The preacher—who is also a pastor—will endeavor to choose a text that meets the needs of the flock he knows so well. He will select a passage of Scripture that has spoken to him, one through which the Holy Spirit has convicted him or given him a new understanding. Thus there are always opportunities to be relevant personally and to the people. The preacher can choose the very text that would, one might say, best suit this Sunday's chariot ride through the desert.

Every veteran preacher can probably recall an occasion when circumstances virtually demanded a particular sermon topic and free text. Perhaps a news item or a specific congregational need suggests special treatment. A few recurring days not handled in the lectionary are so important they deserve attention, such as an annual Sanctity of Life Sunday.[7] In all of these

6 It may be added conversely, of course, that the Gospel and Old Testament reading also caution the preacher against proclaiming "cheap grace" in a sermon on the Epistle. Justifying faith will always lead the believer to do a variety of good works.

7 Noteworthy, however, are the many readings within the lectionary for the Christmas and Epiphany seasons that may be highly appropriate for Life Sunday: Matt. 2:13–18 (Holy Innocents, December 28); Isa. 42:1–7, Acts 10:34–38, and any of the Gospels for the Baptism of our Lord; Isa. 49:1–7 (Epiphany 2, Series A) and 1 Cor. 6:12–20 (Epiphany 2, Series B); Isa. 61:1–6; 1 Cor. 12:12–31a (Epiphany 3, Series C); Mic. 6:1–8, 1 Cor. 1:18–31, Matt. 5:1–12 (Epiphany 4, Series A); Jer. 1:4–10 (Epiphany 4, Series C); Isa. 58:3–9a (Epiphany 5, Series A); and Job 7:1–7.

cases thoughtful preachers will be sure that the text they choose truly does address the need of the moment, rather than using a text as "pretext" for whatever they wish to say.[8]

While free texting is, therefore, a valid possibility, there are indeed significant advantages to a regular program of lectionary preaching. Some are simply practical; one may be crucial to conveying what God actually says through a text.

To begin, the lectionary can save time. An appropriate free text may not present itself quickly each week. By suggesting three usable texts, the lectionary frees up the busy pastor to spend more time in text development rather than in text selection. In many instances, working the lectionary may not be working harder; it may be working smarter!

Second, lectionary preaching helps to assure that a text of proper length is chosen. This can be more important than one might imagine. A text that is too short (that is, less than a complete thought block) can appear to give preaches very wide latitude. Unfortunately, that may cause them to wander from the intended sense. Karl Barth explains:

> We should not choose texts that are too short, since the danger of arrogance is greater with these than with longer passages. For example, we should not detach the first beatitude from the rest of the Sermon on the Mount. When 1 Jn 4:16 ["God is love"] is the text, it is tempting to take this verse in isolation and to exploit its eloquence instead of letting ourselves be guided by it.[9]

To reclaim an analogy used by a contemporary sect: pieces of wood attached by one nail can still shift; two nails make them secure.[10] A text that is too short may not secure the preacher to a line of direction that is really true to the passage. Almost as troublesome, texts that are too long may lead to generic sermons simply because they cannot be covered fully in the allotted time.

While a few pericopes in the modern lectionary only a couple verses in length, the vast majority are of paragraph or multiparagraph length. Only for one Sunday of the church year are they longer than a chapter.[11] Thus

---

8 It should go without saying, too, that a congregation may sometimes wish to transfer or "juggle" lectionary readings. If, as examples, Epiphany, Ascension, or Reformation are not observed on the traditional calendar days, one or more of the readings appointed for those days might be used on a neighboring Sunday.

9 Karl Barth, *Homiletics*, trans. Geoffrey W. Bromiley and Donald E. Daniels (Louisville, KY: Westminster/John Knox, 1991), 93–94.

10 The Reorganized Church of Jesus Christ of the Latter-Day Saints uses this analogy in its evangelism presentations to justify its use of the Book of Mormon alongside the Bible.

11 I.e., Sunday of the Passion, for which the Gospel for each of the three years covers the entire Passion of Jesus, approximately two chapters in length.

as preaching texts they represent complete thoughts but can be developed adequately within the usual time expectations.

A third and very important benefit of lectionary preaching is its assurance that, over time, regular worshipers will hear the full counsel of God. This can, of course, happen through carefully planned free text preaching. However, free text preachers may (quite unknowingly, perhaps) ride "hobby horses" in the pulpit. Too often they will drive home favorite points: the virtues (or decline) of the Christian family, the evil of abortion, the joy of humility, even making cliché a single particular mode of expressing salvation.

Just as dangerous, in an effort to be relevant, the preacher may "choose his text, not from the great spiritual wealth of the Bible, bringing forth treasures old and new, but from the transient happenings of the day."[12] As a result, sensational topics may be addressed, while the sublime truths of the Gospel may be ignored. In either case, God's full counsel is not preached.

The pericopal system protects against hobby-horse riding, assuring that the congregation will hear all the chief doctrines of Scripture on a regular basis. By disciplining oneself to preach, as a rule, on one of the pericopes, the preacher guarantees the people a broad exposure to the Word. Lectionaries have always been designed with this goal.[13]

Some preachers go so far as to commit themselves to preaching all the Old Testament readings one year, all the Epistles the next, and all the Gospels the third, then rotating that cycle in subsequent years so that every pericope will have been used as a sermon text in nine years. While such a schedule will probably seem too confining for most, it certainly would mean that a congregation has heard the full context of Scripture.

A fourth advantage of lectionary preaching is the bond it establishes among believers in different places and of different ages. A pastor in Texas may well choose the same sermon text for the Tenth Sunday after Pentecost as does a fellow pastor in California. And though the lectionary has been adjusted significantly over the centuries, the same pastors preaching on, say, Trinity Sunday, can often turn to Luther or other great preachers of the past for insights on the same text on the same Sunday.[14]

Preaching the lectionary offers other advantages as well. Fred Craddock enumerates: "The readings provide a common ground for discussion in ministerial peer groups; family worship can more easily join public worship

12 Richard C. H. Lenski, *The Sermon: Its Homiletical Construction* (Columbus, OH: The Lutheran Book Concern, 1927; repr., Grand Rapids: Baker, 1968), 20.

13 Lenski, *Sermon*, 30.

14 Compare with the modern lectionaries, for example, the texts used by Luther in *Sermons of Martin Luther*, 8 vols., ed. and trans. John Nicholas Lenker (Minneapolis: Lutherans in All Lands, 1904–9; repr., Grand Rapids: Baker, 1988).

through shared readings; ministers and worship committees can work with common biblical texts to prepare services that have movement and integrity."[15]

The most compelling benefit of pericopal preaching, though, is that it places the text ahead of other priorities in sermon preparation. This, as will be seen, tends to produce sermons that are more likely to be truly textual. And that, we will also see, enables the contemporary preacher to do precisely what Philip did through his "appointed" text. The advantage stems from the initial question preachers may ask as they begin their sermon work.

For the free texter, the sermon task begins not with a portion of Scripture, but with the entire Bible. Presumably a free texter is not yet consciously looking for next Sunday's text. Ideally, such a preacher pursues personal devotional reading with a completely open mind, asking continually, "What is God saying?" At some point, however, a text must be selected. Now the question is, "What do my people need to hear?"

Unfortunately, before preachers have even opened their Bible on Monday, they are exposed to the latter question. Their people are present. The newspaper is open. The pressing realities of a sinful world are all around. Input to the question "What do my people need to hear?" touches the preacher before there is ever the chance to ask, "What is God saying in this passage of Scripture?" It is likely that the preacher, too, will ask the people question before the God question.

Herein arises a risk. If preachers approach reading the Bible with immediate and prior criteria, they may jump to exegetical conclusions. A cursory reading of the text may suggest its relevance to the people's needs. The preacher has "found" what he is looking for! (It has been well said that any competent minister could arrive at any conclusion from any text.) If the preacher who has "found" the answer to his people's needs is superficial in subsequent textual study, he may in all sincerity and with great enthusiasm preach that text on the topic. Unfortunately, he may have found only *his* answer to the needs of his congregation, not *God's* answer.

If instead preachers do their exegetical homework, they may discover that what God has to say only peripherally addresses the need. Then they face a dilemma: To be textual, a preacher may either start over, seek out a new text (no small concern should it be Saturday night), or forget altogether about the reason the text was chosen in the first place. Otherwise, he must preach as his main thrust something that God has made secondary. The preacher faces no excellent option. In short, if texts are to be selected

15 Fred B. Craddock, et al., *Preaching the New Common Lectionary, Series A* (Nashville: Abingdon, 1986), 8.

subjectively based on the needs of the congregation, no final choice can ever be made until the full exegetical process has been completed.

Thus Barth writes: "In picking a text . . . I may reach into the Bible, find something 'nice,' and lift it out. It is dangerous even to address a specific congregational situation or experience in terms of a specific text."[16]

Pericopal preachers, like free texters, brings to their work the influences of the world and congregation. Unlike free text preachers, however, pastors who have resolved to follow the lectionary immediately find before them only one, two, or three passages of Scripture. Likely there will be no obvious (and perhaps superficial) connection to the problems of the listeners. The question "What do my people need to hear?" is therefore of necessity put on hold. The preacher is forced to ask first, "What does the text say?"

From that point, a truly textual study can begin. Craddock observes: "The lectionary encourages more disciplined study and advance preparation."[17] With only a limited selection of texts, the preacher is forced to dig. No main point may be readily apparent. The digging must go deeper. At last the exegetical exercise reveals the message of the text. The preacher can be confident that it is God's message.

Then the preacher may move on to the question of relevance, of application. But even this question has changed. No longer does the preacher ask the subjective question "What do my people need to hear?" Now, with a clear message of Scripture apprehended, the question becomes, "What does this text say to my people?"

Ultimately, the answer will always be relevant—as relevant as was Philip's—because the message will be the same as Philip's. Nothing superficial. Nothing limited to today's news. "Philip began with that very passage of Scripture and told [the Ethiopian] the good news about Jesus." Digging, *really working* a lectionary text, will always reveal its connection to the message behind every page of Scripture, the good news of Jesus Christ. Not just the Suffering Servant song of Isaiah 53, but every Old Testament reading, Epistle, and Gospel finally preaches Christ! And carefully discovering the unique ways each does so opens up to the congregation the rich, diverse, many-splendored beauties of the Savior.

Here, supremely, is what makes lectionary preaching worth the work. Since it presses preachers beyond easy, stock answers and forces them to make God's application rather than any other, preaching the lectionary delivers God's goods. This discipline and the committed work it demands assists the preacher in unveiling Christ.

---

16 Barth, *Homiletics*, 49–50.

17 Craddock, *Preaching the New Common Lectionary*, 8.

Putting the Lectionary to Work

Imagine the possibilities! In the last portion of this essay, we will consider some of the ways a preacher can get the most out of preaching the pericopes.

First, a preacher recognizes that all the readings of the day create a setting for the sermon. The preacher will do well to sit back early in the week and "listen" to all three readings in English, without pause, just as the congregation will hear them on Sunday. Which images stand out? Which familiar phrases bring a knowing nod? Narratives from the Gospel or Old Testament reading—a much-loved Bible story or a parable of Jesus—tend to project. From the Epistle, it may be a verse memorized in Sunday school. Because the lectionary is well-known through years of reading, hearers—especially the pastor—may overlook the obvious. That familiarity, however, is the very asset that may be put to work.

For example, a sermon on Eph. 5:8–14, the Epistle for the Fourth Sunday in Lent, Series A, may focus on a theological abstraction, those who were formerly darkness walking as children of light. The sermon will become more concrete, though, with a brief one or two sentence reference to Jesus opening the eyes of the blind man in the Gospel (John 9:1–41). Had the listeners heard that Gospel story before? Likely. Did they give every detail rapt attention when it was read this morning? Probably not. But might a brief reference to the blind man's restored sight illuminate the theological concept in the Epistle? Yes.

The pericopes as setting for the sermon are especially vivid and, therefore, useful on the festivals. No matter which text is selected for Christmas Eve, the backdrop is Luke 2:1–20. Although the Epistle or Old Testament reading may be chosen as the sermon text for Easter, the hearers see Christ coming out of the tomb. The event of the day is known to all, and the Gospel reading that recounts it is read in the service.

While this may seem limiting to the preacher, it actually invites broad creativity. A Christmas sermon on Heb. 2:14–15 ("Since therefore the children share in flesh and blood, He Himself likewise partook of the same things . . .") might capitalize by laying *us* in the manger, putting *us* among the animals. The hearers know that Jesus was there. Now how would it feel? How low did the Son of God go to "deliver all those who . . . were subject to lifelong slavery"?

The festival Gospel always provides useful subtext. Preaching on Eph. 3:1–12, the Epistle for Epiphany, the preacher has already been given his prime illustration: the wise men illustrate "the mystery" that has now been revealed, that Gentiles are heirs in Christ along with Israel.

A second possibility for putting the lectionary to work is preaching on multiple texts, two or even all three of the pericopes. This can bring highly creative results, though caution must also be added.

The most obvious multiple-text potential is in the connections between Old Testament readings and Gospels. As noted earlier, the lectionary usually provides a natural relationship between these two, such as prophecy-fulfillment, illustrative narrative, or simple parallel. A sermon using both might reflect what Francis Rossow calls "New Testament echoes of an Old Testament text."[18]

For the First Sunday in Lent (Series A) the Gospel is Matt. 4:1–11, the temptation of Christ; this follows the Old Testament reading that recounts the first temptation (Gen. 3:1–21). Not only are the narratives themselves clearly parallel, Satan's words to Jesus also actually echo his enticements to Eve. "Did God actually say, 'You shall not eat of any tree in the garden?'" "Command these stones to become loaves of bread." "You will not surely die." "He will command His angels concerning you . . . lest you strike your foot against a stone." "You will be like God." "All these I will give You." The disaster, of course, is that Eve never answered the devil with firm, definitive words from the Lord. Christ did, and that was the essence of the good news in this text. Where our first parents failed, Jesus succeeded.

By interspersing Satan's words to us (that is, to Eve) with his words to Jesus, a sermon could emphasize that Jesus' success was ours. Jesus' answer to each temptation would then become our answer. After all, for Christ's sake, by faith, God hears Jesus' unwavering response, imputing His Son's perfect obedience as our very own.

Certainly, multiple-text sermons could be developed using the Epistle with one or both of the other readings, and the relationships among them would vary. Rossow suggests a number of further shapes that multiple-text sermons might take: cause and effect, contrast, paradox, question and answer, problem and solution, and multiple aspects of a given truth.[19]

The one caution on multiple-text sermons is this: broadening the text can lead to scattershot, generic sermons. While a Sunday's pericopes are usually related, they also bring different aspects or accents to the day's theme. It is seldom possible to exhaust all of them, and an effort to do so will mean "saying a little about a lot" rather than "a lot about a little."[20] To use again the example of the First Sunday in Lent, a sermon on temptation in general will probably not be very pointed. It will probably offer nothing the congregation

18 Francis C. Rossow, *Preaching the Creative Gospel Creatively* (St. Louis: Concordia, 1983), 91–96.

19 Rossow, *Preaching the Creative Gospel Creatively*, 96–108.

20 Inexperienced—or lazy—preachers may see multiple texts as a convenient way to fill fifteen to twenty minutes. That is not the objective of preaching.

has not heard before. It will likely not explore the depth or unique elements of Matthew's treatment of the temptation. This danger is greater still when the morning's readings are less unified than these.

Multiple text sermons are, therefore, most useful as an occasional "spice" in preaching. They are perhaps best used when the readings have often been preached before individually and need not be explained again. Definitely they should be attempted only when the relationships among the pericopes is cogent.

A third, and very rich, potential for putting the lectionary to work is with sermon series. Given the lectionary's frequent use of continuous readings through Bible books, sermon series become a natural. How appropriate could be a six-week, early-summer series on Luther's favorite book, Galatians (Propers 5–9, Series C). Or a five-week, after-Christmas series from Jesus' Sermon on the Mount (Epiphany 4–8, Series A).

Pericopal series, however, are by no means limited to continuous readings. Often the movement of the season, carried out in the lectionary, suggests series preaching. The Old Testament readings from Isaiah for Advent (Series A) have wonderful commonalities. In each of the four readings, the seer invites his audience to look with him into the future, to visualize the Messiah and the age He will inaugurate. A series on these texts might bear the overall title "Do You See What I See?" Each sermon would seek to be picturesque, to follow the prophet's lead of brilliant and colorful language and images, to let the hearers "see" what in Christ is present reality, even as it remains yet hidden from our eyes.[21]

Conclusion

One Sabbath day in Nazareth, worshipers *were* allowed to see the messianic age with their own eyes. As was His custom, Jesus went into the synagogue and was handed a scroll to read. The pericope of the day—yes, the pericope—just happened to be Isaiah 61: "The Spirit of the Lord is upon Me, because He has anointed Me to proclaim good news to the poor. He has sent Me to proclaim liberty to the captives and recovering of sight to the blind, to set at liberty those who are oppressed, to proclaim the year of the Lord's favor." After sitting down, Jesus announced, "Today this Scripture has been fulfilled in your hearing" (Luke 4:18–21).[22]

As for Philip a few years later, the opportunity could not have been more ideal. Yet preachers every Sunday have opportunities just as promising, just as divinely appointed, in their modern lectionary. For every reading, worked

21 Such a series could also be used for midweek Advent services, using each text the Wednesday following its reading on Sunday and omitting the fourth sermon if need be.

22 Luke 4:16–30, the Gospel, incidentally, for Epiphany 3, Series C.

carefully and thoroughly, yields a message of Christ. When Christ is proclaimed, this Scripture is fulfilled again for today's hearing.

Appendix 1

Some Less-Than-Obvious Themes of the Day

Advent 3, Series C

Readings: Zeph. 3:14–20; Phil. 4:4–7; Luke 7:18–28 (29–35)
Theme: True joy is humble trust in Christ's salvation.

Zephaniah invites the daughters of Zion to rejoice, for the Lord Himself rejoices over them. Paul likewise calls us to "rejoice in the Lord always." John the Baptist's question, "Are You the one?" points us to our only Savior, through whom we have been given the hope of unending joy.

Epiphany 2, Series A

Readings: Isa. 49:1–7; 1 Cor. 1:1–9; John 1:29–42a
Theme: God has called, by name, His Son and all who call upon the Son's name. Therefore, they speak in God's name.

Before His birth, says the Servant of the Lord, Yahweh called Him, mentioning His name and giving Him a "mouth like a sharpened sword," that He might save not only Israel but also all nations. Paul thanks God for calling all in Corinth who call upon the name of Christ and for enriching their speaking. Jesus calls Andrew, who invites his brother Simon, who receives a new name from Christ.

Lent 2, Series C

Readings: Jer. 26:8–15; Phil. 3:17–4:1; Luke 13:31–35
Theme: So deep is God's concern for His beloved children, so serious is His warning, that rejection must bring weeping.

The "weeping prophet," Jeremiah, is nearly killed when he levels the most chilling of warnings against Jerusalem. Paul pleads with his beloved to stand firm in the Lord, for, as he says with tears, those who reject Christ are destined to destruction. Jesus weeps because Jerusalem will now reject God's last loving embrace by killing this prophet too.

Lent 3, Series C

Readings: Ezek. 33:7–20; 1 Cor. 10:1–13; Luke 13:1–9
Theme: God is faithful toward His children, always providing forgiveness and escape, but let them not abuse His faithfulness.

God announces through Ezekiel that judgment is coming, but He promises that the one who does what is "just and right . . . shall surely live." Jesus echoes this same theme in the parable of the fig tree. Paul reminds us that in our trials God provides a way out. Yet if God's people remain in rebellion rather than repentance, His patience has a limit.

Proper 4 (May 29–June 4), Series A

Readings: Deut. 11:18–21, 26–28; Rom. 3:21–28; Matt. 7:15–29
Theme: "Doing the will of the Father" or "obeying the commands of the Lord" is not observing the Law; rather, it is faith in Jesus Christ.

Moses promises blessings for obedience. Christ commends those who bear good fruit, do the will of the Father, or hear His words and put them into practice. But outward actions do not justify. Moses and Jesus, like Paul, are actually calling for faith.

Proper 11 (July 17–23), Series C

Readings: Gen. 18:1–10a (10b–14); Col. 1:21–29; Luke 10:38–42
Theme: Proclaiming and hearing the "one thing needful," the Word of God, provides spiritual nourishment; it is, nevertheless, the message of reconciliation by and for fleshly, physical bodies.

Abraham and Martha serving dinner to their divine guests was certainly of secondary importance to hearing the words they spoke. But the word Paul proclaimed—and that Mary heard—was fleshly indeed: reconciliation of our flesh to God by the physical suffering of Christ.

Proper 17 (August 28–September 3), Series A

Readings: Jer. 15:15–21; Rom. 12:9–21; Matt. 16:21–28
Theme: As Christ out of love went to the cross as the sacrifice for all people, so we are to love others, revealing our faith through our actions. Such loving actions may mean suffering and rejection from the world, but through Christ we "overcome evil with good."

Jeremiah suffers reproach for faithfully following the path God has laid out for him. That is exactly what Christ promises each of us who follow Him. Nevertheless, in view of God's mercy for the sake of Jesus' cross, Christians do offer themselves in loving service to others.

Proper 18 (September 4–10), Series A

Readings: Ezek. 33:7–9; Rom. 13:1–10; Matt. 18:1–20

Theme: While God uses worldly authorities to punish wrongdoers, He commands Christian discipline solely for the purpose of saving the sinner.

Ezekiel is solemnly commanded to warn the wicked of their sin, and, says Paul, disobedience will be punished with the sword. Both the prophet and the secular authorities pose God's own judgment. The kingdom of the left shows by contrast, however, how much more glorious is the kingdom of the Gospel. The secular sword serves only to preserve order. When the church speaks the Law, on the other hand, the goal is always salvation.

Appendix 2

Sermon Series from the Lectionary

Advent 1–4, Series A: "Do You See What I See?"

Isa. 2:1–5:	"Do You See the Nations Walking Together in the Light of the Lord?"
Isa. 11:1–10:	"Do You Behold a Branch That's Growing?"
Isa. 35:1–10:	"Do You See the Redeemed 'Streaming' Down the Highway?"
Isa. 7:10–17:	"Do You See the Sign That God Is with Us?"

Epiphany 4–8, Series A: "The Sermon on the Mount: Not the Sermon You Thought It Was"

Matt. 5:1–12:	"The Beatitudes Are Not a 'How-To' Manual for Happiness" ("Happy," that is, blessed, is what you already are by faith in Christ)
Matt. 5:13–20:	"Jesus Does Not Preach Good News Only" (The Law is indispensable preparation for Christ's Gospel)
Matt. 5:21–37:	"Righteousness Is Not What You Make of It" (True righteousness is in the heart)
Matt. 5:38–48:	"It May Not Be Quite the Way You've Heard It Said" (Try this instead: You will be perfect as your heavenly Father is perfect)
Matt. 6:24–34:	" 'Not to Worry' Is Not Much Help" (The heavenly Father gives all the help we need)

Propers 4–9, Series C: "The Epistle to the Galatians: Luther's 'Katie von Bora' " (This series is based on lectures and sermons by Martin Luther, who referred to Galatians by the above affectionate title)

Gal 1:1–12	"Though Luther Himself or an Angel from Heaven Teaches Otherwise, Let Him Be Accursed."
Gal. 1:11–24:	"For My Doctrine Is God's, Not Mine"
Gal. 2:15–21:	"If We Know This Article, We Are in the Clearest Light"
Gal. 3:23–4:7:	"He Is No Longer His Tutor, but His Good Friend and Companion"
Gal. 5:1, 13–25:	"A Great and Incomprehensible Liberty"
Gal. 6:1–10, 14–18:	"The Only Glory I Have Left Is This: The Cross of Christ"

Propers 10–12, Series A: "Parables of the Kingdom"

Matt. 13:1–9, 18–23: "We Are Living Miracles of God's Word"
Matt. 13:24–30, 36–43: "God Will Harvest No Field until It's/Its Time"
Matt. 13:44–52: "What's the Kingdom of Heaven Worth?"

Propers 13–15, Series B: "Believe It or Not . . ."

John 6:22–35: "Believe It or Not, Faith in Jesus Really Offers Something for Nothing"
John 6:35–51: "Believe It or Not, This Bread of Life Is above All"
John 6:51–69: "Believe It or Not, Christ's Flesh Is Real Food" *or* "Believe Them or Not, Jesus' Words Are Decisive"

Unfolding the Meaning of the Liturgy

William M. Cwirla

A sermon always has a context and a text. The context may be informal or formal. It may take place in a living room or a cathedral. The liturgical context may be a few songs followed by prayer or the elaborate Liturgy of St. Basil. The text will be a selected passage from the Holy Scriptures, determined by some sort of assigned lectionary system, the church year, the occasion for the service, or the personal choice of the preacher. For the purposes of this essay, I will assume that the text of the sermon is determined by the three-year or one-year lectionaries employed by *Lutheran Service Book*. I will also assume that the context is the reformed canon of the Western Catholic Mass, which is characterized by its five traditional texts: Kyrie, Gloria in Excelsis, Creed, Sanctus, Agnus Dei. These texts will also form the backbone of this essay.

A sermon needs to have peripheral vision; otherwise, it will be myopic. With the text squarely in the center of his visual field, the preacher must be keenly aware of context: the context of his hearers and the context of the surrounding texts and actions of the liturgy. The sermon is never an isolated event. It is a part of a greater whole. In a liturgical context, the sermon is closely tied to the readings that preceded it and the Supper that follows. The hearers, too, are linked to their Baptism on the one hand and the forthcoming meal of the Lord's Supper on the other. The sermon is the table talk of the baptized, with the pastor serving as the *paterfamilias*, the head of the family, interpreting the Word of God to the circle of baptized children of God who have come to have table fellowship with Christ. The sermon serves the liturgy by interpreting and applying the Word of God within the greater context of Baptism and the Lord's Supper. The liturgy serves the sermon by providing a stable context for preaching by which the saving acts of God are remembered by the gathered congregation of the baptized.

The liturgy is itself the Word of God. This plain fact is often overlooked by those who are opposed to fixed liturgical forms. The liturgy is not the

Word of God in the sense that God gave a particular form or setting for worship in the New Testament. The New Testament has no ritual book corresponding to the Old Testament Book of Leviticus. There is no divinely established form of worship in the New Testament, nor are there divinely mandated texts. There is only the pattern of teaching and table, Word and Sacrament, apostolic doctrine, the fellowship, that is, the breaking of the bread, and the prayer (Acts 2:42), and the various liturgical traditions that have been handed down to us through the ages. The liturgy is the Word of God because it is almost entirely composed of quotations from the Holy Scriptures. The traditional canticles of the Kyrie, the Gloria, Sanctus, and Agnus Dei are all taken directly from the Holy Scriptures. The creeds are nothing less than a summary of scriptural doctrine concerning the tri-unity of God and the person and work of Jesus Christ.

The liturgy also interprets the Scriptures by applying the passages to the hearers and bringing these passages into interpretive contexts. Why do we pray "Lord, have mercy" at the beginning of a Divine Service? Why do we sing Jesus' birthday song, "Glory to God in the highest," before we hear the Word of God? Why do we chant "Holy, holy, holy" and "Lamb of God" before eating and drinking the Lord's Supper? What does it mean when the death song of Simeon (Luke 2:29–32) becomes our prayer at the close of the day and after receiving the body and blood of Jesus in Holy Communion? The preacher who is open to such questions will be in a good position to unfold the meaning of the liturgy in the ordinary course of his preaching.

Danger lurks close at hand whenever a preacher sets out to expound on the meaning of the liturgy in a sermon. Liturgy is more implicit speech than it is explicit. Deep structure and symbolism invite exploration. The danger of making the liturgy the focus of preaching is precisely the danger that the implicit will become entirely explicit. So-called "narrative" or "teaching" liturgies, however well-intentioned, suffer from the defect of being overly explicit. They are pedantic at best; interminably tedious at worst. The same can be said of the general chit-chat that accompanies most presiding at the liturgy. In a satirical essay on the absence of the implicit on television, semiotician Umberto Eco describes the fictitious Bonga tribe who have no sense of the implicit. A typical Bonga conversation would begin with one saying to another, "Pay attention. I am now speaking, and I will use some words." If a Bonga invites you to dinner, he will seat you with these words: "This is the table, and these are the chairs!"[1] Narrative liturgies tend quickly to go "Bonga" with their endless explanations and elucidations. "We will now make our beginning by invoking the triune name of God." "We will now

1 Umberto Eco, "How to Be a TV Host," in *How to Travel with a Salmon and Other Essays* (New York: Harcourt Brace, 1994), 50–55.

sing a hymn known as the Sanctus, which came into the liturgy in the sixth century but was originally heard by Isaiah in the eighth century BC and later by John the Elder on the island of Patmos in the late first century." The only thing left unsaid is, "And now a word from our sponsor."

Liturgical symbol and sign are meant to be discovered serendipitously, not programmatically. The joy of discovery is undermined by excessive, explicit explanations. Liturgical speech needs to be *al dente*, not overcooked. It should invite conversation and stimulate imaginative catechesis, setting forth biblical treasures, old and new, like an old merchant at a swap meet. Liturgy is better prayed than picked apart; it is intended to be chanted, not dissected. Preaching the liturgy will evoke, allude, connect, and point without turning the liturgy into pedantic pablum.

Unfolding the liturgy means unfolding what God is doing here and now for us and for our salvation. Liturgy goes on in the present, bringing forward the past and propelling us toward the future in Jesus Christ. God is at work in the liturgy making His creative and redemptive presence manifest to us, intruding into our lives, killing us and making us alive with the Law and the Gospel. Liturgical preaching is always Law and Gospel proclamation and is never simply explanation. We are not actors playing roles in some liturgical divine drama. Worship is real life, genuine dying and rising. We are standing as sinner-saints in the presence of our Creator and Redeemer who is revealing Himself to us as once He did to Moses in the burning bush. We stand on holy ground, not to kick off our shoes and put up our feet, but to bow down in worship of the Father in the Spirit and in the Truth who is Jesus Christ. We gather to hear the forgiveness of our sins, to eat and drink Jesus' sacrificial body and blood. Like the Israelite *paterfamilias* of the Old Testament at the Passover table, the preacher unfolds the meaning of the liturgy for the children at the table (Exod. 12:27).

The best way for the preacher to do this is to incorporate little bits of the liturgy into the sermon on a regular basis. A steady diet of liturgical preaching stimulates the liturgical appetite. Sometimes a sentence or two in passing will be sufficient. At other times, a liturgical text may be developed more fully, especially in catechetical preaching. The preacher will always be on the alert for opportunities, even when the appointed reading is not explicitly quoted in the liturgy. Concordance studies are extremely helpful for making the connections. For example, several pericopes that deal with the image of Christ as "lamb" (Acts 8:32; 1 Pet. 1:19; Rev. 5:13; 7:10) provide the opportunity to note our acclamation of Jesus as the Lamb of God who takes away the sin of the world. Sometimes the connection may be topical. The narrative of Abraham and Isaac on Moriah (Gen. 22:1–18; Lent 1, Series B) or the Passover (Exod. 12:1–14; Holy Thursday, alternate and one-year) give the Old Testament content for the Agnus Dei. Familiarity with the structure and texts of the liturgy is indispensable for a preaching on the liturgy that is natural, not forced.

Unfolding the meaning of the liturgy in the sermon invites the hearer to explore the liturgy more deeply, to discover previously unnoticed connections and meaning, and to teach others in the joy of discovery, particularly those who are unfamiliar with the liturgy. Preaching becomes a kind of liturgical catechesis in which even the experienced worshiper is drawn more deeply into the mysteries of God. Instead of being simply an arbitrary "worship service" printed in a disposable bulletin, the liturgy becomes something living and active, which is what it is, the living and active, double-edged word of Law and Gospel at work, killing and making alive, convicting us of our sins and comforting us by our crucified and risen Savior.

Invocation: In the Name

Invocation is calling upon God's name. To invoke the name of God is to lay claim to the power of His promises inherent in His name. God swears by His name and promises to act in His name. God takes the initiative and the responsibility. His name and reputation are on the line. God keeps His promises. Where His name is, there He is mighty to save, to bless, to forgive, and to hear prayer. God tells us His name; we do not invent names for God (Exod. 3:1–14; Transfiguration, one-year). God runs the use of His name. We do not "make our beginning" in the name of God; we invoke God's name in the beginning. We call upon it, lay claim to it, bind it to ourselves, or there will be nothing to begin. We lay claim to His promise that "where two or three are gathered in My name, there am I among them" (Matt. 18:20; Proper 18, Series A).

Invocation is not magic. According to the Small Catechism, the Second Commandment forbids "making magic" (*Zauber machen*) with God's name. We are not conjuring with God's name, as if we could conjure up a God who was not already with us before we called on Him. Nor are we putting a coat of religious varnish on our activity, as though by dropping God's name we are assured of His approval. Invocation presupposes God's presence and His promise to bless us. We are holding God to His promises to be gracious and merciful to us for Jesus' sake. Invoking God's name, we are bold to say that we are coming into the presence of the Father in Spirit and in Truth (John 4:22). God is creatively and redemptively present for us in the flesh of His Son, Jesus, who incarnates the name of God in His human flesh.

By invocation, we are asserting our privilege as the baptized children of God. This is why we make the sign of the cross when we invoke the name of God, according to the Small Catechism. We are baptized into the triune name of God (Matt. 28:16–20; Holy Trinity, Series A). We live in the triune life and love of God, and we are marked as His possession by the cross of the one who bore the world's sin and drew all into His death. The name of God is a holy thing, revealing God's mercy in Christ in a tangible, audible way. Christ is the incarnation of the name of God, for His human name *Jesus* has become, by His dying and rising, the "name that is above every name." It is the only "name by which we must be saved," since He alone has embraced all creatures in His death.

In unfolding the meaning of the Invocation, the preacher will emphasize Baptism, the incarnation, and the close connection between God's name and the Sacraments. The following is a sample from my sermon on Exodus 3 (Transfiguration, one-year) in which God reveals His name to Moses in the burning bush:

> "Sticks and stones can break my bones, but names can never hurt me." So what's in a name, anyway? Why bother with names? Wouldn't numbers be more precise? Yet we don't ask for someone's Social Security number when we want to get to know that person. We ask for a name. Look at how we protect and value our own name. Notice the power of your name signed on the bottom of a contract, a wedding license, or the signature line of a check. Your name stands for everything that you are. Look at how hurt or offended people are when you forget their name. You may as well have forgotten them. You and your name are interchangeable.
>
> Names have power. Drop the right name at the right place and time, and major things can happen. Where your name is, there is your reputation, your authority, your activity, everything that you are and that you represent. Sign your name to a contract and you are committed. Give your name to someone else, and you're asking for trouble. Things done "in your name" are things for which you take responsibility whether you actually do them or not.
>
> The divine service begins with a bit of divine "name dropping." "In the name of the Father and of the Son and of the Holy Spirit." God dropped His name on you when you were baptized. And now you drop His name back. His name tells you that you belong to God, that you belong here among His people. You are sheep of the Good Shepherd's flock. Your life is in Him. He's put His name on you. And now you call upon that name. You invoke it. Not like magic words. This isn't religious hocus pocus. We're not telling God what to do. Nor are we conjuring God out of thin air, as if He wasn't present until we showed up. God was present on the mountain long before Moses ever arrived. And God revealed His presence to Moses. That was Christ in the burning bush,

> a gracious fire that does not consume. And it was Christ who revealed God's gracious, saving name to Moses: Yahweh.
>
> God's name is more of a verb than it is a noun. God acts in His name. "I am who I am" or "He is who He is" or "He will do what He will do." God has acted in Jesus. He stretched out His mighty arm to save. He continues to act, pouring out His Spirit, forgiving sin, baptizing, feeding, and finally raising the dead, which is His specialty. And so when we invoke God's name, "in the name of the Father and of the Son and of the Holy Spirit," this isn't some kind of uncertain wish on our part: "I hope God's around to hear us." Nor is it a religious veneer on our "worship experience": "Lord, aren't You glad we showed up this morning?" We're expecting big things. God's going to be doing burning bush stuff with us this morning. You're standing on holy ground. So don't get comfortable, get ready. Get ready to receive. Get ready to be forgiven and set free. Get ready for those chains of death to come loose. You have God's name, His signature, the power of His promise.

Unfolding the meaning of the liturgy is making connections between the text and action, between what God said and what He is doing. First, I wanted to connect the revelation of God's name in the burning bush to the personal revelation of God's name in the Baptism of the hearer. Second, I wanted to equate the episode of the burning bush with our gathering in the name of God. At the same time I wanted to guard against the notion that the Invocation is something we do to make things happen. The name of God is good news for the sinner, when God acts in His name.

Kyrie: Lord, Have Mercy

Kyrie eleison is the simplest of all prayers. *Kyrie*, Lord. We confess who God is. He is the Lord, Yahweh. *Eleison*, have mercy. We confess what we expect from God. The Kyrie is faith's empty-handed, broken-hearted cry for compassion, the cry of one who has no place to turn but to a compassionate God who has joined us to Himself in His Passion. "Lord, have mercy," David cries out when he had committed adultery and murder (Ps. 51:1; Introit for Ash Wednesday). A Canaanite woman pleads with Jesus for her demonized daughter across the deep chasm of Jewish-Canaanite hostility and separation (Matt. 15:22; Proper 15, Series A). A desperate father intercedes for his epileptic son (Matt. 17:15). A blind beggar sitting on the side of the road outside of Jericho will not be silenced by the embarrassed crowds (Luke 18:38; Quinquagesima, one-year). Ten outcast lepers call out to Jesus from a noncontagious distance, "Lord, have mercy" (Luke 17:13; Proper 23, Series C; Thanksgiving). And mercy they receive from the One who manifests the merciful heart of God in human flesh.

In a world that extols the winners and quickly forgets the losers, the Kyrie joins our voices with the least, lost, lowly, despised, rejected—the very backbone of the kingdom of God. We have nothing to offer God. We come empty-handed and broken-hearted. The liturgy's Kyrie reminds us what Luther recognized so clearly at the end of his life: "We are all beggars." *Kyrie eleison* is the end of prayer as bribery, religious smooth-talking, transaction, or deal-cutting. This is how you pray when you are at the end of your rope, when hope is extinguished, when we cannot do anything, offer anything, promise anything. All we can do is beg. Kyrie is the essence of Luther's last written words: "We are all beggars. That is true."

A way to unfold the meaning of the Kyrie is to take up the topic of prayer. The Kyrie is a graduate course on prayer. It teaches us to pray out of who God is. He is the Lord, Yahweh, Jesus. The Kyrie teaches us what to expect from God: mercy. This example from a sermon on the blind beggar on the road out of Jericho (Luke 18:35; Quinquagesima, one-year) seeks to identify the Sunday morning hearer with the blind beggar:

> Think of the center aisle of the church as the road from Jericho to Jerusalem. Close your eyes for a moment. Imagine that you are a blind man, sitting in darkness. Your ears are your eyes. You are trained to see with your ears. You hear a procession go by. You hear the voices, the clamor, the commotion. It's Jesus, the one you've been waiting for. He's coming your way. He's passing by the place where you are sitting. You can hear Him coming closer. You cry out, "Lord, have mercy!" You say it louder, "Jesus, Son of David, have mercy!" You keep calling it out, louder and louder, so loud that the crowd is embarrassed and tries to quiet you. But you don't care. You won't let them stop you. You can't. Jesus is here, and you can't help but shout your prayer. You know He will hear you; you know He will stop.
>
> Kyrie, eleison. Christe, eleison. Kyrie eleison. Every Sunday, every time we gather for worship, this is our first prayer. Lord, have mercy. And what a dense prayer it is! A beggar's prayer, and one that can hardly be improved. We worry so much about prayer. We worry too much. Do we have the right words? Are we praying with the right attitude? In the right place? For the right things? Let the blind beggar be your teacher. He will teach you the discipline of prayer from the curbside. He is your fellow congregation member, a fellow beggar in need. He sits with you at the curb on the road every Sunday. He sits next to you. Pray along with him. Kyrie, eleison. Lord, have mercy. Jesus is Lord, Yahweh in the flesh come to have mercy on you. Call out to Him. Lord, have mercy upon us.
>
> It isn't the lack of words that keeps us from prayer, but the abundance of pride. The old Adam is proud and religious. He bows the knee to

> no one, and if he does, it's only for flattery and bribery, to butter God up with our words. But sin and death have left us as blind beggars on the curb. Desperate people need simple prayers. Lord, have mercy. Recognize to whom you are praying. Jesus the Lord, who suffered and died for you. Recognize for what you are praying. Mercy from the merciful heart of God. At the end of his life, Luther said, "We are all beggars." That could be said of our beginning too. Beggars we are, and our Lord is a beggar King who has mercy on those who call on Him. Kyrie, eleison.

The Ektene Kyrie[2] puts flesh on the bones of our plea for mercy. It lifts us out of the quagmire of self-diagnosed felt needs into the broader pastures of intercession for the world, the church catholic, and our own congregation. In this sermon on Phil. 4:4–7 (Advent 3, Series C), the petitions of the Kyrie are expanded in prose poetry form. The issue addressed in this sermon is our anxiety over the state of things, amplified over our increased awareness thanks to the variety of communication tools at our disposal. Like the Psalter, preaching on the Kyrie is both prayer and proclamation at the same time.

> We're anxious. We see and hear things that disturb us. A senseless shooting, a tragic accident, a natural disaster, an untimely death. "Grisly details at eleven." The eye of television brings the hard images into our lives. The newspaper blares the headlines in 72-point letters. The Internet floods us with disconnected facts. Anxiety grows. What will we do? St. Paul says, "Stop. Take a deep breath. Pray. Don't be anxious about anything. Talk to God. Tell Him what you want, and thank Him for what brought you to pray. But by all means pray. You'll have peace that goes beyond your understanding, a peace that will keep you whole in Jesus."
>
> And so we pray out of the depths of our anxiety, right at the beginning of worship. We dump on God. The Kyrie of the liturgy is our deacon, bidding the congregation to pray with one voice. Check your anxiety at the door. Bring your petitions before your merciful Lord.
>
> "For the peace from above, and for our salvation, let us pray to the Lord. Kyrie eleison." We want peace—peace in our homes, our communities, our lives. We seek peace but find only unrest. We amuse ourselves to death with mindless entertainment, mind-numbing drugs, and drink. We gather to ourselves paperback prophets who preach "peace, peace" into our ears when there is no peace. We are anxious, isolated, inundated. Peace that lasts is a peace from above, a peace the world cannot give, a peace that passes our understanding, a singular peace that flows

2 The Ektene is a form of the Kyrie prevalent in the Eastern Church in which the words "Lord, have mercy" are spoken in response to a series of petitions or bids.

from the wounds and words of Jesus. To have this peace is to have salvation. Peace and salvation go together, as with the Hebrew word *shalom*. Everything is in order, whole, at peace, in harmony. For this heavenly peace and for our rescue from sin and death; Kyrie eleison.

We pray for the peace of the whole world. For a world riddled by bombs and bullets. For graffiti-covered alleyways and adulterous bedrooms. For warring nations with push-button nuclear warheads and violent streets filled with young men whose notion of manhood is a semiautomatic weapon. For a world filled with prejudice, bigotry, intolerance, and hatred. For a world of broken homes and lives shattered. For peace to the abused and the abuser, to the oppressed and the oppressor. For the world reconciled to God by Jesus' death on the cross; Kyrie eleison.

We pray for the well-being of the Church of God, the visible Body of Christ on the earth. For the persecuted and all who suffer for the name of Jesus. For clergy and laity, for pastors and teachers. For the good news of forgiveness in Jesus, the baptismal bath of His rebirth, the Supper of His body and blood, that they would dwell richly among us and that others would be drawn to them. For the Church, the Bride for whom Jesus died, that she might be spotless, holy, and without blemish; Kyrie eleison.

For the unity of all. For an end to our sectarian schisms and needless divisions. For the killing of all prejudice, hatred, bigotry, and oppression. For the breaking down of every wall that divides and contradicts our unity in Christ; Kyrie eleison.

"For this holy house, and for all who offer here their worship and praise." For our fellow congregation members and for our guests. For those who are like us and for those who are not. For those with whom we have exchanged sharp words at the last church meeting or angry words at the breakfast table. For this little group of sinners who show forth the death of Christ for the life of the world; Kyrie eleison.

The homiletical device of repetition coupled with expanding the petitions draws out what is implicit without making things excessively explicit. The hearers are encouraged to unpack the liturgical sentences for themselves and to incorporate them in their own prayers. In this way the liturgy is catechetical, teaching as it prays and bringing the worshiper into ever broader pastures of prayer.

The Kyrie guards against the misuse of prayer as the bribery of God. Too often, we are inclined to believe that by our prayers we can shift the odds in God's house and obtain the advantage. But prayer does not work that way. *Kyrie eleison* is a cry for mercy, not a bargain or deal. It is prayed on the knees, not atop the high horse. And our Father in heaven knows what we need even before we ask. This is our ultimate freedom to pray, as an empty-handed beggar to a merciful Lord abounding in gifts.

Gloria in Excelsis: Glory to God in the Highest

For most people, Christmas comes but once a year. But the Gloria in Excelsis suggests otherwise. Every Divine Service is a celebration of Christmas! The Word made flesh dwells incarnately among us, enfleshed in the preached Word and Sacraments. Glory to God in the highest. The angelic hosts sang this heavenly song the night of Jesus' birth. And now the church sings Jesus' birthday song anew. Lowly shepherds were the congregation that first worshiped Him on that marvelous night, outcasts and losers, the lowest rung of the working class. And now we join with them. Peace to His people on earth. Peace to the world on whom God's favor rests. God and man are reconciled in this tiny, helpless infant. "In Christ God was reconciling the world to Himself, not counting their trespasses against them" (2 Cor. 5:19; Lent 4, Series C and Good Friday, one-year).

Christmas is a great opportunity to bring the liturgy to life, especially for those who do not experience its joys on a weekly basis. The church is our Bethlehem. We gather with shepherds and angels to celebrate the God who dwells with us. This portion of a sermon on Christmas Eve equates the manger with the Word and the Sacraments.

> Glory to God. Peace among men with whom God is pleased. The song rang out over Bethlehem's fields. Angel hosts rejoiced and sang. Shepherds left their flocks to see God's Lamb, His Son. They heard the great, good news. "A Savior is born to you who is Christ the Lord." Where? In the city of David, the shepherd-king. "There you will find Him. Swaddled in cloths, laid in an animal's feed trough. The baby-God born to save you."
>
> Glory to God in the highest. We sing it every Sunday in the liturgy before we hear the readings from Scripture and the sermon. Every Sunday is a little Christmas minus the lights and the sawed-off tree and all the tinsel and trimmings. We don't hear angel choirs but our own squeaky voices, no less angelic or majestic with the news. Glory to God. Peace to the world. Good news for all. God and sinners are reconciled in this baby born for you.
>
> Join those lowly shepherds. Leave the cares of your work behind. It will all be there when you get back. Drop dead to your life and adore Him who is your life, this child destined to die and rise for you and for the world. Sing His praises with the angels, archangels, and the whole

> company of heaven. And this will be God's sign for you: you will find Him swaddled in the words of Holy Scriptures, in the mouth of the preacher, in the water of Baptism, in the bread and the wine of His Supper. The church is your Bethlehem, now run to it and worship God in the flesh. To you is born a Savior, Christ the Lord.

The hymn that follows the angel's song echoes the invocation of the triune name of God. We worship the Father in the Spirit and in the Truth who is Jesus Christ, the atoning Lamb and our Mediator—three distinct persons, yet only one divine being. The big verbs of worship are summoned to use: praise, blessing, worship, glory, and thanks (Rev. 7:12; Easter 4, Series C). The Father has gathered us in Baptism to worship Him in the Holy Spirit and in the incarnate Truth (John 3). And now we worship the Father through the Son in the Holy Spirit. We stand in the presence of the heavenly King in His throne room. The Father Almighty, the only-begotten Son (John 1:14, 18; Christmas Day), God's Lamb, who takes away the sin of the world, seated in session at the right hand of the Father (Col. 3:1; Rom. 8:34; Heb. 1:3, 13; 8:1; 10:12; 12:2; 1 Pet. 3:22; Rev. 5:7). The Gloria guards against the implicit modalism in much of contemporary praise music, which dwells on one person of the undivided Trinity while ignoring the other two. It also protects us from the casual familiarity that plagues much of modern worship. We are gathered in the presence of an awesome mystery before whom Moses trembled and the seraphim veil themselves in reverence. The Gloria echoes of our Lord's Baptism in the Jordan and the Mount of Transfiguration. "This is My beloved Son, listen to Him" (Matt. 4:12–25; Epiphany 3, Series A; Matt. 17:1–9; Transfiguration, Series A). The glory belongs to God. The peace is ours, a gift from the Father through the Son in the Holy Spirit.

Credo: I Believe

With the heart you believe, with the tongue you confess (Rom. 10:9–10; Lent 1, Series C). To confess is to repeat with the same words what one has heard. The Greek word for confess is *homolegein* (*homo*, "the same," plus *legein*, "to speak words"). *Homolegein*: "to speak with the same words." Confession is a form of baby talk, to say back to Papa and Mama what they said to us. What we have heard from God we repeat. Jesus promises, "Everyone who acknowledges Me before men, I also will acknowledge before My Father who is in heaven" (Matt. 10:32; Proper 7, Series A). Peter confessed Jesus as the Christ, the Son of the living God (Matt. 16:16; Proper 16, Series A). On this confession of Jesus as the Christ, the Son of God, Jesus builds His Church, indestructible against the gates of Hades. In confessing Jesus Christ as Lord, the Church is a preview of the Last Day when every knee will bow and every tongue confess "Lord Jesus Christ" to the glory of God the Father (Phil. 2:1; Proper 21, Series A).

Confession is personal but never private. We neither believe for others nor believe alone nor confess alone. The Apostles', Nicene, and Athanasian Creeds are the confessing tradition of the Church, handed down from generation to generation. They are the Church's confessional heritage. The great baptismal creeds of Rome and Jerusalem and the conciliar creed of Nicaea and Constantinople have become our creeds. We are reminded that we are not the first Christians, nor will we be the last should Jesus delay in His appearing. We believe together with all who have ever confessed the triune name of God. We confess together, as a corporate body, a royal priesthood, a holy nation. The original form of the Nicene Creed began "We believe." Even when we confess "I believe," as in the Apostles' Creed, we confess together as one corporate "I." In Baptism we have been incorporated into the Body of Christ (1 Cor. 12:13). "There is . . . one Lord, one faith, one Baptism, one God and Father of all" (Eph. 4:4–5). The faith confessed by each of us individually is the corporate faith of the whole church at all times and in all places.

At a time when creeds are becoming increasingly individualistic, reflection on the creed is an opportunity to reflect on the corporate nature of faith and confession. Unfolding the creed in the context of the liturgy involves being aware of its place and purpose in the liturgy. Following the reading of the Gospel (Divine Service, Setting Three), the creed is the statement of the apostolic and catholic faith. We are not given to innovate when it comes to the Scriptures. What the preacher says in the sermon will align with the prophets, the apostles, the evangelists, and what believers through the ages have unanimously believed, taught, and confessed. When placed after the sermon (Divine Service, Setting One), the creed is a response to the hearing of the read and preached Word. The creed is therefore both proclamation and response, and the preacher will want to emphasize both aspects.

Preaching on the creeds often can take on an apologetic tone. The creeds are, after all, a summary of the Christian faith, forged at times of controversy. In the following example from a sermon on Matt. 16:13–20 (Proper 16, Series A), I focus on the death and resurrection of Jesus at the heart of the Apostles' Creed. Everything we confess revolves around the historical fact that Jesus died and rose from the dead, which sets apart the Christian confession from all other confessions.

> Who do you say that I am? Jesus speaks to the Twelve, His chosen band of disciples. He also speaks to you. We know what the world says about Jesus, but what are you going to say? Who do you say that Jesus is? A great teacher? Great teachers don't claim to be the Son of God. A

> holy man? Holy men may offer signs and wonders, but none can offer the sign of death and resurrection. A moral example? Moral examples don't die for the sins of others. There is no alternative. Purveyors of religious snake oil there are aplenty. But they don't die and rise from the dead. This Jesus has a death and a resurrection. "Crucified, died, buried, descended to hell. And on the third day rose again from the dead." He said it would happen, right on the heels of Peter's confession. And it ain't bragging if you can do it. He is the Christ, the Son of the living God, crucified and risen. We confess Him every Sunday in the Nicene Creed and every morning and evening in the Apostles' Creed. And in confessing, you and I become a visible (and audible) sign for the world of that great Day to end all days, the day when every knee will bow and every tongue will confess that Jesus Christ is Lord to the glory of God the Father.

Lent is a fine time for catechetical preaching and a perfect time to unpack the fullness of the creed together with the catechism. However, the Sunday sermon can be used to heighten the hearer's awareness of the importance of creedal statements in the corporate life of the church and the individual life of the believer. Here, in a sermon on Matt. 10:32 (Proper 7, Series A), I make the point that confession of the faith is not an option for the baptized believer.

> Confession and denial. There is no third option. You either confess Christ or you deny Him. You either say "Jesus is Lord" or you deny that He is Lord, but there is no middle ground, no third way of speaking. He revealed Himself to you as Lord in your Baptism, and there you, together with the church, confessed Him. Every Sunday you repeat that baptismal confession under the sign of the cross. "I believe; we believe." "I believe, and so I spoke," Paul says to the Corinthians (2 Cor. 4:13). We believe, and so we are compelled to say something. Like a champagne bottle ready to pop its cork, faith cannot be silent. We believe that we know something profound about God. Not that we understand Him any better, but that He has revealed something of Himself to us. We know who He is—Father, Son, and Holy Spirit. We know what He has done for us and for our salvation as our Creator, our Redeemer, and our Sanctifier. We believe that there is good news to tell the world, that God has reconciled the world to Himself in Christ and invites all people everywhere to believe it, trust it, confess it. And so we confess, we say back to God and to each other what we have heard and believed.
>
> Confession begins here, in church, in the divine liturgy, in the company of your fellow believers. This is a safe place to confess what you believe. We all believe the same together, and we say the same words together. When you leave here to confess what you believe in the world, we are still joined together as members of Christ's Body. You are no less the

church when you are at work, at play, mowing your lawn, shopping for groceries, standing in line at the bank. And there you confess or you deny what you believe.

Sanctus: Holy, Holy, Holy

In the midst of the liturgy of Holy Communion comes the Sanctus (Isa. 6:3; Epiphany 5, Series C; Holy Trinity, one-year). The prophet Isaiah first heard this wondrous hymn in that fateful year King Uzziah died. At a time of political uncertainty, the prophet is granted a gracious vision. He saw the six-winged seraphs, fiery angels resembling nothing of the saccharine depictions of angels in popular culture. They are frightful creatures who encircle the throne of God and sing their liturgy of praise without stopping. For these there is no sweet hour of prayer sandwiched between breakfast and kickoff time. They worship without ceasing, day and night. Their liturgy shakes the doorposts and thresholds of the temple and fills it with thick clouds of incense. The vision of God is awesome and terrifying. No one may look on God and live. These angelic beings cover their faces in reverence and hide themselves in modesty. They hover about the throne and call out:

Holy, holy, holy.
Yahweh Sabaoth.
Heaven and earth are full of your glory.

John the Elder saw their faces when he was in the liturgy on the Lord's Day while exiled on the island of Patmos. There were four of them. One had the face of a lion, the king of the wild beasts. Another the face of an ox, the prince of the domestic beasts. A third had the face of an eagle, the most powerful of the birds of the air. The fourth, the face of a man, the foremost of God's visible creatures. They represent the whole creation before God and serve the Creator as creation's acolytes (Rev. 4:6b–8).

Heaven and earth intersect in the liturgy. God's throne room and His footstool come together, and we stand on the threshold of something much greater than we are. We sing the song of the seraphim, the song of creation, three-times holy to the triune God. We sing with the angels, the archangels, and with the whole company of heaven, including the blessed dead who have run the race before us, the patriarchs, the prophets, the apostles, blessed Mary, and also our own dead in the Lord. The pragmatism of attendance figures and head counts is swallowed up by this hymn. Who can count the myriad of angels who are present at every Divine Service? Who can number the saints and martyrs of every nation, tribe, people, and language?

This is not some other-worldly, fantasy adventure into the heavenly realms. Earth does not reach up to heaven, though we are prone to try.

Heaven reaches down to earth, as God always does. In fact, God is ever-present to His creation, so there is no "reaching" at all. Incarnation is no "reach" for God. Here is the mystery of salvation, hidden, though actually present, revealed in the God-man, Jesus Christ. God has revealed the mystery of salvation to the world. He has shown us His face and told us His name: Jesus, the Jewish carpenter from Nazareth, Mary's boy. "Blessed is He who comes in the name of the Lord." He is the God who comes to us to be with us, to save us. We welcome Him with the words of Psalm 118, the victorious Messiah-King comes to His city in peace atop a borrowed donkey. Every Sunday is Palm Sunday. We greet the King who comes to us in His body and blood. He is with us to save us.

Hosanna in the highest! Hosanna is the counterpart to Kyrie.[3] It is a shout for salvation. Lord, save us! Lord, have mercy! We cry out to the king. From the brokenness of our lives. From the ruins of our marriages. From hospital beds. From dangerous streets. Hosanna! Save us, Lord. And He does. With His own body and blood, He comes to save us.

I tried to capture the essence of the cry of Hosanna in this short narrative. While I normally do not use such stories in a sermon, this person was well-known by the congregation, and his story illustrated well our own condition as we come to the Lord's Supper singing "hosanna."

> The doctors said there was nothing they could do. The bleeding couldn't be stopped without surgery, and surgery was not an option for him. And so he lay there, bleeding inside. Bleeding to his death. His wife called. "The doctor said he needs a miracle."
>
> "I can't promise miracles," I said. "But I'll bring Holy Communion."
>
> I arrived about an hour later and proceeded to set up the Lord's Supper on his nightstand. "He's not supposed to eat or drink anything," his wife said, ever obedient to the doctor's orders.
>
> "He'll eat and drink this," I said.
>
> We sang the Sanctus in his hospital room. He sang along with us, quietly but firmly. Hosanna in the highest! I thought of that word. Hosanna! Lord, save us! That's how you greet a king coming home victorious from battle. Lord, save us! And here we were, with our hosannas echoing through the corridors of the hospital. Lord, save us. He already had, by His dying and rising. "The fight is o'er, the battle won." "Death is swallowed up in victory." And yet we must cry *hosanna* as we face death all day long.
>
> I placed a tiny piece of the bread upon his tongue. "Take, eat. The true body of Christ, given for you." I dipped a spoon into the chalice

3 I am personally indebted to the Rev. Dr. Ronald Feuerhahn for this insight.

> and placed it against his parched lips. "Take, drink. The true blood of Christ, shed for you." We prayed and I blessed him, making the sign of the cross on his forehead with a dab of oil in remembrance of his Baptism. I left, hearing the word *hosanna*.
>
> Hosanna! So this is what it means, I thought to myself. You won the victory, now give me a part in it. Hosanna in the highest!
>
> The next day, his wife called me at the church. "We got our miracle," she said. Hosanna! That was an appetizer of the feast to come, the marriage Supper of the Lamb in His kingdom that has no end. Miracles are foretastes, teasers. Resurrection from the dead is the big thing. Hosanna! Save us—from our demons and diseases. Hosanna! Save us—in the hour of our death and in the day of judgment. And He has; He does; He will save us.

The Sanctus affords rich opportunities for the preacher to unfold the richness of worship. Worship is not a transaction or a bargain in which we do and say certain things and conjure up a God who is otherwise really absent. In worship we stand on the threshold between heaven and earth and participate in heaven's liturgy. Heaven is opened to us sacramentally by way of visible signs. The whole earth is full of God's glory, but we have no visible evidence for it. Yet here in the liturgy are the divinely ordained signs that tell us the Word is present in all His creative and redemptive power: the baptismal water, the spoken Word of Christ, the bread and wine of the Supper. You do not need to "go to heaven" to hear angels and worship God. You need only come to the liturgy.

Agnus Dei: Lamb of God

The image of the lamb evokes sacrifice. Its blood poured out at the base of the altar, its body burned up as a "pleasing aroma to the Lord." The image is vivid and lively. The Old Testament teems with lambs: the lambs of the temple by whose blood the children of Israel were forgiven. The Passover lamb by whose blood the children of Israel walked to freedom. The ram caught in the thicket, the substitute sacrifice for Isaac, Abraham's son of the promise. "God will provide for Himself the lamb for a burnt offering, my son" (Gen. 22:7). The ewe lamb slaughtered by the rich man in Nathan's parable to David (2 Sam. 12:3). The Suffering Servant of Isaiah who is led "like a lamb to the slaughter" (Isa. 53:7). The countless lambs sacrificed every morning and every evening in the temple, a continual burnt offering for the sins of Israel. The lamb was a constant reminder that the fallen children of Adam must live vicariously off the death of another. Death is the way of life in a fallen creation. Even the covering of humanity's nakedness and shame comes at the price of blood and death as God made garments from the skins of animals—probably sheep (Gen. 3:21). Fig leaves just won't work; the fig tree was not slaughtered.

Modern life, with its sterile, bloodless religion, has largely forgotten or ignored the lamb's bloody history. We buy our meat from the grocery store in neat, shrink-wrapped plastic containers. There is no notion of sacrifice, of living off the death of another. The death occurs in a meat-packing plant far removed from the suburban sterility of the supermarket. Unless we live in rural areas or work in a meat-packing plant, we neither see the blood nor experience the vicarious deaths upon which we live. Vegetarianism tries to duck the death, but even the carrot and the cabbage must die for us to live. Fruits and nuts may have been our original food in Paradise, but they cannot sustain us in an ecology that lives off of death.

Lamb of God, You take away the sin of the world. Have mercy upon us. We pray to Jesus as God's Lamb who was given into death for the life of the world. John the Baptizer first confessed Him that way. He pointed his finger to the Lamb, dripping wet from His Baptism in the Jordan, and said, "Look, God's Lamb who takes away the world's sin." Listen closely to John's testimony. This is why he was sent. Jesus is not the Lamb who takes some of the sin away from some representative parts of the world, but the sin of the whole world. And He does this not potentially but actually. He isn't a potential lamb who potentially takes away our sin, providing we actualize Him. Jesus actually takes away the actual sin of the whole actual world in His death. God's universal grace in Jesus Christ comes to the forefront here. Nothing short of the world is embraced by the death of this Lamb.

The liturgy brings John's words into a new light. Christ is our Passover Lamb, His sacrificial body broken for the sin of the world, His sacrificial blood poured out for the life of the world. His death proclaimed. "As often as you eat of this bread and drink the cup, you proclaim the Lord's death until He comes" (1 Cor. 11:26). This is the Lord's Passover, the meal that celebrates true freedom. Death passes over the place where the blood is painted. "Christ, our Passover lamb, has been sacrificed" (1 Cor. 5:7). Jesus has gone the way of death ahead of us so that eternal death might pass over us. The blood of the Lamb has been smeared on the doorpost of the world. By this Lamb's blood, poured out for everyone, we walk into blood-bought freedom and life. He is our Redeemer, who purchased and won us from the Egypt of sin and death, not with gold or silver, but with His holy precious blood and with His innocent suffering and death.

This Lamb is God's holocaust, the whole burnt offering par excellence. Spotless, without blemish or defect of sin, He is slain from the foundations of the world (Rev. 13:8), and so His death is once for all time (Rom. 6:10;

Heb. 10:10) and fills the death of all the lambs who pictured Him. In the fullness of time, He laid down His life in the darkness between noon and 3 p.m. on that Friday called "Good." Now we live off His death. The sign of His kingdom is the scavenger birds feeding off another's death (Matt. 24:28; Trinity 25, one-year). His body and blood are our fellowship meal, eaten in communion with God and with one another.

The little liturgical hymn Agnus Dei evokes rich images of sacrifice and blood, death and freedom. As the preacher unfolds the meaning of this text, he will want to expound on the Passover (Exod. 12:1–14; Holy Thursday, alternate; one-year), the sacrifices (Leviticus 1–3), the Day of Atonement (Leviticus 16), and the visions of Christ, the enthroned Lamb, from the Revelation. All come to bear here.

Here is how the Agnus Dei comes into a sermon on John 1:29 (Epiphany 2, Series A).

> John points, and we follow his gaze down to the banks of the Jordan. "Look, God's Lamb who takes away the world's sin." We look. And what do we see? Not a lamb, but a man named Jesus, newly baptized, anointed and ordained by God. He's the one. The Lamb has been washed for sacrifice.
>
> The word "lamb" is used over a hundred times in the Bible. It's almost always used in the context of sacrifice. The lamb that stood in place of Isaac. The Passover lamb. The sin and guilt offerings of the temple. The morning and evening sacrifice. Every morning a lamb is killed; every evening another. Sin and grace were always in the air in Israel. There was the little ewe lamb that the rich man slew for a barbecue in Nathan's little parable to David. And the lamb on the Day of Atonement, his blood carefully poured out in the Most Holy Place. It's dangerous to be a lamb in the Bible. It almost guarantees your death. In view of all this, you'd better be careful about singing, "I am Jesus' little lamb." Isaiah describes the Suffering Servant as one who is led like a lamb to its slaughter. Lamb and sacrifice go together.
>
> The Jews prayed toward the temple. We pray in the direction of the Baptizer's gaze, following his long, bony finger. Lamb of God, You take away the sin of the world. Have mercy on us. We pray to Christ, our Passover, our whole burnt offering, our substitute sacrifice. We sing this prayer, the Agnus Dei, in the context of His Supper, and that's no coincidence. The meal we eat is the meal of His sacrifice. His blood was painted on the wood of the cross as the doorpost of the world. Where the blood is, there death passes over. His body offered up for your sins. There on the altar is the body of the Lamb slain for you and for all. There in the chalice is His blood that washes away your sin and the sin of the world. He is your food and drink. He is your life. Remember how

we prayed for mercy and peace at the beginning of the service? Your kyries are answered. The Lamb has heard your prayer. Mercy and peace are yours in His body and blood.

Nunc Dimittis: Depart in Peace

Old Simeon lived by faith in God's promise. God promised Simeon that he would not die until he saw the Messiah, the salvation of Israel. Day after day he prayed in the temple, waiting, watching, wondering. Then one day a young mother entered the temple courts carrying her 40-day-old baby in her arms. Her husband was with her, carrying a pair of turtledoves in his hands. The poor man's sacrifice. It was for the purification of the mother and for redemption of the boy (Lev. 2:6–8). Simeon took the child into his arms. His cataract-dimmed eyes lifted heavenward. And with strong voice this ancient, Old Testament man laid hold of God's promise: "Now, Master, let Your servant depart in peace, according to Your Word" (Luke 2:29–32; Christmas 1, Series B; Purification of Mary and Presentation of Our Lord).

The Nunc Dimittis is the traditional hymn for Compline, the last prayer of the day. Sleep is a type of death, as awaking is a type of the resurrection. "We go to our sleep as though going to our death, resting in the peace of Jesus, so that we may go to our death as though going to sleep."[4] It is a wonderful contribution of the Lutheran tradition to the development of the liturgy that we sing the Nunc Dimittis after receiving Holy Communion. Like blessed Simeon, we cling to the promise of God incarnate in His holy child, Jesus. We have seen God's salvation, prepared before the face of all people. We behold the hidden glory of God in our Baptisms, in the Word preached, in the body and the blood. And now we, too, are prepared to depart in peace from this valley of tears and sorrow.

The funeral of a dear senior saint, which happened to be on the Presentation of Our Lord (February 2), provided the occasion for a sermon on the Nunc Dimittis and its connection to our death and the Lord's Supper:

> In our Lutheran tradition, we sing Simeon's song as a post-Communion hymn: "Lord, now lettest thou thy servant depart in peace." Some people think it means, "Oh boy, we get to go home now." In a sense it does, but in a much bigger way than they think. It was Simeon's death song. He was ready to die, to go home in peace, just as God had promised. He had held God's salvation, that tiny 40-day-old baby. His life was fulfilled. He could die in peace, trusting God's promises.
>
> We sing this song every Sunday. We sang it in the intensive-care ward the day Marion died. Lord, now lettest thou thy servant, depart in

4 I am deeply indebted to the Rev. Dr. Kenneth Korby for this delightful sentence.

peace. The One who was once presented in the temple and held aloft in Simeon's ancient arms is presented to us here and now under the lowly forms of bread and wine. We, too, see God's salvation, the Light of the nations, the Glory of Israel, perceived through the eyes of faith. We hear His Word, the promise of forgiveness and resurrection. We eat and drink His body and blood. And we, too, depart in peace, as Marion departed in peace. We are all rehearsing that day and are being prepared for it. We go to the Sacrament as though going to our death, so that we might go to our death as though going to the Sacrament.

And so, on this blessed fortieth day after Christmas, the day of our Lord's presentation, His redemption day and His mother's day of purification, we remember also our dear sister and her presentation before the Lord in her death. Jesus was presented to Simeon and Anna in the temple so that you might be presented to His Father holy, spotless, and blameless, as Marion now appears before Him holy, spotless, and blameless. And He will keep you holy, spotless, and blameless in the death of Jesus until the day of your presentation.

Benediction: The Lord Bless You and Keep You

The Divine Service begins with the invocation of the triune name of God, and it ends with the threefold bestowal of His name. "So shall they put My name upon the people of Israel, and I will bless them" (Num. 6:27). How sad it is that some, in a hurry for Sunday brunch, slip out of the liturgy after receiving the Lord's Supper and miss out on the final blessing!

The Aaronic benediction (Num. 6:24–26) is another example of the liturgy interpreting a text of Scripture in a new context. In the Old Testament, this was the priestly blessing upon the priestly people of God. Three times the sacred, covenant name of God is pronounced over them in blessing. In the New Testament, the blessing is pronounced over the church, God's Israel of the end times. The fullness of this priestly blessing has been manifested in Jesus. In Christ, God blesses and keeps us. In Christ, He causes His face to shine on us, and in Christ is He gracious to us. In Christ has He turned His face toward us in favor and granted us peace. This blessing propels God's priestly people into their vocations. The church, which has been visibly gathered around the Gospel and the sacraments, now resumes her hidden character in the world as the scattered priests of God. The Benediction is the last sacramental act of the Divine Service, one more blessing for God to impart before sending the church back into the world for priestly service. Benediction is a return once again to Baptism. God reiterates His naming us; He traces over His signature. In Baptism God named us with His name.

In the Benediction we are named again, set on a hill to be a light for the city, sprinkled as grains of salt on the earth. God has turned His face toward us graciously in Christ, and now we turn our faces toward the world, reflecting His glory and His goodness into the darkness of our present age.

Unfortunately, the text of the Aaronic benediction is assigned only as a text for New Year's Day in the three-year lectionary. This is a tremendous oversight that fails to do justice to its importance. Nevertheless, the topic of blessing and benediction—for example, Jesus blessing the little children (Mark 10:16; Proper 22, Series B) and His blessing the disciples prior to His ascension (Luke 24:50; Ascension)—affords the preacher opportunity for incorporating the Benediction in the sermon.

Here, by way of conclusion, is a short sample of what might be done with the Benediction in preaching:

> "Bless you." We say it when someone sneezes. It's short for "God bless you." The usual response is "Thank you." The better response would be "Amen." That's what you say when you are blessed by one of God's priests. You say, "Amen," blessing received.
>
> "Bless you" is what you hear before you leave the liturgy. "The Lord bless you and keep you." This isn't some fond wish before we part ways for another week. This is blessing, benediction. The words do what they say, for they are God's words spoken in His name. With these words God puts His name on you, just as He did in your Baptism. Every Benediction is a return and reminder of Baptism.
>
> "Why bother?" you may ask. I've been forgiven in the Absolution, I've had the Word preached to me, I've had the Lord's Supper. What more could I possibly need? Such a silly question. You don't say that about dessert, do you? I've eaten all I can, but then the dessert tray comes around. Surely there's room for a little bit more. And there's always more with God when it comes to blessing.
>
> The Lord bless you and keep you. His name guards and protects you from all evil—from the devil, from the world, from your own sinful self. The Lord make His face shine upon you and be gracious to you. By grace we are saved, and in His grace we live. His grace shines upon us in the radiant face of Jesus. The Lord lift up His countenance upon you and give you peace. He looks up at you, He turns His face toward you. He is not ashamed nor angered to look at you. You are His child, forgiven and free in Jesus. He gives you *shalom*. Peace. You asked for it at the start of this service with your Kyrie. He delivers it in abundance in Jesus. You are blessed. And all you can say to such gifts is "Amen."

LITURGICAL TEXTS	Texts	3-Year Lectionary	1-Year Lectionary
Kyrie	Ps. 51:1		
	Matt. 15:22	Proper 15 (A)	Lent 2
	Matt. 17:15		
	Matt. 20:31		
	Mark 10:47–48	Proper 25 (B)	
	Luke 18:38–39		Quinquagesima
Gloria in Excelsis	Luke 2:14	Christmas Eve/Day	Christmas Day
Creed	Matt. 10:32	Proper 7 (A)	
	Luke 12:8		
	John 9:22		
	Rom. 10:9	Lent 1 (C); Proper 14 (A)	
	1 Tim. 6:12	Proper 21 (C)	Tuesday in Holy Week
	Heb. 13:15	Proper 17 (C)	
	1 John 2:23; 4:2, 3, 15	Christmas Eve; Easter 5 (B)	Christmas Eve
Sanctus	Isa. 6:3	Holy Trinity (B) Epiphany 5 (C)	Holy Trinity
	Rev. 4:8		
	Matt. 21:9		Advent 1 Palm Sunday Procession
	Mark 11:9	Advent 1 (B)	
	Matt. 23:39		
	Luke 13:35	Lent 2 (C)	
	John 12:13	Palm Sunday Procession	Palm Sunday Procession
	Ps. 118:25–26		
Agnus Dei	John 1:29, 36		
	Exod. 12:1–13	Holy Thursday (alternate)	Holy Thursday

LITURICAL ACTIVITIES			
Invocation/Benediction	Matt. 28:19	Holy Trinity (A)	
	Num. 6:22–27	Circumcision and Name of Jesus	
Intercessory Prayer	1 Tim. 2:1–4	Proper 20 (C)	Easter 6
	Phil. 4:1–7	Proper 23 (A); Advent 3 (C)	Advent 4
Offering/Offertory			
Consecration/ Distribution	1 Cor. 11:23–25, 26	Holy Thursday (alter-nate)	Holy Thursday
Praise/Hymnody	Col. 3:6	Easter Wednesday	Easter Wednesday
Peace	Matt. 5:23–24	Epiphany 6 (A)	Trinity 6
	John 20:19, 21, 26	Easter 2	Easter 2
OTHER LITURGICAL TEXTS			
Nunc Dimittis	Luke 2:29–32	Christmas 1 (C)	Christmas 1
Magnificat	Luke 1:46–55	Advent 4 (C)	
Benedictus	Luke 1:67–79		
"This Is the Feast"	Rev. 5:12–13; 7:12	Easter 3 (C); Easter 4 (C)	
"What Shall I Render	Ps. 116:12–14		
"Thank the Lord"	Psalm 107		
"Create in Me"	Ps. 51:10–12		

Hymnody and Preaching: A Gold Mine of Opportunities

Paul J. Grime

Most of us probably remember the day when pastors regularly concluded their sermons with one or more stanzas of an appropriate hymn. In many cases the hymn was a familiar one, perhaps one that many in the congregation could quietly recite with the pastor. Familiarity with that hymn provided congregational members a means by which they could call to mind the sermon throughout the following week.

While the practice of reciting hymn stanzas in the sermon has not fallen into complete disuse, it has certainly become the exception to the rule. Among the reasons is the steady decline in learning hymns by heart that has occurred during the past several generations. If a hymn is not committed to memory, it is much more difficult to grasp its meaning and relevance, especially when one has only the ears with which to grasp it. Furthermore, because of a general decline in the study and enjoyment of poetry in our culture, the public reading of hymns is much more foreign to the average person than it once was.

The purpose of this essay is not necessarily to suggest that preachers return to the former practice of quoting hymn stanzas in the sermon, even though carefully selected texts can from time to time marvelously illustrate a point. The primary purpose of this essay is to propose another way in which hymns can serve the preaching task, namely, by providing ideas, imagery, and language to assist the preacher in developing and writing the sermon. To accomplish this task, we will focus on the person and work of Christ. Jesus Christ is the main thrust not only of Lutheran preaching but also of its hymnody. Looking at both together will provide the preacher with new material to help carry out his primary task of proclaiming the Gospel. Before undertaking this study, however, we will briefly consider the example of Martin Luther's own hymns.

The Hymns of Martin Luther

When the first hymnal of the Reformation was published in Wittenberg in 1524, Luther not only took an active role in determining its contents but also provided a brief preface to the hymnal that supplied the rationale for its publication. Using examples of singing from both the Old and New Testaments, Luther wrote, "Like Moses in his song [Exod. 15:2], we may now boast that Christ is our praise and song and say with St. Paul, 1 Cor. 2[:2], that *we should know nothing to sing or say, save Jesus Christ our Savior*."[1]

That the Son of God should figure prominently in Luther's three dozen or so hymns is not surprising. In his linguistic study of Luther's hymns, Patrice Veit compiled a list of 126 references to Christ.[2] What is so instructive about this list is not only the frequency with which Luther speaks of Christ but also the diverse ways in which he does so. Of these 126 references, only 11 use the name "Jesus" or "Christ." The remaining 115 speak of Christ in terms of His relationship to others and of His work as Savior.

Notice the rich and nuanced language that Luther employs in his hymns. For example, he employs a number of words to speak of Jesus' divinity. He calls Him God,[3] God's Son, the Father's Son, the Only-begotten, and so on. The word "Lord" is also frequently used, perhaps the most familiar example being these words from "A Mighty Fortress":

> Ask ye, Who is this?
> Jesus Christ it is,
> Of Sabaoth Lord,
> And there's none other God. (*LSB* 656:2)

Other terminology that confesses Jesus' divinity includes words that describe Him as equal to the Father, eternal, God by nature, and the Creator. The paradox inherent in these terms is that the almighty God takes on human frailty in the incarnation, a theme that is also quite prominent in Luther's hymns, especially in the Christmas hymns. In addition to words that express the physical reality of the incarnation—words such as *born*, *birth*, *child*, *body*, *flesh*, and *blood*—Luther uses expressions that vividly depict the significance of the incarnation for us. For example, Jesus is referred to as our Shepherd, our noble Guest in this world, our Brother, our Life, our eternal Good, and the right Man.

---

1 AE 53:316, emphasis added.

2 Patrice Veit, *Das Kirchenlied in der Reformation Martin Luthers: Eine thematische und semantische Untersuchung*, Veröffentlichungen des Institutes für europäische Geschichte Mainz 120 (Stuttgart: Franz Steiner, 1986), 186–87.

3 Luther frequently refers to Christ as "God" in the Christmas hymns, yet always keeps His human nature in view, thus reflecting the confession that Jesus is both God and man; see Veit, *Das Kirchenlied in der Reformation Martin Luthers*, 95.

Intimately connected to the person of Christ is His work for our redemption. Luther again uses rich imagery to set forth the full biblical witness. Jesus is our Savior, our Mediator, and the Lamb of God. His work was to reconcile us, to satisfy God's wrath, and to pay for our release. Throughout, Luther emphasizes the personal dimension of Christ's work, using the familiar phrase "for you" several times.[4] Interestingly, large segments in the life of Christ that are recorded in the Scriptures are not encountered in Luther's hymns; rather, Luther focuses his witness to Christ on the redemptive acts of His incarnation, death, and resurrection.[5]

Clearly, Luther's hymns follow his own advice that "we should know nothing to sing or say, save Jesus Christ our Savior." For the preacher this emphasis is a salutary reminder that the sermon must, above all else, bear witness to the redemptive, salvific work of Christ. Beyond this material principle, Luther's rich and vivid vocabulary can serve as a model for preachers who fear getting stuck in the rut of proclaiming the Gospel the same way week after week. Following the lead of Luther, attention to the biblical and dogmatic language concerning the person and work of Jesus Christ can prove quite fruitful.

Hymnody as a Treasury for the Preacher

Every worshiper has undoubtedly had the experience of pausing during the singing of a hymn to take note of some phrase that invites, and even demands, further reflection. The nature of hymn singing in corporate worship, however, presents the worshiper with an unfortunate choice: either keep on singing or miss out on the rest of the hymn as one reflects on that choice phrase or sentence. Of course, it is this depth and richness of expression that not only invites one to return to a particular hymn again and again but also helps to separate hymns that are worth learning and repeating from those that are not.

If one considers a hymn to be a sermon in miniature, then the church's vast treasury of hymns presents the preacher with a considerable amount of material to be put into the service of the homiletical task. On a rudimentary level, hymns can serve as a source for evocative sermon titles. For example, a sermon on St. Paul's invitation to sing "psalms and hymns and spiritual songs" (Eph. 5:6–21; Proper 15, Series B) might bear the title "Through

---

4 Veit, *Das Kirchenlied in der Reformation Martin Luthers*, 107.

5 Veit, *Das Kirchenlied in der Reformation Martin Luthers*, 110.

the Church the Song Goes On."[6] Equally fitting might be the title "A New Dimension in the World of Sound."[7]

A catchy sermon title, however, goes only so far. The real benefit derived from turning to the church's hymns is found in the ideas, images, and language of the hymns that can shape how the preacher approaches his task. The remainder of this essay will do just that, namely, examine evocative language in our hymnody with an eye toward the use of this language in preaching. To limit the scope of this study, I will use Luther's explanation of the Second Article of the Apostles' Creed from the Small Catechism as a lens or filter by which to examine the hymns. My choice of Luther's explanation is twofold. First, it is quite comprehensive and invites a variety of topics to be addressed under a unified topic. Second, as stated in the introduction, my ulterior motive is to revisit what is unquestionably the chief article of the Christian faith, thus giving preachers an opportunity to be refreshed in their preaching of the Gospel.[8]

Before launching into our examination of hymn texts, there are several preliminary matters that must be considered. The first concerns translations of hymn texts. Anyone who has carefully compared hymn translations with their original language versions is aware that the two can say very different things. It can hardly be otherwise, given that a literal and accurate translation must conform both to the demands of meter and rhyme. It is, in fact, a tribute to translators that hymn translations frequently are very faithful to their originals. Nevertheless, for purposes of this study, the precision of the translation is not a crucial factor. Even a translation that is better classified as a paraphrase can provide rich imagery and language for the preaching task. Additionally, different translations of the same hymn might yield differing, yet equally valid, ideas to include in the sermon.[9]

Another matter to consider before beginning concerns the source of the hymns. The majority of examples that follow are taken from *Lutheran Service Book* (2006), the primary worship book of the LCMS.[10] For purposes of sermonic preparation, however, preachers need not be limited only to the particular hymnals of their church body. Included in the citations that

6 Cf. "Holy God, We Praise Thy Name," *LSB* 940:3.

7 Fred Pratt Green, "When in Our Music God Is Glorified," *LSB* 796:2.

8 For an examination of the rich, biblical metaphors for the Gospel, see J. A. O. Preus, *Just Words: Understanding the Fullness of the Gospel* (St. Louis: Concordia, 2000). See also Francis C. Rossow, *Preaching the Creative Gospel Creatively* (St. Louis: Concordia, 1983), 32–49.

9 Because this essay was originally written prior to the publication of *LSB*, some examples of different translations have been retained from earlier hymnals.

10 As hymn texts are quoted in the remainder of this essay, references to *LSB* will be provided immediately following the quotation, rather than in the footnotes. Both the hymn and stanza numbers will be given, separated by a colon.

follow, for example, are several hymns that appear elsewhere. The curious preacher who is always in search of new expressions and ideas will, in fact, want to take advantage of the virtual explosion in hymn writing that has occurred during the last several decades.[11] While the doctrinal faithfulness of many of these hymns requires careful scrutiny, they can, nevertheless, serve as a rich treasure trove of new ideas.[12]

Opening Some Windows to the Second Article of the Creed

The Second Article of the Apostles' Creed contains the heart and core of the church's Christological confession. Parts of it are expanded in the Nicene Creed, and other parts are quoted verbatim in the Athanasian Creed. Luther's explanation in the Small Catechism is, perhaps, one of the most exquisite, not to mention concise, summaries ever written. In just one, albeit Germanic, sentence, Luther captures the essence of Christ's person and His work and masterfully demonstrates what this all means for the believer.

The following citation of Luther's explanation is given in poetic fashion, with indentations to assist in recognizing the structure and progression of thought.

I believe that Jesus Christ,
  true God,
    begotten of the Father from eternity,
  and also true man,
    born of the Virgin Mary,
is my Lord,

  who has redeemed me,
    a lost and condemned person,
  purchased and won me
    from all sins,
    from death,
    and from the power of the devil;
  not with gold or silver,
  but with His holy, precious blood
    and with His innocent suffering and death,
  that I may be His own,
    and live under Him in His kingdom,

11 See Paul Westermeyer, *With Tongues of Fire: Profiles in 20th-Century Hymn Writing* (St. Louis: Concordia, 1995).

12 In addition to denominational hymnals published in the last two decades, there are many hymn collections containing hymns that have never been included in official hymnals. An appendix at the conclusion of this essay lists several of these collections.

and serve Him in everlasting
righteousness,
innocence,
and blessedness,
just as He is risen from the dead,
lives and reigns to all eternity.
This is most certainly true.[13]

True God . . . True Man . . . My Lord

The Christological controversies of the fourth and fifth centuries focused in large part on the question of who, exactly, this Jesus of Nazareth was. Luther's explanation, obviously intended for the average layperson, marvelously cuts through all of the technical language and simply confesses that "Jesus is Lord" (1 Cor. 12:3). Not discounting the theological battles that were waged and martyrs' blood that was shed, Luther masterfully explains the Lord's two natures in simple and direct language: He is true God and true man.

While the celebration of Christ's nativity provides an obvious opportunity to preach on the mystery of the incarnation, there is virtually no Sunday in the year when the preacher does not have the chance to proclaim the divinity and humanity of the Savior. Whether the text speaks of His miracles, His wise teachings, or His victory over death and the grave, the opportunity exists for the preacher to hold high the divinity of Christ. Likewise, the humanity of Jesus figures prominently in Christian preaching as we are directed to the one who "became flesh and dwelt among us" (John 1:14).

It is, most appropriately, in the Christmas hymns that images for the incarnation can be found in abundance. The most evocative images are those that speak to the mystery of the true God coming in human flesh. In Luther's Christmas hymn "We Praise, O Christ, Your Holy Name," he writes:

> The virgin mother lulls to sleep
> Him who rules the cosmic deep. (*LW* 35:3; cf. *LSB* 382:3)

The preacher might use this image to develop an illustration like the following:[14]

> Taking care of the Son of God was really no different than what any mother willingly does for her newborn child. And the same goes for fathers too. When the diaper is dirty, you change it. When baby is

13 *Luther's Small Catechism*, 16–17.

14 I do not intend to provide homiletical examples for each of the hymns that are quoted. The following is simply given to demonstrate how the hymn text can serve as a springboard. Hereafter, I will provide the raw material from the hymns—ideas and illustrations—and allow the reader the "joy" of working that material into the sermon.

crying with hunger, you provide nourishment. When the poor child is in desperate need of sleep, you sit in the rocking chair and softly sing sweet lullabies. No doubt, Mary did the same.

And yet the great mystery of the incarnation—of God coming in our flesh—is that this child whom Mary lulled to sleep in her lap is the Lord of all creation. Even as He would fall into that peaceful sleep that every parent has seen on a child's face, this infant—Jesus—was at the same time directing the course of the sun and moon. Even as He nursed at His mother's breast, this little child, who was true God, was feeding the birds of the air and the great creatures of the sea. All our wisdom and human reason can never fathom this mystery. Only faith is able to take hold of this word from God and trust that the child of Bethlehem is truly human—made like us in every way—and truly God, the one who came to bring us salvation.

There are other hymns that address the paradox of the incarnation. In the English carol "See amid the Winter's Snow," Edward Caswall (1814–78) writes:

Lo, within a stable lies
He who built the starry skies. (*LSB* 373:2)

Richard Wilbur (b. 1921), a poet laureate of the United States in 1987–88, uses a similar image in his hymn "A Stable Lamp Is Lighted":

A barn will harbor heaven,
A stall become a shrine. (*HS98* 810:1)[15]

There is, of course, language in our hymnody that speaks specifically of Jesus' divinity. For example, Elizabeth Cruciger (ca. 1500–35), an early-Reformation hymn writer, speaks of Jesus' divine nature in her hymn "The Only Son from Heaven":

No sphere His light confining,
No star so brightly shining
As He, our Morning Star. (*LSB* 402:1)

The image of light is an obvious choice for a hymn on Jesus' transfiguration:

O wondrous type! O vision fair
Of glory that the Church may share,
Which Christ upon the mountain shows,
Where brighter than the sun He glows! (*LSB* 413:1)

15 Richard Wilbur, *Advice to a Prophet and Other Poems* (New York: Harcourt Brace, 1961).

Similarly, speaking of the journey of the Wise Men, the fifth-century hymn writer Coelius Sedulius alludes to the paradox of following a light, the star, in order to see the true light, Jesus.

And, led by light to light they trod
And by their gifts confessed their God. (*LSB* 399:2)

In his hymn "Dear Christians, One and All, Rejoice," Luther uses the following picturesque phrase to illustrate the divinity of Christ:

Then go, bright jewel of My crown,
And bring to all salvation. (*LSB* 556:5)

These words, which are spoken by the Father in the hymn, serve as a colorful way of saying what Luther confesses so simply in the Small Catechism: that Jesus is true God.

The preceding quotation highlights another feature of the church's theology of the incarnation, namely, that at the birth of Jesus His redemptive work is already in view. One cannot, in fact, preach the incarnation without also preaching the death and resurrection of Christ. This quickly becomes evident in the church's song. In "Voices Raised to You We Offer," Herman Stuempfle (1923–2007) pens a simple description of Christ's purpose for coming, which is to bring "heaven's grace" (*LSB* 795:3).

Jaroslav Vajda (1919–2008) provides an exquisite image that draws us to the reality of Jesus' humanity while at the same time reminding us of the purpose for His coming.

A still, small voice to cry one day for me. (*LSB* 369:3)

Charles Wesley (1707–88) makes the same point in "Hark! The Herald Angels Sing":

Born that man no more may die. (*LSB* 380:3)

In the hymn "Have No Fear, Little Flock," Marjorie Jillson (b. 1931) draws a marvelous contrast between the divine and human and still maintains an emphasis on the work of Christ.

Praise the Lord high above;
Praise the Lord high above,
  For He stoops down to heal you,
  Uplift and restore you;
Praise the Lord high above! (*LSB* 735:3)

Turning again to the hymn "Dear Christians, One and All, Rejoice," we find that Luther describes the incarnation—God becoming flesh—in terms that intimately bind us to Him and, more importantly, to the work that He came to accomplish on our behalf.

His royal pow'r disguised He bore;
A servant's form, like mine, He wore
To lead the devil captive. (*LSB* 556:6)

In later stanzas Luther explains the meaning of this imagery:

For I am yours, and you are Mine. (*LSB* 556:7)

My innocence shall bear your sin,
And you are blest forever. (*LSB* 556:8)

This joyful exchange between Christ and the sinner is found in other hymns as well. In Nikolaus Herman's (ca. 1480–1561) Christmas hymn "Let All Together Praise Our God," he makes the image very explicit.

He undertakes a great exchange,
Puts on our human frame,
And in return gives us His realm,
His glory, and His name. (*LSB* 389:4)

As Christ takes on our guilt and shame, He puts on us His robe of righteousness. This image of the "joyful exchange" is vividly expressed in "To Mock Your Reign, O Dearest Lord," a hymn by Fred Pratt Green (1903–2000):

They did not know, as we do now,
That though we merit blame
You will your robe of mercy throw
around our naked shame.[16]

A Lost and Condemned Person

In the preceding discussion concerning Christ's incarnation, the purpose for our Lord's coming is already evident. As Luther explains, Jesus is "my Lord, who has redeemed me." But before Luther moves on to the issue of Christ's redemptive work, he first deals with the thorny issue of who it is that Christ has redeemed. The reality is that Christ came to redeem me, "a lost and condemned person."

In contrast to the modern tendency to downplay any emphasis on sin and punishment, much of the church's hymnic heritage is replete with vivid images that portray human sinfulness. In some cases, the description is simple and to the point, as in Isaac Watt's (1674–1748) famous line in the hymn "Alas! And Did My Savior Bleed":

Would He devote that sacred head

16 Fred Pratt Green, *The Hymns and Ballads of Fred Pratt Green* (Carol Stream, IL: Hope Publishing Company, 1982), 43.

For such a worm as I? (*LSB* 437:1)[17]

In the American folk hymn "What Wondrous Love Is This," the image of our sinfulness is also very simply expressed:

When I was sinking down, sinking down, sinking down,
When I was sinking down, sinking down,
When I was sinking down,
Beneath God's righteous frown,
Christ laid aside His crown for my soul, for my soul,
Christ laid aside His crown for my soul. (*LSB* 543:2)

The repetition of "sinking down," coupled with the plaintive character of the melody, very powerfully highlights the sinner's helplessness in the face of God's righteous judgment.

Turning again to the hymn "Dear Christians, One and All, Rejoice," Luther provides a very comprehensive description of the sinner.

Fast bound in Satan's chains I lay,
    Death brooded darkly o'er me.
Sin was my torment night and day;
    In sin my mother bore me.
But daily deeper still I fell;
My life became a living hell,
    So firmly sin possessed me. (*LSB* 556:2)

Luther doesn't worry about details regarding particular sins; rather, he goes for the jugular. With each line, he places another nail into the coffin of our condemnation. We are bound, tormented, born in sin, firmly possessed. Without God, life is a living hell. He leaves no room for escape, which truly is a model for how the preacher needs to apply the Law in all its fury.

In contrast, some hymns portray human sinfulness using specific themes or concepts. For example, Ronald Klug (b. 1939) focuses on the concept of guilt in his hymn "Rise, Shine, You People." Clearly, the people of God would benefit by hearing the preacher unpack the concept of being driven by guilt and how God has forgiven them and set them free from that taskmaster. In Eliza Alderson's (1818–89) hymn "Lord of Glory, You Have Bought Us," the issue of our thanklessness is succinctly and vividly expressed:

Melt our thankless hearts of stone. (*LSB* 851:2)

Or consider the hymn "Forgive Us, Lord, for Shallow Thankfulness" (*LSB* 788) by William Reid Sr. (1890–1983), where he addresses the temptations of our materialistic world. The image of a feast that knows nothing of

17 Sadly, most modern hymnal editors "smooth out" this uncomfortable language, using alternates like "For sinners such as I." The editors of *LSB* chose to return to Watt's original phrase.

fasting in stanza 5 sounds very much like the eating, drinking, and merry-making about which the Scriptures warn. Likewise, taking a few minutes in the sermon to warn God's people that they run the risk of starving their own souls would probably uncover the sin in not a few people.

Some hymn writers choose to highlight sin by placing us within the biblical narrative. From Samuel Crossman's (ca. 1624–83) hymn "My Song Is Love Unknown," come these thoughts:

> Then "Crucify!"
> Is all their breath,
> And for His death
> They thirst and cry.
>
> A murderer they save,
> The Prince of Life they slay. (*LSB* 430:3, 5)

Martin Franzmann (1907–76) accomplishes the same objective by uniting us with Adam and Eve, who attempted to hide their sin from God.

> We all have fled that evening voice
> That sought us as we ran. (*LSB* 569:1)

Franzmann extends the image as he alludes to the altercation between Cain and Abel.

> We fled Thee, and in losing Thee
> We lost our brother too;
> Each singly sought and claimed his own;
> Each man his brother slew. (*LSB* 569:2)

Understandably, this theological use of the Law is often inseparably bound to the proclamation of the Gospel of forgiveness and life in Christ. A good example is found in the hymn "O Dearest Jesus" by Johann Heermann (1585–1647):

> What punishment so strange is suffered yonder!
> The Shepherd dies for sheep that loved to wander. (*LSB* 439:4)

The imagery of our sinfulness is captured marvelously in description of sheep who love to wander. At the same time, Heermann fuses this image to another, namely, that of a shepherd willing to die for his wandering sheep. A similar theme can be found in the fifth stanza of "The Night Will Soon Be Ending" by Jochem Klepper (1903–42), which reminds us that God in His grace does not leave us, even when we leave Him for a time.

In "O God, O Lord of Heaven and Earth," Martin Franzmann provides the preacher with rich images that describe the effects of sin. Throughout this hymn, however, the Gospel continually breaks through the darkness of our condemnation. With words like these, the preacher can paint a mental picture that depicts the consequences of sin: futile birth, house of doom, poisoned air, reluctant breath. But equally vivid is the Gospel, with Christ breaking down the walls that separate us from the Father and drinking our deep despair. This last example, perhaps better than any other, demonstrates how specific Law and specific Gospel can work together to expose the ugly truth of our sinful condition and also proclaim very clearly our release from the bondage of sin and the curse of death. Additionally, Franzmann's example demonstrates that when the Law is presented in all of its fury, we are incapable of finding any peace except in the redemptive work of Christ.

Purchased and Won Me

Having faced God's truth about the sinner—that we are corrupt through and through—Luther now turns to the heart and core of the Second Article: our redemption. In the Large Catechism Luther provides a simple explanation of what it means to be redeemed by Christ:

> Let this, then, be the sum of this article: the little word *Lord* means simply the same as *redeemer*. It means the One who has brought us from Satan to God, from death to life, from sin to righteousness, and who preserves us in the same.[18]

Likewise, in the Small Catechism Luther's explanation is not only succinct but also carefully constructed. There is an inner logic that very clearly unfolds the work of Christ on our behalf.

> Jesus Christ, my Lord, "has redeemed me,"
> *meaning* . . . He has "purchased and won me."
>
> Purchased and won me from what?
>
> "from all sins,
> from death,
> and from the power of the devil."
>
> How has He done this?
>
> "Not with gold or silver,
> but with His holy precious blood and with His innocent suffering and death."

Christian hymnody is replete with images that unpack and develop these themes and insights. We begin by looking at several examples that address God's desire to save his fallen children. Once again, Luther's hymn "Dear Christians, One and All, Rejoice" goes to the heart of the matter.

18 LC II 31 (*Concordia*, 402).

God said to His beloved Son:
  "It's time to have compassion.
Then go, bright jewel of My crown,
  And bring to all salvation.
From sin and sorrow set them free;
Slay bitter death for them that they
  May live with You forever." (*LSB* 556:5)

In the stanza preceding this one, Luther unpacks the depth of God's compassion:

He turned to me a father's heart;
He did not choose the easy part
But gave His dearest treasure. (*LSB* 556:4)[19]

In his hymn "Love Divine, All Loves Excelling," Charles Wesley describes God's compassion in very expansive language:

Jesus, Thou art all compassion,
Pure, unbounded love Thou art. (*LSB* 700:1)

The depth of God's compassion is masterfully portrayed in these words from "A Lamb Goes Uncomplaining Forth" by Paul Gerhardt (1607–76):

O wondrous Love, what have You done!
The Father offers up His Son,
  Desiring our salvation.
O Love, how strong You are to save!
You lay the One into the grave
  Who built the earth's foundation. (*LSB* 438:3)

Likewise, in his Advent hymn "O Lord, How Shall I Meet You," Gerhardt writes:

Your thirst for my salvation
Procured my liberty. (*LSB* 334:4)

Samuel Crossman addresses the same motivation for God's plan of salvation with these evocative words from his hymn "My Song Is Love Unknown":

Love to the loveless shown
That they might lovely be. (*LSB* 430:1)

---

19 Note the similarity to Luther's conclusion to the Creed in the Large Catechism: "In all three articles God has revealed Himself and opened the deepest abyss of His fatherly heart and his pure, inexpressable love [Ephesians 3:18–19]. . . . We could never grasp the knowledge of the Father's grace and favor except through the Lord Christ. Jesus is a mirror of the fatherly heart" (LC II 64, 65 [*Concordia*, 406]).

And from the familiar hymn "The Church's One Foundation," by Samuel Stone (1839–1900), these words:

From heav'n He came and sought her
To be His holy bride. (*LSB* 644:1)

To redeem means to buy back. To that concept Luther adds another: Christ has purchased and won us. It is especially the latter expression that receives special attention in our hymnody. In Luther's Easter hymn "Christ Jesus Lay in Death's Strong Bands," he portrays Jesus' redemptive work in terms of a conflict:

It was a strange and dreadful strife
When life and death contended. (*LSB* 458:4)

This battle imagery is often quite vivid. From Kaspar Stolshagen's (1550–94) Easter hymn "Today in Triumph Christ Arose" come these words:

Now hell has lost its pow'r and might;
Our Lord puts all its hosts to flight. . .
He brings the end of all our woe;
He routs our foes and lays them low. . .

Our strong Defender hurls him down
And wins for us a heav'nly crown. (*LW* 136:2, 3)

Again, in the hymn "Jesus Has Come and Brings Pleasure" by Johann Allendorf (1693–1773) a similar image is provided.

Jesus breaks down all the walls of death's fortress,
Brings forth the pris'ners triumphant, unharmed. (*LSB* 533:3)

In the Bohemian hymn "Lo, Judah's Lion Wins the Strife," the author draws on Old Testament events to portray the victory won by Christ.

As David, so our David too
The jeering huge Goliath slew. Alleluia!...

Our Samson storms death's citadel
And carries off the gates of hell. Alleluia!
Oh, praise him for his conquest! (*LW* 146:2, 4)

Stephen Starke (b. 1955) also draws on Old Testament images in his hymn, "When Time Was Full, God Sent His Son":

This holy Jonah undecayed
    Lay still within the whale;
This Lord of Life on death then preyed,
    Hell's titan to impale;
From gaping jaws came forth this King,

With death the casualty!
Colossal foe, where now your sting?
Where, grave, your victory?[20]

Images so rich in biblical language can provide the preacher with ready-made sermon illustrations. Rather than limiting one's vocabulary to a few stock phrases like "Jesus died for you" or "Jesus has saved you," the preacher can proclaim this great truth in all of its multifaceted splendor and thus assist the congregation in gaining an ever deeper understanding of and appreciation for God's gift of salvation.

The "how" of Christ's work of salvation is, of course, also richly portrayed in hymns. For example, Thomas Kelly (1769–1854) directly connects the cross to God's intent to save in his hymn "We Sing the Praise of Him Who Died":

Inscribed upon the cross we see
In shining letters, "God is love." (*LSB* 429:2)

Again, in his Palm Sunday hymn "Ride On, Ride On in Majesty," Henry Milman (1791–1868) writes:

Ride on, ride on in majesty!
In lowly pomp ride on to die. (*LSB* 441:2)

In his hymn "Nature with Open Volume Stands," Isaac Watts also demonstrates that despite obvious appearances, the cross and Jesus' death upon it are not defeat but the very means of our salvation.

But in the grace that rescued us
God's brightest form of glory shines;
'Tis fairest drawn here on the cross
In precious blood and crimson lines.[21]

The details regarding Jesus' death are handled in a variety of ways in the hymns. This powerful image comes from "The Royal Banners Forward Go" by Venantius Honorius Fortunatus (530–609):

On whose hard arms, so widely flung,
The weight of this world's ransom hung. (*LSB* 455:4)

Paul Gerhardt uses the image of the lamb being led to slaughter in "A Lamb Goes Uncomplaining Forth":

A Lamb goes uncomplaining forth,
The guilt of sinners bearing

20 *O Sing of Christ: The Hymns of Stephen P. Starke* (St. Louis: Concordia, 2005), no. 28.

21 *A New Hymnal for Colleges and Schools*, ed. Jeffery Rowthorn and Russell Schulz-Widmar (New Haven, CT: Yale University Press, 1992), 34:2.

And, laden with the sins of earth,
None else the burden sharing;
Goes patient on, grows weak and faint,
To slaughter led without complaint,
That spotless life to offer.
He bears the stripes, the wounds, the lies,
The mockery, and yet replies,
"All this I gladly suffer." (*LSB* 438:1)

Werner Franzmann (1905–96), brother of Martin Franzmann, has written an Easter hymn, "Triumphant from the Grave," that uses rich language to depict the death of Christ.

Fierce though God's wrath had been,
Afflicting him for men,
The fi'ry judgment burned no more;
Its fury had passed o'er....

Nailed fast to yonder tree
See your iniquity!
His cross has banished all your sin,
Your pardon has brought in. (*LW* 144:3, 4)

In a unique twist on the events leading up to Jesus' death, Timothy Dudley-Smith (b. 1926) offers the Palm Sunday hymn "No Tramp of Soldiers' Marching Feet" (*LSB* 444) that in stanza 3 describes the transition from a roadway covered in palms to a crown of thorns.

Fred Pratt Green focuses on the treatment Jesus received at the hand of the soldiers in his hymn "To Mock Your Reign, O Dearest Lord."

In mock acclaim, O gracious Lord,
They snatched a purple cloak,
Your passion turned, for all they cared,
Into a soldier's joke.[22]

And regarding Jesus' burial, Samuel Crossman offers this insight:

In death no friendly tomb
But what a stranger gave. (*LSB* 430:6)

The means by which Christ accomplished our salvation is, as Luther explains, "not with gold or silver, but with His holy, precious blood and with his innocent suffering and death." In "Dear Christians, One and All, Rejoice," Luther repeatedly emphasizes the great cost of this sacrifice:

What price our ransom cost Him! . . .

22 Green, *Hymns and Ballads*, 43.

He did not choose the easy part
But gave His dearest treasure. . . .

"Your ransom I Myself will be;
For you I strive and wrestle. . . ."

"Though he [the devil] will shed My precious blood,
Me of My life bereaving,
All this I suffer for your good." (*LSB* 556:1, 4, 7, 8)

Other hymns are more specific in describing the ransom price. From the seventeenth-century office hymn "At the Lamb's High Feast We Sing" come these words:

Where the paschal blood is poured,
Death's dread angel sheathes the sword. (*LSB* 633:3)

A more recent hymn by Christopher Idle (b. 1938), "In Silent Pain the Eternal Son," offers the graphic description of the earth stained with the blood of the Lamb, which was shed to cleanse us (*LSB* 432:2).

The following example from "O Darkest Woe" by Friedrich von Spee (1591–1635) and Johann Rist (1607–67) places very vivid images in close juxtaposition:

The Bridegroom dead!
God's Lamb has bled
    Upon thy sin forever. (*LSB* 448:4)

A stunning contrast to these images is provided by Timothy Dudley-Smith in his hymn "No Weight of Gold or Silver."

No weight of gold or silver
    Can measure human worth;
No soul secures its ransom,
    With all the wealth of earth;
No sinner finds his freedom
    But by the gift unpriced,
The Lamb of God unblemished,
    The precious blood of Christ.[23]

Dudley-Smith's text clearly reflects Luther's catechism explanation, which, of course, is but an appeal to 1 Pet. 1:18–19: "You were ransomed from the futile ways inherited from your forefathers, not with perishable things such as silver or gold, but with the precious blood of Christ, like that of a lamb without blemish or spot."

---

23 Timothy Dudley-Smith, *Lift Every Heart: Collected Hymns 1961–1983 and Some Early Poems* (Carol Stream, IL: Hope Publishing Company, 1984), 118.

That I May Be His Own

In explaining the redemptive work of Christ, Luther is not content simply to state what Christ has done; rather, he also proceeds to explain what it means for the Christian:

> Why has He done this?
>
> "That I may be His own,
> and live under Him in His kingdom,
> and serve Him in everlasting
> righteousness,
> innocence,
> and blessedness."

Obviously, there are countless quotations from the church's hymnody that elucidate the meaning of these words. A few examples are all that we can consider.

To "be His own" means to belong to Christ and to share in all His benefits. This emphasis is similar to Luther's teaching of the joyful exchange between Christ and the sinner: He takes on Himself all our sin and shame and gives us what is His—life and salvation. Luther expresses this image most directly in "Dear Christians, One and All, Rejoice."

> For I am yours, and you are Mine,
> And where I am you may remain;
> The foe shall not divide us. (*LSB* 556:7)

In his hymn "Jesus, Thy Boundless Love to Me," Paul Gerhardt expresses union with Christ in this way:

> Unite my thankful heart to Thee,
> And reign without a rival there! (*LSB* 683:1)

In his baptismal hymn "God's Own Child, I Gladly Say It," Erdmann Neumeister (1671–1756) expresses the benefit of being Christ's own: the devil no longer has power over God's child because in Baptism Christ is united with the baptized (see *LSB* 594:3).

The consequence of belonging to Christ is wonderfully portrayed by Jaroslav Vajda in his hymn "Holy Spirit, Gift of God."

> One is nevermore alone
> Who is kin to God's dear Son. (*HS98* 835:7)

A thorough discussion of what it means to live under Christ in His kingdom would require an entire chapter, if not a book, covering topics like spiritual warfare, the Sacraments, trust, hope, death, and so on. For our purposes, we begin with several references to the Sacraments. In Erdmann

Neumeister's baptismal hymn we hear of the release granted to a guilty conscience because in this Sacrament we are sprinkled with Jesus' blood (see *LSB* 594:2).

From the Communion hymn "Here, O My Lord, I See Thee Face to Face," by Horatius Bonar (1808–89):

> Here grasp with firmer hand eternal grace,
> And all my weariness upon Thee lean. . . .
> The feast, though not the love, is past and gone. (*LSB* 631:1, 6)

Haquin Spegel's (1645–1714) hymn "The Death of Jesus Christ, Our Lord" offers this insight:

> A heav'nly manna for our soul
> Until we safely reach our goal. (*LW* 107:5)

Other hymns also focus on the goal of remaining faithful until one's death. Again, Erdmann Neumeister makes clear that we need not fear death because we will "sleep secure" (*LSB* 594:5).

Stephen Starke offers this vivid description of those who have suffered for the faith in his hymn "Saints, See the Cloud of Witnesses":

> Through faith they conquered flame and sword and gallows,
> God's name to hallow. . . .
>
> Our lives unfold, embraced within Your story. (*LSB* 667:2, 6)

Luther's point about serving God "in everlasting righteousness, innocence, and blessedness" also finds a place in the hymns. From "Come Down, O Love Divine," by medieval Italian poet Bianco da Siena (d. 1434), come these descriptive words:

> Let holy charity
> Mine outward vesture be
> And lowliness become mine inner clothing. (*LSB* 501:3)

Other hymns become more specific in describing how our service takes concrete form. For example, Dorothy Schultz (b. 1934) writes the following in "Love in Christ Is Strong and Living":

> Love is patient and forbearing,
> Clothed in Christ's humility,
> Gentle, selfless, kind, and caring,
> Reaching out in charity. (*LSB* 706:2)

William Reid Sr. writes in "Forgive Us, Lord, for Shallow Thankfulness" (*LSB* 788) that true thankfulness does not count the cost, but gives freely. Eliza Alderson also speaks to the issue of how one who belongs to Christ gives himself or herself in service to the neighbor:

Grant us hearts, dear Lord, to give You
Gladly, freely of Your own.
With the sunshine of Your goodness
Melt our thankless hearts of stone
Till our cold and selfish natures,
Warmed by You, at length believe
That more happy and more blessed
'Tis to give than to receive. (*LSB* 851:2)

For the Christian, serving God also means speaking of the glories of His work of salvation. In his hymn "Thy Strong Word," Martin Franzmann thoroughly explores the imagery associated with oral proclamation to make his point:

Give us lips to sing Thy glory,
Tongues Thy mercy to proclaim,
Throats that shout the hope that fills us,
Mouths to speak Thy holy name. (*LSB* 578:5)

Risen from the Dead

Interestingly, Luther does not address the resurrection of Jesus until the very end of his explanation. Rather than placing it immediately after his discussion of Jesus' suffering and death, Luther prefers to conclude with it. In this position the reference to Jesus' resurrection adds emphasis and also shows that the entire life of the Christian—the one who belongs to Christ, lives in His kingdom, and serves Him—has as its basis the resurrection of Jesus. By implication, the Christian's hope is in the final resurrection of all flesh, of which Jesus' own resurrection is the first fruit.

The hymns are rich in resurrection imagery. In the hymn "I Bind unto Myself Today," which is attributed to St. Patrick, this evocative line describes Jesus' resurrection:

His bursting from the spiced tomb. (*LSB* 604:2)

In his Easter hymn "All the Earth with Joy Is Sounding," Stephen Starke uses several striking biblical images to highlight the resurrection.

He, the greater Jonah, bounding
From the grave, His three-day bed . . . .

Christ, the devil's might unwinding,
Leaves behind His borrowed tomb. (*LSB* 462:1, 2)

The hymn "Long before the World Is Waking" (*LSB* 485) is based on John 21:1–17, the post-resurrection appearance of Jesus on the seashore. Hymn writer Timothy Dudley-Smith describes Peter as plunging into the water to come to Jesus, thus communicating his joy when he recognized that it was the risen Lord who was speaking.

This striking image from Werner Franzmann's hymn "Triumphant from the Grave" incorporates the prophecy that Jesus' body would not see decay (cf. Ps. 16:10; Acts 2:28, 31):

> Buried like sinful man
> Who ends his mortal span,
> Our Lord could not for long lie there,
> Decay of men to share. (*LW* 144:2)

John of Damascus (ca. 696–ca. 754) draws the parallel between the crossing of the Red Sea by the children of Israel with Jesus' resurrection in his hymn "Come, You Faithful, Raise the Strain."

> Come, you faithful, raise the strain
> Of triumphant gladness!
> God has brought His Israel
> Into joy from sadness,
> Loosed from Pharaoh's bitter yoke
> Jacob's sons and daughters,
> Led them with unmoistened foot
> Through the Red Sea waters. (*LSB* 487:1)

Perhaps one of the most graphic portrayals of the resurrected Christ is found in Thomas Troeger's hymn "These Things Did Thomas Count as Real" (*LSB* 472:1, 3). As Troeger addresses Thomas's need to see Jesus for himself, the senses are engaged in reflection on blood and steel, wood and stone, flesh and bone—and the way actually touching our Savior's wounds stopped Thomas's doubts.

As with many of the preceding examples, this text could provide the preacher with an abundance of images and illustrations to assist the hearers to get into the mind of Thomas and to understand how we may often face similar doubts.

Conclusion

As I have stated many times, the examples provided above are by no means exhaustive. Even so, they present an almost bewildering array of ideas and images from which the preacher might draw to aid in sermon preparation. It is important, however, to note an inherent danger in this exercise, namely, that the preacher may be tempted to heap one illustration upon another. In the end this will only serve to confuse those who hear the sermon. Rather than juxtaposing several contrasting images, the preacher and hearers alike will be better served by focusing on a single image and developing it in a way that brings the biblical text to life. Like salt, such rich images are best used in small doses.

The purpose of this study was to demonstrate that the countless hymns in our hymnals and other resources provide a rich resource for enlivening the preached word. Of course, there are many other resources that do the same thing, such as published sermons. A benefit of turning to the church's hymnody is that at least some of these images will be familiar to those who hear the sermon and thus can reinforce the proclamation.

Those who immerse themselves in the church's hymns—hymns that span the centuries—will quickly come to realize that these poetic and musical expressions of the Christian faith wonderfully complement the doctrinal writings of the faith. They provide a living, breathing expression of the truths of Holy Scripture, and they employ vivid imagery to bring nuance to the proclamation of the Word. And, not infrequently, our hymns provide words that describe what will only be fully known on the day when our Lord returns.

> Alleluia, alleluia!
> Oh, to breathe the Spirit's grace!
> Alleluia, alleluia!
> Oh, to see the Father's face!
> Alleluia, alleluia!
> Oh, to feel the Son's embrace! (*LSB* 491:4)[24]

Appendix: Hymn Collections

Daw, Carl P., Jr. *New Psalms and Hymns and Spiritual Songs*. Carol Stream, IL: Hope Publishing Company, 1996.

———. *A Year of Grace: Hymns for the Church Year*. Carol Stream, IL: Hope Publishing Company, 1990.

Dudley-Smith, Timothy. *A Door for the Word: Thirty-six New Hymns 2002–2005*. Carol Stream, IL: Hope Publishing Company, 2006.

———. *A House of Praise: Collected Hymns 1961–2001*. Carol Stream, IL: Hope Publishing Company, 2004.

———. *Praise to the Name: 36 New Hymns Written between 2005 and 2008*. Carol Stream, IL: Hope Publishing Company, 2009.

Green, Fred Pratt. *The Hymns and Ballads of Fred Pratt Green*. Carol Stream, IL: Hope Publishing Company, 1982.

———. *Later Hymns and Ballads and Fifty Poems*. Carol Stream, IL: Hope Publishing Company, 1989.

Idle, Christopher M. *Light upon the River: Hymn Texts by Christopher M. Idle*. Carol Stream, IL: Hope Publishing Company, 1998.

---

24 Jaroslav Vajda, "Up through Endless Ranks of Angels."

Starke, Stephen. *O Sing of Christ: The Hymns of Stephen P. Starke*. St. Louis: Concordia, 2005.

Stuempfle, Herman. *Awake Our Hearts to Praise*. Chicago: GIA Publications, 2000.

———. *Redeeming the Time: A Cycle of Song for the Christian Year*. Chicago: GIA Publications, 1997.

———. *Wondrous Love Has Called Us: Hymns, Songs, and Carols*. Chicago: GIA Publications, 2006.

———. *The Word Goes Forth: Hymns, Songs, and Carols*. Chicago: GIA Publications, 1993.

Troeger, Thomas H. *Borrowed Light: Hymn Texts, Prayers, and Poems*. New York: Oxford University Press, 1994.

Troeger, Thomas, and Carol Doran. *New Hymns for the Lectionary to Glorify the Maker's Name*. New York: Oxford University Press, 1986.

Vajda, Jaroslav J. *Sing Peace, Sing Gift of Peace*. St. Louis: Concordia, 2003.

Preaching and the Visual Arts: "I Heard a Voice, and I Turned to See"

Dean W. Nadasdy

Word and Image

Over the altar in the church of my childhood is a life-size sculpture of Jesus Christ.[1] The sculpture replicates Thorvaldsen's famous image of Christ, His arms extended in welcome. The story goes that Thorvaldsen originally intended to show a glorious Christ, arms raised in triumph. The studio was very warm that day, however, and the tired model let his arms drop. The result was a Christ with arms in the welcoming position. Thorvaldsen stayed with the latter.

All these years later, when I think of Christ, trying to picture Him in my mind, I am brought back to that sculpture. In no small measure this is the result of my childhood pastor's frequent use of the sculpture in his preaching. It was nothing that profound. My pastor simply and frequently pointed to the sculpture from the pulpit at the mention of Jesus' name. For a child that gesture, repetitive and natural, created an inescapable link between word and image, between the Word incarnate and the word ensculptured.

Art is not a substitute for preaching. But as medieval cathedrals were called "sermons in stone," so works of art can enhance and illustrate the Word of God as proclaimed from the pulpit. It can give the preacher a visual vocabulary. Lutheran preachers can be open to imagination and the arts in a way that others, confined to right-brain ratiocination, cannot.

The Visual and the Word

One of the most engaging verses of the New Testament comes at the beginning of the Revelation to St. John as the evangelist is encountered by the glorified Christ. He has just heard a voice tell him to write down the letters

1 The church is St. Martini Lutheran Church in Chicago, and the sculpture still stands.

to the seven churches. Then, John writes, "I turned to see the voice" (Rev. 1:12). What is heard begs for what is seen. It is that way with apocalyptic—and with all effective—preaching. The oral and the visual must merge. Good preaching is both heard and seen. It goes all the way back to the *dabar* of the Hebrew.[2] *Dabar* entails both word and event. God utters the word, for example, and things come into being, things that can be seen. So the *logos* of the Greek is both word and person. In Jesus, God speaks; in Jesus, God can be seen. The visual makes oral composition memorable. We may write sermons, but we must deliver them to make them seen and heard and experienced. Otherwise, they will not be remembered. Certain Greeks came, wanting to see Jesus. It meant they wanted to hear Him and speak with Him as well. What is more, neglecting the visual in preaching leaves behind the theological force of the word that is *dabar* and *logos*. People will turn to "see the voice" and find only spoken word, not event. Strong, visual preaching makes appropriate to preaching the confidence of Emily Dickinson's cherished little verse "A Word," in which she points out that speakers give life to words.[3] Only an artist or a poet can have that confidence, someone who understands the visual load of a single word. Preachers, as we will see, are nothing less than artist or poet when serious about their craft.

Jesus makes use of the visual on at least two levels. In an immediate sense, Jesus appears to have used what was visually at hand as medium. Birds in flight, lilies in a field, a woman making an offering at the temple, a child at His knee, a shepherd and his flock—these and other images became the visual vehicles for lessons of the kingdom. Jesus told His hearers, but He also showed them. As such, He taught like the prophets who used the visual to make a point, ranging from Amos's basket of ripe fruit (Amos 8:1–14) to Jeremiah's burying of his loincloth (Jer. 13:1–11). Jesus took the familiar images of His culture—temple, crop, cleaning house, feasting—and taught from them.

At a second level, Jesus' use of the visual involved engaging the imagination via narrative. That engagement came most often in Jesus' use of extended metaphor or parable. Story creates images in the mind. If I say, "prodigal son," immediate images, not necessarily words, come to your mind—a Jewish boy in a pig pen, a father running through a village to greet his long-lost son. The same is true for "lost sheep" and "the pearl of great price." These extended metaphors for the kingdom create pictures. Word and image are fused.

---

2 For an excellent discussion of *dabar* and its merging of word and event, see Calvin Miller, *Spirit, Word, and Story* (Grand Rapids: Baker, 1989), 120–21.

3 Emily Dickinson, "A Word," in *Collected Poems of Emily Dickinson* (New York: Avenal, 1982), 23. Quoted in Miller, *Spirit, Word, and Story*, 115.

These two levels have characterized the preaching of the church for centuries. On the one hand, preachers tap the visual symbols of worship for their immediacy and power to carry truth. Among those visuals in the face of the worshiper are the Bible, the font, the altar, and the cross. Like my childhood pastor, preachers point to or hold up or turn to look at these holy things, and there they are. Why merely talk about the Lord's Table when you have one ten feet away? Why just stand for the authority of the Word in words alone when a Bible sits on the pulpit desk in front of you? Why not preach a sermon on the Baptism of our Lord from the font? So we show them. In the words of Gordon Lathrop, we "break open" these holy things.[4] Lathrop catches something of the power of visual things in worship, even without interpretation. He points out that "the things around which we gather in church are matters of concern, events, objects put to use." Many of these things give profound meaning to the human experience in a way that cannot be described in "scientific" terms. The "experience" of all these things in their appointed places points to the reality of some central point of focus. Then the words employed in worship seek to name this center and impress it upon our memory.[5] The preacher's task is to bring words—the Word—to these things. The words we use are themselves symbols, but they give meaning; again, they break open the visual, make sense of it. They set it into context, giving it a fresh yet eternal spin. Book, font, table, and cross are all available for the preacher's use, not now and again, but often.

Just as engaging is the preacher's reference to the architecture of the worship place. Many churches send the eyes upward toward heaven. There is something to that image. It provides the visual content of a word on reverence or hope, and it begs the participation of the hearer the moment you mention it. How can a worship space in the semiround serve a sermon on Christian community? How does worship in a gymnasium present a visual for a word on pressing on toward the prize? How can the arches of a Gothic church bring the visual to a word on transition or support?

It goes even further, this breaking open of the church's symbols. Some churches are rich in visual images in stained glass, altar pieces, paraments, and so forth. These art forms can be brought into sermons periodically. As a teenager, I heard a sermon in which the preacher pointed out a stained-glass window right next to my pew. The stained glass showed the all-seeing eye of God. Hundreds of sets of eyes turned my way to look at that penetrating eye, alive with color from the sun outside. Decades later, I still remember the preacher's move. A teenager does not forget the God whose eye sees all,

---

4 Gordon Lathrop, *Holy Things: A Liturgical Theology* (Minneapolis: Fortress, 1993), 104.

5 Lathrop, *Holy Things*, 90.

especially when the eye is three feet away on a Sunday morning. I heard a voice, you might say, and I turned to see.

A parish I served sponsored a Christian art festival every year. The art was juried and actually hung and displayed in the sanctuary. It included paintings, sculpture, weavings, ceramics, and other media from artists around the country. Each year on the Sunday the festival opened, we incorporated several of the pieces into our liturgy. The pastor would circle the room and stop at five or six pieces, briefly describe each, and offer a collect at each one. The art pieces were broken open in worship, and then one or two were picked up again as visuals in the sermon.

Also available to the preacher are the visuals of the culture, waiting to be broken open, given meaning, a fresh spin in the light of the Gospel. In Athens Paul caught sight of the Altar to the Unknown God. It was not a Christian symbol, but Paul used it as a bridge to the truth of the Gospel.

> Paul, standing in the midst of the Areopagus, said, "Men of Athens, I perceive that in every way you are very religious. For as I passed along and observed the objects of your worship, I found also an altar with this inscription, 'To the unknown god.' What therefore you worship as unknown, this I proclaim to you." (Acts 17:22–23)

It is similar to a preacher in St. Louis raising the image of the Gateway Arch to introduce the subject of Christ as Mediator or the gate to heaven. The preacher might say, "We're all impressed with the Arch downtown, showing St. Louis to be the Gateway to the West. Yet consider Jesus Christ, the Gateway to heaven, spanning time and space, and opening the way to all who believe!" A cultural image becomes a vehicle for the Gospel as words are added and new meanings provided. The result? Hearers of the sermon have a new "in your face" icon from the culture, broken open by the Gospel. The next time they see the Arch, they will see it in a Gospel light.

At another level, the preacher creates images in the hearer's mind via the use of extended metaphor or narrative. For the hearer, a narrative, biblical or otherwise, is received as a series of images. The hearer's imagination is engaged. Like a filmmaker using a story board to establish plot line, the preacher moves from scene to scene, offering one image after another. Story—a sequence of interconnected events with a beginning, a middle, and an end[6]—forms a series of visual images in the hearer's mind. Those images, as much or perhaps more than the story's words, make the story memorable. If we remember stories, we likely recall an image or images associated with the story, then the words. The first stories we ever heard, perhaps stories from the Bible, may have come to us via images in a picture Bible.

---

6 I owe this definition to Thomas Long, *Preaching and the Literary Forms of the Bible* (Philadelphia: Fortress, 1989), 70–71.

This comes through most powerfully in a scene from the film *Amistad*, the story of a group of nineteenth-century Africans fighting for freedom from slavery in the American courts. Some abolitionists have given a Bible to one of the slaves, who shows the book to his friend. These two do not speak or read English, but the Bible is illustrated with pictures of Jesus. Amazingly, they piece together many of the basic elements of the Gospel just looking at and interpreting the images of Jesus in those pen-and-ink drawings. They see His love, the injustice done to Him, His death, His resurrection, and His ascension. They add their own words from their language as the story unfolds from picture to picture. What is more, they connect with this man in the pictures. Like Him, they know injustice and suffering. They seem to find hope in Him. True, it may not be saving hope as yet, but the story in its beginning, middle, and end is there. Repeatedly, the pictures show Jesus with a corona about His head. "Wherever He goes," says the one imprisoned African, "the sun shines." Once having seen the cross in those pictures, the Africans now see the cross everywhere, even in the masts of ships. I showed this excerpt of *Amistad* to a group of missionaries once. They watched it differently than others I had observed. They watched knowingly, because they had seen it again and again. They had experienced the power of image to tell the Gospel story and rivet it to the mind and heart.

The Preacher as Artist and Poet

The New Homiletic, discussed in another essay in this book, speaks of the preaching task as that of the artist or the poet. In addition to traditional persuasive logic, the preacher can employ participatory evocation. The artistry comes in the preacher's careful use of simile, metaphor, and synecdoche.[7] *Simile* provides a tight comparison between two things, offering clarity and fuller understanding. Something unfamiliar is set against something more familiar. For instance, Jesus said, "The kingdom of heaven is like a mustard seed."

Metaphor makes comparisons in a different way. Metaphor takes the familiar and sets it over against the unfamiliar. Here, though, the connections may be many and varied, not always tight. Hearers are turned loose to make their connections. Some of Jesus' parables were like this—metaphors in narrative form, complex, with levels of meaning. Consider this sermonic metaphor:

> When I was a boy, life on my city block was not always easy. It was a noisy place. Mrs. Pfeiffer was constantly yelling for people to get off

7 For a thorough discussion of these three tools, see Thomas Long, *The Witness of Preaching* (Louisville: Westminister Press, 1989), 161–76.

> her grass. The bully, Jimmy Ringbauer, was always after someone to lay out flat on the pavement. Stumpy's dad, Mr. Lovsosky, could be heard bellowing in a drunken stupor. Dogs barked, and the elevated trains howled by. Yet there was a tree in the park, and twelve feet up in that tree, I could look down on my world and feel safe and secure and quiet and at peace. I loved that tree the way I love Christ's Church.

Here, the safe tree in the park is a metaphor for the Church, connecting with many images in the Bible, including the tree of life in Genesis and the saving tree upon which Christ was crucified.

Finally, *synecdoche* makes no comparisons at all but invites the hearer in to experience a part of the whole, a "slice of life," as Thomas Long calls it.[8] In synecdoche, the part stands for the whole, as in a news item "the White House" stands for the U.S. government. We are showing them a piece of the truth we preach, saying, "Here it is. Come on into this truth and experience at least a part of it." So if the message concerns the folly of building one's life on an accumulation of things, the preacher can spin a yarn (as Jesus did) of someone whose business grows and grows, only to be lost when suddenly that person dies. Images of amassed wealth will be carefully woven, and the image of sudden death carefully set into a sequence of scenes, showing the heart of the matter, gain and loss. The mind of the hearer makes the inevitable connection.

All three of these tools—simile, metaphor, and synecdoche—are the tools of poetry, the artistry of words. Jesus the master communicator used them all. Why shouldn't we? We ask more of the language here than we may when writing something to be read. This asking more of the language is crucial in preaching on two counts. First, oral composition demands such visual imagery. Unless one distributes copies of the sermon as people leave the sanctuary, the sermon is heard, not read. It is oral, not literary composition. Much of poetry is oral. Both preacher and poet rely heavily on the engagement of the imagination, showing hearers, not just telling them. Second, sermons seek to evoke a response, to move to action. That calls for more than logic and a well-structured argument. It calls for language that interests, engages, and invites participation. That language in our culture today is visual language, language that paints pictures and tells stories, carefully, richly, even with levels of meaning.

The Liturgy as *Dabar*

The liturgy is rich in visual imagery. Its words carry images. For instance, we sing the Gloria in Excelsis, imaging in our minds the angels over Bethlehem.

8 Long, *Witness of Preaching*, 173.

We sing any setting of the Nunc Dimittis, envisioning an old man cradling a baby in his arms with a look on his face that says, "I can go now." And if a teacher or pastor has taken the time to break it open, we cannot sing the Sanctus without picturing Isaiah in the temple or the singing living creatures of Revelation.[9]

Truthfully, many people do sing the liturgy without these images in mind and heart because no one has ever turned the projector on. Words are only words then, not to be seen. One of the beauties of the historic liturgy, in whatever specific setting, is its linkage with biblical narrative. As we have seen, where there is narrative, the imagination is engaged. Pictures are formed in the mind.

Like the Bible, font, table, and cross, therefore, the pastor's sermon will no doubt frequently break open a portion of the liturgy for its visual value. In a sermon on the healing of the leper, the pastor suddenly reaches for the Kyrie, and the listener has a picture to go with the words, "Lord, have mercy." On All Saints' Day or St. Michael and All Angels, in preaching on Heb. 12:1–2, why would a preacher not tap the cherished words of the Preface: "Therefore with angels and archangels and with all company of heaven . . ."? Liturgy is word and event, word and narrative, word and imagination. Or, if left to its words alone, never broken open, never visualized, liturgy can be heard and spoken, but never seen. It will be less evocative then, this imageless liturgy of words, less engaging to the young, less real. To place the liturgy in its aesthetic, biblical, and often narrative context maximizes its impact and enhances its memorability. Here the preacher becomes teacher, interpreter, and, once again, artist.

The Use of the Visual Arts

Missed today by many preachers is the power of an art piece to help engage the imagination in preaching. Most pastors have at one time or another shown slides of a variety of artistic depictions of Christ. Perhaps their text was Jesus' question, "Who do people say that the Son of Man is?" (Matt. 16:13). Or perhaps at a Good Friday service, one image after another of the Passion of our Lord was displayed as the congregation sang "O Sacred Head Now Wounded." Whatever the application of the art pieces, hearers became seers, and they will likely never forget the experience.

In some worship settings, the use of art images can powerfully enhance the preacher's words. Projection screens that are not intrusive and yet visible to all offer a great tool for worship and preaching. Such technology is hardly inexpensive. It is not uncommon for larger churches to spend $30,000 for a

9 *Imaging the Word: An Arts and Lectionary Resource*, ed. Susan A. Blain, 3 vols. (Cleveland: United Church Press, 1995), 2:205.

screen and projection system. In many, perhaps most, churches, a folding screen set up near the chancel is more than adequate. However sophisticated the technology, images accompany the preacher's words. The sermon is seen, not just heard. Imagine a sermon based on 1 Pet. 5:7, "Casting all your anxieties on Him . . ." Throughout the sermon, projected on a screen before the congregation, is one of Pablo Picasso's several paintings titled *Woman Crying*. The colors the woman wears are black and purple. She bites anxiously into a blue handkerchief. Her skin is green. Her face and hands are distorted with pain. Tears flow. As one commentary on the painting puts it: "Picasso painted this woman with intense, shocking colors and distorted forms to express her profound emotion. He painted her emotion rather than her outward appearance."[10] Again, we can talk about anxiety, terror, or loss, or we can show them. The painting can provide a haunting image for the anxieties we carry. A little research reveals that these paintings by Picasso, this one from 1937, came at a time when Spain had known war and loss. This image in particular, from a Christian perspective, is a *Kyrie eleison*. As such, it may suggest another application. Accompanying a narrative Communion service, in which worshipers are taught the scriptural roots and meanings of the language of the liturgy, could be visuals, works of art that capture the essence and mood of the various versicles and canticles of the liturgy. How fitting Picasso's weeping woman becomes as an accompanying image for the Kyrie. Or imagine, for instance, singing the Agnus Dei while viewing the image of Jan van Eyck's *Adoration of the Mystic Lamb* (1432). This central panel of the altarpiece at Vijd Chapel, Cathedral St. Bavo, Ghent, Belgium, depicts Christ as the Passover Lamb atop an altar, the Lamb's blood flowing into a chalice. Angels and archangels and the saints of God adore Him.

Many pastors are uncomfortable using art projected on a screen to augment preaching, the singing of a hymn, or the liturgy. A screen may seem intrusive to some, even when used periodically. For others, anything that smacks of audio-visual can spell threat or disaster for the technologically challenged. What is more, pastors face some ambiguity concerning the permissions necessary for screening fine art pieces. Yet this is no reason to run from art as a preaching and worship enhancement. Preachers can find themselves stretched and their hearers engaged by orally describing a piece of art, breaking it open for the light it brings to the truth of the sermon. An excellent writing exercise asks the writer to help the reader experience a painting without ever seeing it. The writing student is asked to put the painting into words. A piece of art asks much of any writer—and of any preacher. Yet without ever projecting the art piece on a screen, many pastors do well

10 Three of these are drawn from the excellent resource *Imaging the Word*. This valuable three-volume resource includes many paintings and other works of art and often provides a brief commentary, opening the painting from a Christian perspective.

incorporating a description of the piece into their sermon as an enhancement of a sermonic move or as the move itself. In what follows, four art pieces will be cited for their value as sermonic images.[11]

Frank Dicksee, an English painter of the nineteenth century, put vivid oils on canvas in a painting titled *Two Crowns*. The painting is exhibited in the Tate Gallery in London. At its center is a medieval king in triumphant procession atop his royal mount. Ladies-in-waiting drop petals of flowers before him. Banners are unfurled. Trumpets are raised. The bright colors depict the opulence and pageantry of a monarch. Atop his head rests a jeweled crown. As one first views the painting, all seems centered on the king. It is a masterful misdirection by Dicksee. Some will walk on and never really see the painting. If you stop long enough you will look into the face of that king and see that he is utterly distracted. His eyes look piercingly and humbly to his left. There, in dark tones at the far right of the painting, is a crucifix. And on that cross, suspended, is another king who wears a crown of thorns. The king at the center of the painting, his face full of wonder, seems to defer to the one on the cross. The painting, when described as above, can serve not only to illustrate but also to make the primary move of a sermon on humility (Phil. 2:5–11) or on losing oneself for the sake of Christ (Mark 8:35). Even without seeing the painting on a screen, the hearer's imagination has been engaged. Having used this piece before, I can assure you that a few hearers will run to the Internet after worship and find the painting to see it for themselves. I saw a copy of *Two Crowns* posted on a refrigerator a few weeks after the sermon! I once referenced the painting in a chapel sermon at the seminary. By mid-morning a student had copies for everyone in our homiletics class.

The fresco paintings by early Christians provide a mother-lode of images that carry significant theological messages easily wrapped into a sermon. Often said to be the first depicted image of Jesus, the Good Shepherd image appears as early as mid-third century. The Vatican has a restored sculpture of the Good Shepherd image dating from the late third century. The statuette shows the familiar image of the young shepherd with a sheep over his shoulders, his hands grasping the sheep's legs.[12] This ancient image can be found in many settings and media. Easily described in a sermon, though, is the image of the Good Shepherd fresco on the ceiling of a family tomb room in Rome

---

11 Helpful here is artcyclopedia.com, with its many links to museums, galleries, and other sources of fine art. Often just entering the artist's name will get you to the piece. Visual tours are available in many galleries and museums. A place to start is entering the keyword "art" and seeing where your browser takes you.

12 For an excellent photograph and interpretation of the sculpture, see *The Vatican Collections: The Papacy and Art* (New York: The Metropolitan Museum of Art, 1982), 218–19.

Cubiculum Velatio, Catacomb of Priscilla).[13] Here again, an oral description of the painting can engage the imagination of the hearer and help move the sermon along on several counts. The young shepherd's short tunic is suited to the task of chasing stray sheep. His right shoulder and arm are free of the tunic for freedom of movement. A leather pouch is strapped across his shoulder. This particular shepherd's tunic is enhanced with purple stripes, signaling riches and authority. His right hand is extended in welcome. A rescued sheep is atop his shoulders. Other sheep, the Church, surround him. Trees in the background have doves with olive branches in their beaks, representing perhaps the peace and rescue the shepherd brings. A little research shows that not all interpreters see this ancient image as a depiction of Jesus (the shepherd, after all, is hardly more than a boy) but rather a representation of the rescue and saving grace the shepherd brings. This may explain its appropriate use in adorning family tomb rooms. It would be easy to wed aspects of this image to the language of John 10, where Jesus describes Himself as the Good Shepherd. The early date of this typical representation gives the hearer a sense of being closer to the words and images of the text.

Some works of art bring a narrative with them. A sermon on Rom. 5:1–5, for instance, might get at the narrative behind John Biggers's painting titled *Shotgun: Third Ward #1*.[14] Biggers grew up in the rough third ward of Houston. His painting depicts dilapidated "shotgun" homes (common among poor Southern blacks, with three rooms on one side of a hallway: you can fire a shotgun from the front door and out the back without hitting anything). In the background, a church has clearly been gutted by fire. In the foreground of the painting stand five adults, three of whom have their backs turned to the viewer. They are drawn to the burnt-out church, to tragedy, loss, and, no doubt, hatred. Yet at the middleground of the painting, one sees children at play. A clergy figure at the center of the painting faces away from the gutted church, bearing a lantern with a burning candle. A young woman holding a baby turns from the church as well to face the direction of the man of God. The candle, the man of God (so highly respected in African-American culture), the playing children, and the woman with an infant all spell hope for the future despite the loss of a beloved place and the pull of despair. Biggers invites the viewer of his work (and the preacher) to fill in the details of the narrative, to give the painting depth of meaning by probing its narrative clues. Particularly when preaching on a text from the Epistles, this merger of visual and narrative can greatly enhance the sermon.

This narrative quality of some art pieces is seen particularly in depictions of biblical narratives. Describing the paintings in detail often

---

13 *Imaging the Word*, 2:216–17.

14 The fresco with commentary is presented in *Imaging the Word*, 1:197.

provides a visual structure for telling the biblical story. Consider Duccio di Buoninsegna's *Jesus Opens the Eyes of the Man Born Blind* (ca. 1310),[15] based on John 9. Gestures, costume, color, and movement tell us a story. Or look closely at Rembrandt's *The Return of the Prodigal Son* (1636).[16] The father graciously leans into his son, who kneels in exhaustion at his father's knees. These paintings based on biblical narratives often hold great potential for structuring the telling of the story in a sermon or for finding the deeper meaning in the narrative.

The neglect of the visual arts in preaching and worship wastes an invaluable resource. Art can serve both Law and Gospel well and need not be relegated to the stuff of museums and tours of cathedrals. In preaching especially, cherished works of art can bring narrative and image to the listener, two aspects of the New Homiletic that need not be "started from scratch" in every sermon. It takes practice, though, especially when your only tool for describing the work to your hearer is language. The time invested in learning this craft, though, yields more memorable and engaging sermons.

The Use of Film

Film presents another visual medium ripe for use in the pulpit. Some cautions, however, are in order regarding the use of film as a preaching resource.

1. Consider the appropriateness of the film as a resource for preaching. What is the film's rating? Do I need to put some sort of disclaimer on the film (e.g., "This is not a recommendation that you see the film")?
2. Be careful with copyright permissions. If I plan on showing an excerpt from a film, do I have the necessary permissions?[17] Again, most preachers today prefer to describe the excerpt rather than run it on a screen.
3. Beware of becoming too enamored with film as a preaching resource. People do not come to worship for film reviews, and not all listeners are engaged by film (just as not all listeners are engaged by references to sports events).

Some preachers will run from film as a tainted medium. Truthfully, some films, because they are so tainted by violence, sexual aberrations, or

15 At the National Gallery of Art in London.

16 At the Hermitage Museum in St. Petersburg, Russia.

17 Although some film excerpts may be shown for educational purposes, generally the use of a film excerpt in a public forum (even though no fee is charged) requires the permission of the production company. These permissions can often be received via fax or even phone.

filthy language, have no redemptive value in the pulpit. *Pulp Fiction*, for example, has an inherent and amazing affirmation of the dynamic power of the Word, but the film is so replete with the above immoralities that most preachers will take a pass on using it in the pulpit. Still, given the immense popularity of film, the preacher does well to be on the prowl for tapping this cultural resource. Walking into a movie theater is not unlike walking through Athens to Mars Hill. It just may be that the screens in our theaters are the new altars to an unknown god, waiting to be broken open with the Gospel. When looking for sermon material in a film, preachers watch for the following:

- *Depiction of the culture.* What does the film say about the values and "truth" of our culture? This may be the most salutary use of film as a preaching resource.
- *Character development.* Are there characters who stand out for their representative attributes?
- *Character pronouncement.* Does a character say something deeply significant?
- *Metaphor.* Does the film present a metaphor for theological truth?
- *Message.* Does the film say something affirming biblical truth or antithetical to it?
- *Foil.* Does the film beg for the Gospel, offering itself, therefore, as a second use of the Law exposé of sin?
- *Parallel narrative.* Does the storyline of the film in any way reflect the narrative sequence of a biblical story?

The power of metaphor in film, actually bordering on synecdoche, can be seen in the film *The Mission*. The film actually tells the story of the struggle of Jesuits to carry on a mission in Peru in the eighteenth century. This commercial film carries an amazing 12-minute scene focusing on sin, guilt, redemption, grace, and forgiveness. The scene depicts the redemption of a former slave trader and murderer. He has taken slaves from their homes for years and now has killed his own brother. A penance is designed by a Jesuit missionary who will be returning to work among the very native people from whom the man has taken slaves. The guilt-ridden man will accompany the Jesuit company, dragging behind him in a net the armor and tools of his slave trade. These heavy symbols of his guilt will be his burden all the way back to the scene of his crimes. We watch him struggle with the weight of that rusting iron, climbing cliffs and crossing rivers. He refuses any help. When one Jesuit cuts the rope that connects the man to his burden, he reties the knot. He will not be released. With the patience of a novelist, the filmmaker shows us the pain of bearing one's own sins, the ordeal of it. Then the party arrives at the village. The people recognize him. One of them approaches with a knife. The native lifts the man's head. Will he slit his throat in revenge? He sees the man's pain and remorse. In an act of grace, he cuts the rope that connects the man to his past. The bundle of rusted iron rolls into the water below, splashing into the water with a blood-red stain. Only one who had been wronged by the man could forgive him. It is an act of sheer grace, and the forgiven man weeps for joy as the natives about him celebrate his freedom.

You can show that excerpt or you can tell it in detail. It is more than a strong sermon illustration. I have used that excerpt in homiletics classes to show the care that must be given to the use of imagery in preaching. A series of seven or eight hastily told stories from an illustration book hardly compares in value to one strong, image-laden narrative that offers evocative meaning at a variety of levels. Students who view this excerpt see in its parade of images everything from grace to Baptism, from blood atonement to church. For many preachers, one of their first and best moves to more engaging preaching will be the move away from stringing illustrations together toward well-crafted, visual imagery in narrative form. We learn that from this scene in *The Mission*, but we are also given a strong narrative that engages the imagination when preaching on guilt, grace, and forgiveness.

Culture depiction abounds in films. Sometimes film represents the Hollywood culture and not much more. At other times, though, a film is exactly on target in depicting the culture's values and questions. Postmodernism's denial of reality can be seen vividly in *The Truman Show*, where the protagonist discovers that his whole life has been a show. As Truman prepares to leave his world, really a sound stage, the director (sounding very much like a surrogate creator) says that he will find no more truth out there than what he has found here. Truman disagrees and walks into the real world for the first time.

In *Groundhog Day* a selfish man keeps reliving a day until he finally gets it right. This magical realism is very much a part of postmodernism. Phil, Bill Murray's character, presents another spin for the preacher, though—the challenge to make *kairos* (meaningful time that is ripe with good) our *chronos* (the mere passing of calendaric time [Eph. 5:15–16]). *The Matrix* takes on the myth of virtual reality and does so with an array of Christian nomenclature and events. The film traces the redemption of reality by one chosen for the task, Neo, accompanied by none other than Trinity. Like *The Truman Show*, *The Matrix* may reflect postmodernism's questioning of truth and reality, but in the end what is real wins out. That in itself offers fuel for a sermon on Jesus Christ as ultimate reality and truth (John 14:6).

Character pronouncements worthy of mention in sermons abound in film. Two come to mind immediately. *Chariots of Fire* tells the story of the 1924 British Olympics team. One of the runners, Eric Liddell, is arguing with his sister. She thinks he should go to China immediately as a missionary. He wants to stay behind to continue his training for the Olympics. As Eric walks with his sister in the highlands, he assures her that he will go to China. But he adds, "God made me for China, but he also made me fast. And I feel his pleasure when I run." The pronouncement can provide an image and narrative for an Epistle text such as Phil. 2:13 or Eph. 5:17, both on understanding God's will.

A second character pronouncement comes at the end of the film *Schindler's List*. The film traces the work of industrialist Oscar Schindler in saving hundreds of Jews from extermination in death camps. Schindler would bribe officials and hire the Jews as workers in his factories, even though they were barely skilled. As the film ends, we see the workers gathered to present Schindler with a ring made from the gold dental work of one of their own. The war has ended. The workers are free, and Schindler must move on. It hits him just there in looking at the crowd of workers, how many more could have been saved. He says that he could have saved more, that he wasted so much money that could have saved so many more. He weeps in regret. The scene serves up a vivid memoir of time wasted, opportunities for witness lost, and the reality of time running out (John 9:4). From the perspective of the Law these are strong realities regarding Christian witness, but ultimately the Gospel is the sole motivation.

This brief look at the use of film as an imaging tool in preaching encourages preachers to have a pad of paper handy the next time they see a film. On several counts, films offer strong visual material for the preaching task.

Conclusion

It was C. S. Lewis who said that the first responsibility of art is to spark interest.[18] Lewis, perhaps as much as anyone in the last hundred years, understood the function of art, the responsibility of the spoken word and visual image to interest or engage. We have all preached sermons that fall short not only of the glory of God but also of the simple goal of interesting our hearer. When the visual is added to the spoken, in liturgy or in preaching, the imagination is engaged. That happens when a skilled preacher uses both the tools of oral composition that tap the imagination and the visual arts of church

18 C. S. Lewis, "Hamlet: The Prince or the Poem" (1942), in *Selected Literary Essays*, ed. Walter Hooper (Cambridge: Cambridge University Press, 1979), 103.

and culture. Word is given light, texture, and story. Like Michelangelo's *Awakening Prisoner*,[19] truth breaks free from the rock. It was there all along, but now it is visible. It is the stuff of incarnation, making us aware of One who was not only heard but seen.

19 Sculpture in Accademia in Florence, Italy.

Liturgy as Story

James A. Wetzstein

William Willimon, dean of the Chapel at Duke University and author of several books and articles on preaching, has written a pair of seemingly contradictory statements, published only eight years apart. In *Peculiar Speech: Preaching to the Baptized*, Willimon is critical of the position taken by Fred Craddock in *As One without Authority*. He describes Craddock's position as one that identifies freedom to choose for oneself as the highest American ideal. Craddock says, "No longer can the preacher presuppose . . . the authority of Scripture."[1] "It requires of the preacher that he resist the temptation to tyranny of ideas rather than democratic sharing."[2] Willimon can barely hide his contempt: "Nothing is said here about the tyranny of sin, the tyranny of the cultural status quo, the tyranny of the congregation."[3] On the other hand, in "Five Minute Preaching Workshop," a regular feature of *Pulpit Resource*, a preaching journal that he edits, Willimon states: "Much of our violence [against the text] begins with our modern lust for one 'right' interpretation . . . I now honor [a] diversity of reading."[4] How we reconcile these apparently contradictory statements from the same writer will provide insight for the task of this essay, namely, an analysis of the so-called New Homiletic and its strengths and weaknesses for liturgical preaching.

It may come as a shock to regular preachers who spend their time considering biblical texts in the context of blank paper or computer screen and the nagging question, "What will I say about this?" that the role of the text in preaching is somewhat controversial. We, whose chief aim is to plan for coherent, Law-Gospel speech that is grounded in the text, negotiate this

1 William Willimon, *Peculiar Speech: Preaching to the Baptized* (Grand Rapids: Eerdmans, 1992), 49.

2 Willimon, *Peculiar Speech*, 49.

3 Willimon, *Peculiar Speech*, 49.

4 William Willimon, "Five Minute Preaching Workshop," *Pulpit Resource* 28, no. 1 (January 2000): 60.

controversy intuitively, without formal thought, seeking to connect the timeless truths of Scripture in a timely fashion. We want to make a connection between the text on the page and the congregant in the pew. It seems obvious to us that this is the task.

We do well, however, to stop for a few minutes and consider the controversy and our personal, preaching position in the debate. What is the role of the text in this task and what is the role of the hearer (or reader) of the text? This may seem like an exercise in sophistry, like the question of a tree falling in the forest—if no one is there to hear it, does it make a sound? But the issue is more than a philosophical joke. The issue is one of the role of truth in the text and the role of the reader/hearer in making that truth real.

For centuries it has been assumed that truth is "of itself," namely, that some things are true, period. It follows, then, that descriptions of these truths become statements of truth, or true statements. These are true "of themselves"—in the forest—with no one to hear or read them. In this last century (i.e., the twentieth century), however, this question of absolute and objective truth has come under fire. There are many critics of such a relativistic view (and most preachers of the Gospel fall into this category, certainly in the LCMS, my own church body). They point out that this questioning of absolute truth is spawned by a desire to evade the clear dictates of truth, particularly ethical or theological truth, in order to refashion a world in one's own image. While it is certainly possible for this approach to be employed by those looking for an ethical dodge, the motive behind the question is purer than this. It derives from a serious epistemological question. It comes from the attempt to understand the nature of understanding and meaning. Who makes meaning? How is it grounded? What role does the hearer/reader play in the task? There is clearly some role. Even those who assert that the truth is the truth in the midst of the empty forest must concede that the truth in the empty forest doesn't mean anything if no one is there to consider it. And it is in this consideration of the truth that the question becomes complicated. Words have meaning both individually and collectively, this is sure. But what do they mean, and who decides? It is a question that sparks debate.

The New Homiletic rises from this hermeneutical debate (sometimes called the "New Hermeneutic"). It strives to help a preacher convey truth with sensitivity both to the reality that the reader/hearer has a part to play in arriving at the meaning of a text and with an awareness that many hearers are aware, if viscerally, that they do have a part to play. The New Homiletic (at its best) seeks to give the preacher a means to invite the hearer on the quest for the truth in the context of life and the text.

Classical preaching is often described as "deductive," that is, it is an effort to identify the meaning presented in the text (the general principle) and apply that meaning to the lives of one's hearers. This is the core motivation behind what Willimon describes as the preacher's appeal: "Give me 20 minutes and I can explain this to you."[5]

It is not hard to recognize the weakness behind such a statement. Hopefully preaching is more than just the explication of complicated texts. What is harder to recognize is the inability of such an approach to take seriously the real role of the reader/hearer in the communication of the text.[6] An example of this took place in TV commentator Bill Moyers's book on Genesis. The account being discussed was Abraham's sojourn in Egypt (Genesis 12) and the moral tension coming from his decision to pass his wife off as his sister and so avoid the possibility of death, while in so doing essentially ensuring that Sarah will sleep with the Pharaoh. While the whole group is debating the ethical ramifications of this story and struggling with Abraham and Sarah's roles, one participant offers this reflection: "I studied this narrative with a group of bankers, lawyers, and business executives. One of the lawyers said, 'Wait, let's look at the beginning of the story. God takes this shepherd, and he's got nothing, right? Morality aside, look what happens. By the end the chapter, Abraham is talking one on one with a head of state. Leave aside how he sold Sarah. Well, here he is, talking with Pharaoh. He's supposed to become the head of a great nation. He's earned start-up costs. Let's face it—nobody likes the fact that he sold his wife, but hey, it worked.' "[7] The analysis hit the conversation like a bombshell. Was this attorney's assessment of Abraham's performance and the meaning of the story correct? Is this the truth? Who is to say? How do we decide? Certainly, Scripture interprets Scripture, but what will be the role of the reader? Has this man simply gotten it wrong?

The New Homiletic, an approach espoused to varying degrees by such notables as Craddock, Buttrick, Long, and others, seeks to give attention to the role of the reader/hearer through what is described as an inductive approach to the text. Inductive logic seeks to draw an inference of a generalized conclusion from particular instances. That is, having personally observed several cows giving milk, I draw the inference (without seeing all the cows in the world or even talking to their owners) that all cows give milk. Craddock in his book *As One without Authority* rightly points out that this is

---

5 Willimon, "Five Minute Preaching Workshop," 60.

6 This is especially true for preachers who have been raised on the idea that every text has a "central thought," the main truth, which is then applied to the congregation through an assessment of malady and means on the way to a goal, which is the application of the truth of the text into the lives of the hearers.

7 Bill Moyers, ed., *Genesis: A Living Conversation* (New York: Doubleday, 1996), 166.

the way people learn in everyday life.[8] While we might like to suppose that I know that this cow before me gives milk because I have deduced it from the true universal statement "all cows give milk," the truth of the matter is that I have induced that statement of principle from my series of experiences with a variety of milk-giving cows or have taken on faith the induction of others based upon their experience.

How does this difference of approach between deduction and induction work in a specific biblical text? Consider the visit of Nicodemus, as recorded in John 3:

> Now there was a man of the Pharisees named Nicodemus, a ruler of the Jews. This man came to Jesus by night and said to Him, "Rabbi, we know that You are a teacher come from God, for no one can do these signs that you do unless God is with Him."
>
> Jesus answered him, "Truly, truly, I say to you, unless one is born again he cannot see the kingdom of God."
>
> Nicodemus said to Him, "How can a man be born when he is old? Can he enter a second time into his mother's womb and be born!"
>
> Jesus answered, "Truly, truly, I say to you, unless one is born of water and the Spirit, he cannot enter the kingdom of God. That which is born of flesh is flesh, and that which is born of the Spirit is spirit. Do not marvel that I said to you, 'You must be born again.' The wind blows where it wishes, and you hear its sound, but you do not know where it comes from or where it goes. So it is with everyone who is born of the Spirit."
>
> Nicodemus said to Him, "How can these things be?"
>
> Jesus answered him, "Are you the teacher of Israel and yet you do not understand these things? Truly, truly, I say to you, we speak of what we know, and bear witness to what we have seen, but you do not receive our testimony. If I have told you earthly things and you do not believe, how can you believe if I tell you heavenly things? No one has ascended into heaven except he who descended from heaven, the Son of Man. And as Moses lifted up the serpent in the wilderness, so must the Son of Man be lifted up, that whoever believes in Him may have eternal life.
>
> "For God so loved the world that He gave His only Son, that whoever believes in Him shall not perish but have eternal life. For God did not send His Son into the world to condemn the world, but in order that the world might be saved through Him. Whoever believes in Him is not condemned, but whoever does not believe is condemned already, because he has not believed in the name of the only Son of God. And

8 Fred B. Craddock, *As One without Authority: Essays on Inductive Preaching* (Enid, OK: Phillips University Press, 1971), 66.

> this is the judgment: the light has come into the world, and people loved the darkness rather than the light because their works were evil. For everyone who does wicked things hates the light and does not come to the light, lest his works should be exposed. But whoever does what is true comes to the light, so that it may be clearly seen that his works have been carried out in God." (John 3:1–21)

A deductive approach to this text will see this as a text about the universalism of God's grace in Jesus Christ (v. 16). It communicates the need for Baptism as the means for entering into the kingdom of heaven (v. 5). It shows the crucifixion of Jesus as the basis for grace made personal in Baptism (v. 14). This might even seem like a first-year homiletics exercise, it is so straightforward. In fact, at this point it might look like the most challenging task will be how to limit the number of truths to be told in a 12–20 minute sermon, especially if one sees the need to present refresher information on the position of Nicodemus and the story of Moses and the bronze serpent.

An inductive approach to this text would point out that the text actually says nothing propositionally about the doctrines of universal grace, Baptism, or the crucifixion of Christ. In fact, the church has induced this meaning from this and several other biblical texts through the combined efforts of exegetes and systematicians. Further, the text is thick with meaning and nuance. An inductive approach would call us back to the reality that this text from the Gospel according to John is a story. It is a story about one man, Nicodemus, and his quest for information regarding the nature of the kingdom of heaven. Such an approach would then go on to assert that this story has a primary audience, the people of the early church who recalled these stories prior to John's writing, and a secondary audience, John's community of initial readers and hearers. The text comes alongside the hearer and comes aboard with its set of particulars, engages the particulars of the audience, and then leaves behind an audience that is changed.

The challenge then is to lead hearers into a consideration of their circumstances in light of those of Nicodemus, the first hearers of the story, and John's community of hearers. Thomas Boomershine[9] encourages people to memorize the stories of the Bible. He calls people to remember, both factually and emotionally, moments in their lives when they were in circumstances similar to the character in the story.

In the context of John 3, this might be done through a connection to our own experiences of fear in the face of change. Change makes most people uncomfortable, and the fear that change inspires is often enough for us to

---

9 Thomas E. Boomershine, *Story Journey: An Invitation to the Gospel as Storytelling* (Nashville: Abingdon, 1988).

remain in an unsatisfying or unhealthy situation. "The devil you know is better than the devil you don't know," goes the proverb. Psychologists and counselors tell us that it is fear of change and the unknown that, apart from any chemical addictions, keeps most dysfunctional situations going, despite the admission of all involved that the situation, as presently experienced, is unacceptable. Having drawn up inside of us the recollection of that level of uncertainty and fear, we can see how Nicodemus, who comes alongside of us, is in the same boat. Aware that this Jesus may be all that he has hoped for and anticipated, he comes in the shadows, hiding himself not just from his colleagues but also from the truth that Jesus will tell. Jesus confronts Nicodemus. He doesn't let him hide, but flushes him out with talk of radically new beginnings, as new as being born again. And then, while Nicodemus is struggling to put this new talk into familiar old categories (struggling because they will not fit), Jesus comes again with the assurance of His presence for Nicodemus through the change. This presence is made no more real than in His crucifixion where Jesus is lifted up for the sake of those in need of new life in the kingdom of heaven, just as the bronze serpent was lifted up for new life in the wilderness with Moses. The truths of the text in this approach are not imposed from above; rather, they bubble up around us, engaging us in our own lives and using those lives to bring intentional meaning to the text. In a time when the church strives to be relevant in a changing world, such an approach virtually assures relevance. What is more, it gives an opportunity to orthodoxy in a manner that declarative and deductive preaching cannot. As Gordon Lathrop puts it, "to say an old thing in the old way in a new situation is to inevitably distort its meaning."[10] An inductive approach, by definition, says old things in new ways.

The inductive approach, however, presents several dangers. The first is its temptation to deflate the authority of Scripture (as Willimon points out in his critique of Craddock) to but one of a series of collected specific experiences or points of view. The New Homiletic seems to come out of denominations that are weak on the doctrine of Scripture. The response to this misunderstanding is to maintain the authority of Scripture in all its parts as source and norm of teaching such that we will never allow ourselves to dismiss the message of the biblical text as a troublesome and somewhat outdated opinion.

A second danger lies in the susceptibility of the inductive method to the control of a weak sample of specifics (what Willimon calls the "tyranny of the cultural status quo"). An antidote to this danger is to ensure that the sample of experiences that are brought alongside of Scripture are of such breadth—different times, places, cultures—that the preacher, in a quest for

10 Gordon Lathrop, *Holy Things* (Minneapolis: Augsburg Fortress, 1993), 5.

relevance to the audience, does not disengage from relevance to the kingdom of heaven. The assumption behind this suggestion is that while individual experiences may present a view of human life that is at odds with the truths of Scripture (e.g., the presence of sin, the quest for immortality, the need for redemption), the broader sweep of human experience is consistent with these truths. Of course, outside of the revealed word of Scripture there is no ability to present or proclaim the work of Jesus the Christ. *A nearly guaranteed means of enriching such a sample is to be sure to include in the gathering of specific experiences the ancient voice of the historic liturgy.*

"Our Lord speaks and we listen . . . Saying back to him what he has said to us, we repeat what is most true and sure."[11] In the context of our topic, it is helpful to add, "and we have been repeating this for centuries." For the preacher, especially in the inductive task, the depth of the experience and the formative nature of the liturgy are a gold mine of blessed meaning-making.

The liturgy, taking its cues from Scripture, tells stories and tells them well. The liturgical script tells the great story of creation, redemption, and sanctification among the people of God who have come to say back to God what He has said to them. The freight that the liturgy must carry is the freight of the story of God. The great wonder and blessing are that, as the liturgy goes about this task, the people of God experience not just the recollection of the stories of God or "the gift of shared memory," as one particularly insipid homily put it. No, in telling the story of God in the words of God, the liturgy delivers the Word of God Himself. In the midst of the telling—as the Words of Institution demonstrate—Christ Himself is present. In His presence, He is about the task of making a people or rescuing them from their time-bound specificity.

Christ Himself is present (and again we look to the liturgy to teach us) *for you*. The location of Christ's presence among His people in the liturgical event not only says something about Christ—that He is gracious and true to His promises to be with us and bless us with life and salvation—but also about us. We who gather for the liturgical event, follow the liturgical script, and participate in receiving the gifts of Christ's presence in the liturgical story are a peculiar (that is, unique) people. Like any good story, the liturgy tells us things not only about the protagonist (in this case God: Father, Son, and Holy Spirit) but also about ourselves, the listeners to the story. And it is in this "people-producing power" that we often overlook the gift of liturgy. The story of the liturgy *changes* us. It changes us by calling us to be identified with the story, to see ourselves in the story. The power of every story, from Aesop's fables to the latest film, is in its ability to bring us to compare ourselves to the characters and find ourselves in one of the characters and

11 *LW*, p. 6.

so see ourselves in a new light. The reason Jesus' parables recorded in Luke 15 (the lost sheep, the lost coin, the father with two sons) get His hearers so upset is because they can tell that Jesus is telling stories about *them*! They, the people who listen, are being made into the surly older brother of the prodigal son while they listen. And they know it. Stories don't just remind us of who we are. They make us who we are. Ask a child around the holiday dinner table who has been blessed with the patient ability to listen in on the old stories that the grown-ups tell again and again. Such a child will tell you: this is one of the places that she discovers herself and learns the things that are true about life.

So it is that the liturgy, well-practiced as the vehicle for the stories of God, actually makes a people. It makes a people who are at odds with the world, for the story that they share in the liturgy, if it is scriptural, is at odds with the stories of the world. In that people-making work, the liturgy becomes the context for good, inductive preaching. What meaning will we "who are surrounded by such a cloud of witnesses" (Hebrews 12) find in the day's preaching text?

Since the purpose of this essay is to present the preacher's task in the context of this liturgical story, it might be helpful to review briefly the content of the liturgical story as it is classically scripted.

Arthur Just suggests that the Emmaus road experience (Luke 24:13–35) forms an outline of the liturgical event as the early church had drawn it from their roots in the weekly Passover seder and synagogue service.[12] He makes a compelling case. We do well, however, to recall that the Emmaus story is not the exclusive informer or reflector of the shape and story content of the Divine Service. All of the great stories of encounter with the divine share in framing the events of the liturgy of God's people: the story of Moses at the burning bush, the account of the first Passover, Elijah hiding in the cave, the visit of the three strangers to Abraham and Sarah, the call of Isaiah, the confrontation between Nathan and David, the visit of the angel Gabriel to Mary, the Last Supper, the conversion of Paul, and the vision given to John the Evangelist. The themes are the same. God's people are confronted where they are by the divine presence. This confrontation takes place in the larger context of God's covenant promises. The confrontation requires of God's children a radical rethinking of who they are and who God is. The tension of the confrontation is resolved through the gracious act of God, which is part and parcel of His presence and which, in its blessing, calls us to carry His message into the world.

That is what happens every Sunday morning. And it happens—for God has promised it to happen—in the context of the retelling of these

12 Arthur Just, *Luke*, vol. 2 (St. Louis: Concordia, 1996), 972–1020.

great stories of God's action for His people in their presence. An irony of Sunday morning is that so much of what is told and celebrated in church is not, in fact, about church; rather, it is about life. The great stories and songs derived from these stories shape the historic liturgy and are from and about events that are as far from Sunday as possible. Journalist Richard Rodriguez states that the significant moments of our lives take place "in the Tuesdays and Thursdays of life."[13] What we celebrate Sunday morning are the great Tuesday and Thursday encounters with God. To push Rodriguez's observation further, it is worth noting that as a liturgical people, that is, a people whose lives are framed, defined, and interpreted in our regular encounters with the divine mystery through a scripted rite, we discover that the Tuesdays and Thursdays of life are a living out of the great celebratory Sunday encounters with God.

It starts before the church doors are unlocked, in the homes of those who prepare to come. The liturgy begins as God's people make the choice to rise and seek the presence of God where He has promised to be. They are making a peculiar choice. In fact, they are being summoned.[14] Competing calls vie for their attention: the bed and much needed sleep, the Sunday paper and its informing relaxation, the yard and its promise of return on real estate investment. As usual, the greatest temptations that plague the people of God are not evils but misplaced "goods." Against these competing calls God's people still come. Are all those who dress and drive this conscious of the motive behind their action? Not likely, not all the time. But the gifts of God are not dependent upon the frame of mind of either people or presiding minister; rather, they are assured by the promise of God's presence.

One might expect that those who make sanctified choices on weekends would be rewarded with a warm welcome and praise from those who lead them in the life that they are so faithfully achieving. Indeed, mission practitioners tell us that we do well to give a warm greeting to all of the assembled as a sign of the hospitality of God's people in God's house—a reward for good behavior, so to speak. But such greetings—what a colleague refers to with contempt as "the Holy Howdy"[15]—are conspicuous by their absence from most published forms in the Lutheran Church. Instead, these who seek to do well are confronted first by the direct naming of God as Father, Son, and Holy Spirit, and then by the brusque allegation of their own sinfulness. Is this the way we win friends and influence people? Not likely. But it is the way a people are made. One recalls the demand made upon Moses to remove

---

13 Richard Rodriguez, *The Newshour with Jim Lehrer*, 12/30/99 http://www.pbs.org/newshour/essays/2000 essays/rodriguez_2000.htm 1.

14 Willimon, *Peculiar Speech*, ix.

15 With thanks and apologies to Rev. Arthur Burkman, Redeemer Lutheran Church, Highland, Indiana.

his shoes. The question to Elijah, "What are you doing?" The absolute terror of Isaiah, "Woe to me! I am ruined!" God has been named and so is present among His people. God's holy presence for people living in a stumbling but self-important world is always an indictment. Like a child whose mother walks unexpectedly into the kitchen, our hands are caught in the proverbial cookie jar. We are "busted"! And so the morning's liturgical story is prepared for by rubbing our nose in our failure.

The brief order of Confession and Absolution functions as a summary of all that is to follow: presence of God, confrontation, then gifts of blessing and forgiveness. Absolution always follows confession.

"Lord have mercy" and "Glory to God" or "This is the feast" help us begin again. We are the kids on the parade route, waiting for the big float. We are the supplicant subjects awaiting the king's arrival and the "pork" that such local politicking is sure to bring with it. In Mark, the blind man was the only one to see it and say it: "Son of [King] David! Have mercy on me!" Could he see what was coming? No. But like the subjects who would cry, "Lord, have mercy!" before the king's entourage, he knew it would be good. It would be "the goods." So it is with all those who make this cry of hopefulness. We have come into the presence of the King of the universe. We speak the words of those who await His arrival.

Then the word comes. Tied to the actions of God down through the ages in the experience of the people of the first covenants (Old Testament readings) and the teachings of the early Easter-witnessing church (Epistles), we stand to see the Word of God Himself in the reading of the Gospel. "This is the Word of the Lord!" proclaims the presiding minister. Is he talking about the sound, the book, the invisible but real presence of Christ? Yes to all.

Then come the sermon and the creed and the blessing of fellowship with God. There is an invitation to dine with the divine. God has come among us, and, like all of the old stories of God's coming, His faithful presence has created and strengthened a faithful bond between Him and us. Those who came from separate homes and were confronted by their separate sins are now swept up together with all the faithful.

"Lift up your hearts!" calls the minister. "Let's go to heaven!" he might as well be saying.

"We're already there," comes the reply. "We lift them [our hearts] up to the Lord."

The stories of the presence of God are always awe-inspiring. Even Elijah's still, small voice makes a maximum impact. These stories are mustered together in the telling of God's presence in the reality of Jesus' Holy Supper. "Holy is God the Lord of Hosts." Isaiah's story is our story. "Hosanna in the highest." We join the people on the Palm Sunday parade route. The one who comes is Jesus Himself. He has come to win the victory!

But His victory looks like no victory to be televised and analyzed on ESPN. He comes not with shouts of triumph. He comes to make right. Turning over the tables of our plans to get ahead, Jesus comes to bless with His presence. There we are, victorious.

Simeon was a man who was promised a vision of the Savior. When he saw Jesus, his life was fulfilled. Likewise, having tasted and seen that the Lord is good, we go, complete and fulfilled. Curiously, our fulfillment will have nothing to do with the success of the preacher or the preparation of the choir, though this is no excuse for bad preaching and thoughtless singing. We will leave fulfilled because God has made Himself present for us. The presence of God doesn't just bring blessing. The presence of God is blessing. The blessings do not depend on the people. The blessings depend on the presence of God, made real in the story He has told, which we now tell back to Him. In the telling we find our identity and calling as carriers of His message of grace into the world for the life of the world (John 6:51). Further, in this retelling we are connected to countless lives across the ages, and in this connection we find the meaning in the text.

Such an approach assumes familiarity with the liturgy and its references. What good is a good story if the hearer doesn't connect with its references? How can the cloud of witnesses inform me if I do not see them? The *Lutheran Service Book* seeks to overcome this problem, listing the specific Scripture passages that inspire the elements of the liturgy. At the very least, the average worshiper who takes the time to read the fine print will know that the composers of liturgical texts have not just been making it up.

Extra-narrative references are a basic part of good storytelling. Often these references, while oblique, are clearly understood. The story moves along, carrying with it the whole content of another story that has never been explicitly told in this telling, but benefiting from the presence of the content all the same. Popular animated films make a regular practice of extra-narrative references. Situations and quotations from older films pepper the dialogue to the delight of the parents obliged to accompany their children to the movieplex.

This is not to suggest that the preacher's task is best spent leading weekly workshops on the narrative history of the liturgy. If the preacher is involved in biblical preaching, he will, by necessity, be telling the same stories as the liturgy. He will, in fact, be delivering to the people—"for them" in the way that the Lord's Supper is distributed "for them"—the stories of the liturgy that are, by definition, the stories of Scripture.

The importance of this task is evident in the reflections of most liturgical Christians on the format of the Sunday liturgy. Typically, liturgical scholars will point to the reading of the Gospel and the Words of Institution (both proclamations of our Lord's own words) as the climax of the Service of the Word and Service of the Sacrament, respectively. Presumably, if the liturgy is about the presence of Christ, then the words of Christ are most important. When the folk in the pew are asked the same question, however, the answers are different.[16] Constantly, when asked to reflect on this question, the majority of individuals cite the sermon as the climax to the Service of the Word. This could be disposed of as an example of the dominance of a nonsacramental, sermon-based theological bias in U.S. culture except for the following fact: these same respondents cite the distribution of the elements of Communion as the highpoint of the Service of the Sacrament. The parallels are striking, for it is in both events that the Word of God is made personal. The sermon joins the distribution in proclaiming the gifts of God "for you." While earlier in this essay we were calling for the liturgy to inform the sermon, the reverse is true as well.

It is in the sermon that the story of the people of Scripture is identified as the story of God and then, most wonderfully, as the hearer's story as well. Their story is His story which becomes now my story. The liturgy, if the preacher will exploit its storytelling potential and draw its references into the text of the day, can become a powerful reinforcement for the hearer.

Rather than disposing of the texts of the liturgy as altogether too irrelevant to contemporary life, we ought to be searching for ways to make their relevance as parts of the story plain to those who sing them. This is the liturgical equivalent of an actor discovering his character's motivation. It is in this discovery that he "becomes" the character. This is no less the goal of the liturgical participant: in a sense to "become" the blind man, the angels, King David, Isaiah, Simeon—to find in their stories our own story. It is perhaps in this sense that St. Paul exhorts us to "put on" Christ.

So the text, the liturgy, and the experiences of the hearers are mutually informative. This is the best conclusion of the inductive approach. All three have their stories. All three come together in the preaching event. The goal of a good preacher of the Word will be to help the hearers see that the stories are, in essence, all the same. Not because the preacher says so, but because they "see so." For they are all involved in the great saving story of God.

---

16 This assertion is based on the author's experience as a liturgical consultant in the context of workshops on the nature of the liturgy and the space that houses it.

Preaching within the Faith Community

John Arthur Nunes

Public Faith

The public character of Christianity is inevitable. This faith brims. It resists any closeting. All attempts at privatizing fail. For centuries this faith has vigorously demanded to be published—literally, to be made public. Contrasted with the vagaries of mystical meditation or New Age personal spiritual exploration, there is always some sort of quest to be known in Christianity—seeking for human community. That community is formed primarily when God's redeemed people gather to hear a word from the Lord.

Assembling in the name of Jesus is essentially public. For example, Holy Communion apart from community is an anomaly. Believers have no real identity apart from this public community. Through the means of the Spirit, God retrieves us from sin, death, and the devil and weaves us into a faith community—the nurturing vine that gives life. Apart from that web of relationships—pastor, altar, pulpit, and pew—growth in grace will slow or die.

God's eternal things are public things. The splashing of Holy Baptism, the homiletical speaking of God's Word, the solemnizing of vows for marriage, the promises of confirmation spoken at an altar, the breaking of bread and the sipping from the cup at the Lord's Table—these happen "in church," that is, in close relation to the pastoral office and a regularly functioning assembly, because holy things belong first to God.

The eternal plan starts in the heart of the Father (John 3:16). The Holy Spirit transacts salvation, creating faith, applying the promises of God and the benefits of Christ to the human heart. That's His priority. Preaching confers precisely what God's Word promises. Whether punishment or promise, preachers can be sure that what they declare will be delivered. God's Word works. Likewise, the Sacraments communicate an audible and visible word of hope and healing. What follows involves the mouth (Rom.

10:9–10). Confession is made. Praise is sung. Jesus is celebrated publicly. The transaction continues.

Every expression of the confession "Jesus Christ is Lord" flows from worship. Human care ministries are living branches of the primary healing from the vine of worship. For example, during the Pentecost time of the church year, there is ample chance to preach and sing through the relationship between healing and salvation (Matt. 9:22; Mark 5:34; Luke 8:48).[1] The church then does what it says, or, best yet, what it is. But the direction of this human care trail is formed from God's surplus at the altar and pulpit toward human need, not vice versa. Recall John's apocalyptic insight of the new garden with a tree of life, bearing fruit and producing leaves with power to heal the nations. Literally, it is a tree for the therapy of the ethnics (Rev. 22:2). But the focus is on the Lamb at the center—it is first about Jesus, not us.

The Divine Service is viewed as the hub from which all spokes of ministry emanate. From this the work of the congregation goes forth. Worship leaders will be sensitive to the context in which the preaching and the Divine Service occur. From the 1998 Consultation on Orthodox Liturgical Renewal at the New Skete Monastery in Cambridge, New York, we hear this good instruction:

> . . . worship sometimes has been compared to language. Through worship we communicate with God. But just as languages have their own peculiarities of syntax, grammar, and vocabulary and change through time, so also our ways of worship vary and change. Consequently, the gestures, symbols and styles of a given time or place may not be immediately understandable in another context. Within Christianity, variety in the "language" of worship is evident from the beginnings of the Church, as local communities developed their own forms for expression and celebrating their faith. Through the centuries, in order to carry out its mission of spreading the Gospel to all nations and all peoples, the Church has continued to adapt its ways of worshipping to new contexts.[2]

Meaning and Maximal Actions

Among my non-Lutheran clergy friends, there is a mutual exchange of playful teasing. We all occasionally chuckle at the caricatures of each other's preaching and worship traditions. One fraternal jibe leveled directly toward

1 See Garth D. Ludwig, *Order Restored: A Biblical Interpretation of Health, Medicine and Healing* (St. Louis: Concordia, 1999).

2 "Consultation on Orthodox Liturgical Renewal and Visible Unity," *St. Vladimir's Theological Quarterly* 42, nos. 3–4 (1998).

Lutherans—and indirectly upon many liturgical churches—is what we might call "worship minimalism." Here, though the liturgy itself bespeaks the Lutheran belief in grace, our practice of liturgy can betray what we say. Some forms of historic liturgy seem so succinct as to be truncated. When it comes to water: a sprinkle, preferably from a small shell. When it comes to bread and wine: small portions are distributed. When it comes to preaching: no more than a dozen minutes is widely appreciated, if not encouraged. When it comes to the volume of sound: smooth, mild, frequent periods of pianissimo interspersed with ample silence. When it comes to time at worship: the "59/59 rule" applies. (The "59/59 rule" is a colloquial comment in some urban Lutheran circles referring to the maximum of 59 minutes and 59 seconds allocated for the Divine Service.)

The irony for some consists in this: how can we be so speedy in completing the Divine Service on the one hand, and speak doctrinally at such length on the other. Our theology overflows with the Gospel. Why does our preaching and liturgical practice actually seem cheerfully and willfully curtailed? We're glad to get to the end. Is this merely a varying view of time and timing? Is it deeply systemic? Is this simply a matter of taste, as one person resonates with a quick scherzo, while another loves the slow, soulful blues?

Not that quantity ever substitutes for quality, or that substance and style can be bifurcated, but what constitutes precise expression in some communities can be interpreted as a paucity of content in others: "He must not have much to say about Jesus," "He must be in such a hurry he can't enjoy the joy of the Lord," or "This must not matter much to him."

Can we learn from new communities (new to Lutherans, that is) to do the same old thing in new and different ways? Can actions more clearly connect with what is observed and what is meant. Currently, St. Paul Lutheran Church in Dallas, Texas, is planning the construction of a new worship facility. The team designing the worship space has lengthily considered what mode or modes of Baptism will be offered. Their planning process involves more than the architectural preparation. They have returned to primary questions. What is sacred space? What are the theological implications for theater-style seating? Does being in the inner city make any difference? David Benke, LCMS Atlantic District president, has wisely advised that communities such as St. Paul Church (characterized by multicultural, multiclass, mission-oriented worship) must be measured by the standards of confessional Lutheran theology and at the same time must speak idiomatically in the language of the people.[3]

---

3 David H. Benke, "Multicultural Worship: Urban LCMS Mission Perspectives," *Lutheran Worship Notes* 31 (1994): 1.

St. Paul is mulling over what sort of structure surfaces when theology, locality, and functionality come together. What messages are sent? How is meaning connoted and denoted within this faith community and for the sake of the larger community? What are the precedents in the history of the congregation, in the denomination, and in Christendom? Or more local questions: What does brick signify to those living in a virtual concrete jungle? Is there value in the use of Kente fabric for paraments? How can the visual aspects of the Sacraments be most legible or sensible to this local community without compromising their timeless nature or jettisoning the tried practice of the wider church? In other words, how does physical space serve to communicate the Gospel?

Deep River

"Deep River" is a mellifluous African-American spiritual. It movingly sings of the homeward and heavenward trek through Jordan. These slaves knew they were saved through water. A healthy, path-breaking conversation is emerging around St. Paul Church's core confessional value of Baptism. Romans 6:3–6 and Colossians 2:11–12 have been instructive with their epistolary evocations of baptismal death and resurrection, violently killing off, cutting off, and drowning the "sinful nature" and powerfully being rescued and raised for a brand-new discipled living. As such, the committee is planning the construction of a facility that will afford both the sprinkling and immersion options for Baptism. In the inner city, life is often lived on the hard edge, indeed sometimes bleeding edges. In Baptism, God offers salvation in trinitarian words that claim the candidate as God's own. In Baptism, water and Word flow, bestowing a change for life, now and forever. In Baptism, God gives life so people can live and live out their faith, freed and forgiven. This life is much more than a biological, vegetative repetitive existence (John 10:10). As in the act of baptizing, this life in Christ is much more than just going through the motions. In some communities some might find immersion a more accessible way to signify participation in the death and resurrection of Jesus Christ—God snatching us from the jaws of hell and keeping us safe from the enemy (John 10:28). The biblical and confessional language is dramatic. So can be the delivery of God's promise whether one is baptizing by immersion or sprinkling. The outward form is a matter of adiaphora. Luther baptized infants by immersion.

Further, immersion can well demonstrate that the amount of water does not determine the efficacy of Baptism as long as both forms are equally offered, accompanied by clear teaching without binding consciences. As profoundly as immersion may maximize the gesture, careful communication must be exercised. The Dallas region of Texas is a virtual Baptist belt.

On full-immersion Sundays, pastorally responsible preaching will take on strong catechetical tones. It must counter false allusions to Baptist or Reformed practices. It must disassociate with Pentecostal groups inasmuch as they hold faulty understandings of Baptism. While full immersion maximizes the significant action in those churches, their theological stances minimize the potency of God's saving grace operating by faith in this Sacrament. St. Paul Church is concluding that whenever infants are baptized by full (and careful) immersion—as they are in Orthodox fellowships—the sacramental character of the sign will be enhanced first from the pulpit. Evidence of household texts can be preached (1 Cor. 1:16; Acts 16:15; 16:33; 18:8). Covenantal correlation to the rite of circumcision can also be proclaimed (Col. 2:11–12; Rom. 4:11; Eph. 1:13; 4:30).

An Ongoing Conversation

The pioneering hymnal supplement *This Far by Faith: An African-American Resource for Worship* was released by Augsburg Fortress in 1999. Besides being the first black Lutheran hymnal, it provides a model for how a specific ethnic group can join the ongoing goal of unity in worship. All communities of faith should keep their senses attuned not only toward their own indigenous gifts but also toward what other practices have proven themselves for the sake of the whole church. The title of this volume is intended to reflect this goal. Thus it is *not* subtitled *A Worship Resource for African-Americans*! Although it primarily emerges from Lutherans of the African diaspora, from Accra to Canada to Caracas, it is intended as a gift to the church catholic. The developers viewed it as an investment in the evolving project of the Western liturgy. Any notions that the church's rites are rigidly fixed are mistaken historically and theologically. The Holy Spirit guides the church through the ages.

One processional service in *This Far by Faith* is called a "public liturgy." This "Way of the Cross" is recommended for use especially on the Fridays in Lent. It amounts to eight evangelical stations of the cross—all clearly recorded in the Passion narrative. An opportunity is given in the service notes for stations to "be made outside the church walls as a public witness. Outdoor stations may be made at significant locations in the immediate neighborhood where healing is needed and where associations between the contemporary struggles of life and the events of Christ's suffering can be made (for example, sites where crimes have occurred, abandoned buildings, or other places of human struggle)."[4]

---

4 *This Far by Faith: An African-American Resource for Worship* (Minneapolis: Augsburg Fortress, 1999), 102.

When God's people pray at a meaningful site they extend the possibility for witness. Outdoor liturgy can be a concrete form of Lutheran spirituality. An aim of mission is the people outside, that is, outside the building and outside the Body of Christ. God's church cannot be contained within a stained-glass ghetto. In view of God's compassion, His servant people are called into pilgrimage in their Father's world. Moved by mercy, they follow the world's groaning and yearning. In their hearts, on their lips, and with their hands, they share the gift of redemption. Lives are transformed. Mission is extended. Neighborhoods are revitalized. Weak knees are strengthened. Such service toward sister or brother, stranger or convict, or even enemy, could be called the church's outdoor liturgy.

Some liturgical adjustments are unfortunate but necessary accessions. In some inner-city communities, more than half the children are being reared in non-nuclear households. To affirm the rearing, nurture, and catechetical support provided by single parents, grandparents, or other guardians, consideration should be given to the language used in preaching. Community is not built when public commentary is coldhearted or careless. Never should someone doing their best in the worst of circumstances be made to feel inadequate. Never should someone enduring the consequences of a mistake from which they have turned in repentance be made to feel as though they are a mistake. As well, the language that accompanies baptismal and confirmation services needs to be considered. How does the wider community function as a "village of the Word" in raising a child in the way of the Lord?

Dr. Bill Rojas, superintendent of schools in Dallas, openly attributes his professional success to the formative influence of the Lutheran faith community. In humble circumstances, his mother was his primary parent. She would not have "made it" without the Rev. Albert Paul Abel and Atonement Lutheran Church in New York City. That participation led to his "learning for life" on Concordia campuses in Bronxville, New York, and River Forest, Illinois. His opinion of this faith community is that they are "caring, compassionate people."[5]

Believe Globally—Speak Locally

Sermons do not proceed nakedly from the pages of Scripture to the lips of the preacher. They are first cradled in the embryo of tradition. They emerge from within a web of historic relationships, preserved by the Holy Spirit. Although sermons start with an event, an image, a persisting idea, a song in the soul, none are completely original. Sermonizing is a craft carried along

5 Related to the writer by Dr. Rojas at his office on January 25, 2000.

by the momentum of tradition. It speaks to the faith of Christ-confessing ancestors. Ancient is our local word.

Yet it must take on the sound of the local community. Because preaching strives after excellence does not mean it takes on the verbiage of exclusive esotericism. Because a liturgical action is polished does not mean it takes on the mien of being posh. Jesus never considered Himself too important to go to small places to do great things for ordinary people. His touring through "backwater" Galilee evidences Jesus' aim to do the Good News with ordinary mud, ordinary loaves and fish, ordinary water, ordinary stories, even amid bad-news situations. Likewise, God imbues our liturgy and preaching with extraordinary forgiving power as we take on the ordinary earthen forms wherever we are. We cast our buckets, like Booker T. Washington said, precisely where we are. Liturgy and preaching may be most catholic where and when they are most local. Believe globally, worship locally.

Two Voices from the City

A fruit of faith is kindness and justice for all. This is more than a lofty sentiment. It is divinely mandated. Without concern for the wholeness of the whole community, the church is out of step with God. Empowered by the outpouring of God's grace, justified believers will also be doers of justice and lovers of mercy as they walk with God (Mic. 6:6–8). This means substantive preaching that takes seriously divinely driven hopes and dreams. The "ear candy" of quick-fix Christianity is unable to nurture and sustain faith. Ear-candy religion is preferred. It delights in sweet sounds that gush with feigned depth but are unable to satisfy the soul for eternity. Ear-candy religion turns away from truth, ultimately trusting nothing as it dabbles in a mixture of myths, choosing what is pleasing or pragmatic for the moment. Ear-candy religionists gather around themselves "teachers to suit their own passions" because they have "itching ears" (2 Tim. 4:3). Purifying this fluffy amalgam takes both patience and a commitment to truth. To swing God's judgment like a sledgehammer rarely hits the target. The apologetic task in this new millennium is aggressive, not wild. It is always accompanied by a defense of the faith that defines truth in deeds of love, not just words.

Preachers are prophets of truth who desire growth while affirming individuals in love—people, created in God's image, preciously redeemed by Christ. Communities are not commodities; people are not pawns or projects to be studied or, worse, statistical growth sectors. The race is not given to the fastest, but to the faithful. Apparent winners—growing churches—can be losers if they exchange worldly popularity for biblical fidelity.

These following urban sermon excerpts from two distinct Christian faith traditions speak their views coherently.

Dr. James Perkins, Detroit (Baptist)

> Being a prophet on God's behalf is an awesome assignment. Anyone who takes the assignment need not look for popularity. Prophetic ministry does not allow for participation in popularity contests. I fear that the so-called church-growth movement has seduced a whole generation of preachers into believing that the most authentic prophet is one who has the greatest number of followers. This warped understanding leads to watering down the word and sensationalizing religion. This kind of preaching tends to ignore thorny and troublesome social issues. Such prophets lower their voices in order to raise their budgets. And they make those who sincerely want to be faithful proclaimers of God's whole Gospel feel like they have failed. True success in ministry cannot be determined by numbers and masses. Success in prophetic ministry is determined by faithfulness to God's Word.[6]

Pastor Brad Beckman, St. Louis (Lutheran)

> God's love, His mercy and forgiveness lived out through us should break down every racial, ethnic, and economic barrier. So we must abandon the 20th-century marketing strategies incorporated by many Christians that church growth can only happen in homogeneous settings, settings where people are of like ethnic and economic realities. In the 21st century, the Christian church on earth (particularly in the urban areas of the United States) needs to get back to the Lord's original plan—that it reflect and be composed of professing people from all nations.[7]

The rich mélange of ethnic identity that is gaining attention in the U.S. church is not new to Christianity. Jesus customarily worshiped in a congregation with more than one language. Even in the obscure, small town of Nazareth, the Scriptures were translated from Hebrew, the liturgical language, to Aramaic, the people's language—from the language of the theology and tradition, to the language of the heart and the "hood"—same meaning, different words. Martin Luther recaptured this principle by placing the Bible into the hands of the people. (Check the interesting explanatory footnote for Luke 4:16 in the *Concordia Self-Study Bible* [St. Louis: Concordia, 1984], 1553.)

---

6 James Perkins, "The Burden of the Lord: The Need for a Prophetic Voice," preached at Andover Newton Divinity School, Alumni Day, May 23, 1995.

7 Bradley Beckman, "Can Anything Good Come from the 'Hood'?" preached at Messiah Lutheran Church, St. Louis, Missouri, December 12, 1999.

Seeking the Seeking

In his seminary courses on liturgy, Gordon Lathrop often refers to the summons inscribed on the old bell of a village church in Wisconsin: "To the bath and the table, to the prayers and the Word, I call every seeking soul."[8] God is for us and for our salvation. But God is also for everyone. There is no place on earth (catholicity) to which the message of the Gospel need not go (apostolicity).

In May 1999 six African-Americans (I among them) participated in a mission trip to the largely Afro-Caribbean island nation of Jamaica. We went preaching, teaching, and reaching people in this Third World setting. We went to seek the seeking. The group returned to the United States deeply impacted by the sense of shared destiny among those with whom they worked in the slums of Kingston. Most people in this forgotten area not only knew their neighbors' names (rare in most North American metropolitan areas) but also shared their neighbors' pain (Gal. 6:2). Despite material lack, their lives fulfilled the Law of Christ.

A second striking spiritual attitude concerned each evening's service. Those who during the day wore no shoes—we, in fact, doubt some owned a pair—showed up at the place of worship in their "Sunday best." Whereas the trend among North American Christians is to dress more casually at worship (which we are not implying is, in itself, wrong), in Jamaica those with less than us sought to honor God with their best attire. Their hopes may have been put on hold, their dreams all but dashed by harsh economic realities, yet their faith in Christ gave them a sense of personal dignity. God indeed gathers the hopes and dreams of all, uniting them with the prayers of all people from all races, all places, all times, all climes—diverse faces, one faith (Eph. 4:4).

Human Service—Divine Service

There is a strong correlation between God's saving service to us in Christ as it is related in the Scripture and Sacraments and our service to humankind. Today's church rightly concerns itself with doctrinal purity. The proclamation of divine truth ought be at the top of our preaching priorities. Our worship helps defend the faith.

The Scriptures are rich in their concern for the horizontal dimensions of the faith.[9] Throughout, concern for the rights of others is expressed. Human dignity and personhood are avidly maintained. Provisions are made

8 Lecture notes, Lutheran Theological Seminary at Philadelphia, 1986.

9 For example, see the chart entitled "Major Social Concerns in the Covenant," *Concordia Self-Study Bible* (St. Louis: Concordia, 1984), 270.

to care for widows, orphans, aliens, and the sick. Workers should be fairly compensated. Disabled people are not to be taunted. No one, no matter how weak or disabled, is to be exploited or taken advantage of, but every life has value because all of life is a gift of God.

In earlier eras the crisis of violence was ascribed most specifically to the inner-city communities. Now, the crumbling ethical infrastructure pervades at all levels. Witness the nine school shootings in the late 1990s, occurring in middle-class, suburban communities.

The hubris of postmodern people is to be pitied. Here he is "stewing in the muck of his own dechristianized anthropology, claiming to be the captain of his own soul and riding for destruction."[10] Where authority and community are both disintegrating as moral realities, churches with good theology and good liturgy have the opportunity to teach good living and community building. We need each other much more than our pride permits us to admit. God by grace has bound us together in what Reinhold Niebuhr often referred to as a "bundle of life." God gives us grace to depend on one another within the Body of Christ.

Living Well, Living Good

By some measures, in the United States, these are spoken of as the best of times. Yet the poor we will have with us always (John 12:8). The pervasive and persisting problem of poverty does not provide an escape or an excuse, but to the person of faith it is an invitation to action. A pervasive moral concern of the Old Testament is the treatment of those at the margins of society. These "treasures of the church" (cf. St. Laurence) should find a voice in the homiletical life of the church. Our current time has been termed a decade of economic prosperity. The expansion is unprecedented in U.S. history. Yet some are still limping. Some have slipped, or they have been pushed between the cracks during this period of relative affluence. The Gospel, in turn, pushes the church into a retrieval mode.

The Spirit who calls us by the Gospel and unites us as one body in the one saving faith is the same Spirit who seeks the lost. The challenge for urban ministry is to make churches bases for rescue and recovery missions, places where wounds are healed, souls are satisfied, and broken spirits are made whole. God calls churches to be places where goodness and kindness are shared, places where His grace in Christ and joy in the Holy Spirit abound. Churches are the environment of authentic Christian community.[11]

---

10 Herman A. Preus, *A Theology to Live By: The Practical Luther for the Practicing Christian* (St. Louis: Concordia, 1977), 63.

11 John Nunes, *Voices from the City: Issues and Images of Urban Preaching* (St. Louis: Concordia, 1999), 69.

From the malformed to the unborn without any opportunity to ever form, God's Word directly links the liturgy with how we live among the least, last, lost, and the left-behind in society. Embraced by God's grace, the church embraces the human debris of our throwaway society and calls it sister, brother, friend. Otherwise, warns Amos, the Divine Service sinks to the level of noise pollution (Amos 5:21–23).

The liturgy reaches its zenith with that proleptic feast that anticipates eternal union with a holy God. In this eschatological picture, we see health, ecological balance, harmonious relationships, ethnic healing (not ethnic cleansing), and a resolution of all tensions in God's perfect glory.

Closing the Gap

Divine Service gives rise to human service done in the name of Jesus. Specifically, the context of conscientious preaching can serve to build a whole community. The words of preaching have implications for the faithful. Worshipers are impelled by the Gospel toward closing the gap between the words of the liturgy and the deeds of love carried out within the community. As this happens, the liturgy becomes more than sung, poetic expression derived from Scripture, but is seen as a source that sustains faith active in love. "The ministry of word and sacraments, therefore, is addressed to the whole person, not merely to body or to soul."[12]

Here are some themes that arise from the liturgy:

> **Kyrie:** A plaintive plea emerges from all (and for all) who need God's mercy and forgiveness. Supplicants pray for mercy in a merciless world (Isaiah 40).
>
> **Gloria in Excelsis:** God dwells "in the highest," yet has regard for the lowest, lowliest, and the lonely. God's omnipotence does not preclude His taking away the sin of the world, having mercy, and hearing human need—"receive our prayer."
>
> **Creed:** The very words "Father" and "Maker" reveal a relationship with creation. Note the salvific interplay among the First, Second, and Third Articles. God's plan of salvation redeems and affirms creation. "God has so structured His world that the reality of salvation which His Word effects is delivered and brought into being through selected elements of the created order."[13]

---

12 *Faith Active in Love: Human Care in the Church's Life*, A Report of the Commission on Theology and Church Relations, The Lutheran Church—Missouri Synod (February 1999), 6.

13 "What Benefit Does the Soul Receive from a Handful of Water? Luther's Preaching on Baptism, 1528–39," *Concordia Journal* (October 1999): 358.

Unity: The Church is one, striving for unity in love and truth.

Catholicity: The aphorism of St. Vincent defines the inclusive and timeless character of being in Christ: "We should hold fast to what has been believed everywhere, always and by everyone" [*Quod semper, quod ubique, quod ab omnibus creditum est*].[14]

Apostolicity: This implies not only a continuity of orthodox teaching but also a missionary dynamism that undergirds all ministry, the essential sentness of the church.

The Lord's Prayer: Given by Jesus and always prayed by the Church in the first-person plural grammatical forms ("our," "us," "we"), the prayer strongly suggests the corporate character of Christianity. God's kingdom and God's will are for all people. This down-to-earth dimension provides a glimpse of the *civitas Dei.*

Sanctus: This speaks to the relationship between God's absolute holiness and the human quest for wholeness. Heaven and earth are full of God's glory—the incarnation is the glory of God coming to the ordinary, which has been broken by sin.

Agnus Dei: This presents the theology of the cross for those who bear crosses. God in Christ bestows real peace, removing the sin that infects life and condemns humanity. Peace is the presence of God's shalom, not merely the absence of conflict. Jesus Christ is our bridge-builder between God and humanity (1 Tim. 2:5). Between brother and sister believers, He is our peace (Eph. 2:14). He breaks down the walls that tear people apart.

14 St. Vincent of Lerins, *Commonitorium Primum* 2:3 (50:640).

Speaking FOR, Not Just TO, the Church

Ronald R. Feuerhahn

Preaching is a rather peculiar undertaking—in both senses of the word: unique and strange. In the Christian church it is a very particular office with a very particular form and even a very specific location, the pulpit. In the world outside the church, preaching is peculiar—strange. At least, that would seem to be the case today. It's unreal. It's even offensive. There was a time, not so long ago, and perhaps in some places still today, when the two senses of preaching as peculiar seemed to overlap. This occurred, for instance, in Germany in the post-World War II era when churchmen spoke about the *Predigtnot*, the "problem of preaching." While they knew of preaching, in the sense of the church, as a particular office, they had come, like the outside world, to view this venture as rather strange if not offensive. It seemed obsolete.

What the so-called *Predigtnot* announced was that the world was being allowed, even called upon, to critique the church. Young pastors, we are to understand, questioned the sermon, traditionally understood. It was a monologue! It was an assertion of authority. Thus it was authoritarian! It was archaic. This view was illustrated, for instance, in the very location of the sermon—the pulpit. The pulpit became unacceptable. It was the focal place, literally, a place, of this authoritarian monologue. Churchmen were to engage the world in a dialogue rather than a monologue. They asked by what authority we address the world from such an aloof place.

The answer to this *Not*, this problem of preaching as authoritative, comes in the words of our Lord: "All *authority* in heaven and on earth has been given . . ." (Matt. 28:18, emphasis added). Perhaps even more serious was the "problem" of misunderstanding what this authority really was. It was neither aloofness nor superiority nor power over others. For Jesus and His apostles it was service; that is the same for His preachers. This is, after all, the "authority on earth to forgive sins" (Matt. 9:6).

This is the authority of ministry to "all nations" (Matt. 28:19), no longer confined to Israel. It is difficult for the church to visualize this responsibility. The church is small, weak, or insignificant in the eyes of the world. Israel was the least among the nations. Yet would the church dare to address the world? For very practical reasons it seems inconceivable that the church would undertake to "preach" to the world—after all, the world is not there, in church, when the preacher is preaching! Nevertheless, the church does, because it has God's message for the whole world. In this awareness the church regularly sings with Simeon: "For my eyes have seen Your salvation that You have prepared in the presence of all peoples, *a light for revelation to the Gentiles*, and for glory to Your people Israel" (Nunc Dimittis, Luke 2:30–32, citing Isa. 42:6; 49:6; emphasis added).

Likewise, St. Paul and St. Barnabas found themselves under the mandate of the Lord who said: "I have made you a light for the Gentiles, that you may bring salvation to the end of the earth" (Acts 13:47).

We preach as if we know what is wrong with the world—and we do!

Fallenness

Some people may still remember the title of the hymn "The World Is Very Evil."[1] Indeed, it is! And so we have confessed that the three great enemies of the Christian are the devil, the world, and the flesh.

For clarity, however, a distinction is required at the outset: when we speak of the "world," we do not mean the creation. The world here is the *kosmos* as identified by the evangelist St. John.[2] It might be described as the state of humans in their fallenness:

- people without God;
- people in need of God;
- people in rebellion against God;
- people who have decided against God.

For this world, Jesus is always "a sign that is opposed" (Luke 2:34). It "knew Him not" (John 1:10). "God made foolish the wisdom of the world"

---

1 See, for instance, *TLH* 605. The original by Bernard of Morlas, a monk of Cluny, and written around 1140, was translated by John M. Neale. The original verse was *Hora novissima; tempora pessima sunt*, "The hour is very late / The times are very bad." The translation in *LBW* 322 and *LW* 463 is "The Clouds of Judgment Gather." The title of Bernard's lengthy (3,000 lines) poem was *De Contemptu Mundi* ("Concerning Disdaining of the World," trans. Wayne Schmidt).

2 On *kosmos* in John's Gospel, see Donald Heinz, "Kosmos-Men or Men of the Kosmos," *Concordia Theological Monthly* 41, no. 6 (June 1970): 360–65.

(1 Cor. 1:20). It is this world that the Spirit of God will "convict . . . concerning sin and righteousness and judgment" (John 16:8).

Deception

This world lives a lie, the lie of its own making and of the devil's encouragement (John 8:44). In its association with the devil, the deceiver, it has not the truth. It is thoroughly a realm of doubt and uncertainty. Living under the Law, it knows not the things of God nor of its redemption. It lives the lie of self-Law (*autonomos*) and thus of self-salvation, as if in control of its living and of its fate.

Everything in the world seems turned around. It is full of contradictions. For the world the Gospel is an alien word. "For the word of the cross is folly to those who are perishing, but to us who are being saved it is the power of God" (1 Cor. 1:18). The cross is foolishness and a scandal, while for those who are called it is the power and wisdom of God (1 Cor. 1:23–24). Rather, "through the folly of what we preach" those who believe are saved (1 Cor. 1:21). So that while the world hears the Gospel as an alien word and the Law as the proper or natural word, the church knows that the Gospel is God's proper word and the Law His alien word.

Isolation and Alienation

The world has no true sense of community. Each person lives for himself or herself. In postmodernity as in modernity, the chief authority is the "I." The identity is defined in terms of self. For the Christian, self-knowledge means knowledge of the relationship to God. Our *worth* is relational. Ours is an alien dignity. Ironically, the view of modernity, what we might normally call a very *worldly* view, takes one out of the world. It means in effect that the person becomes a worldless *spectateur* or *voyeur* rather than *acteur*.[3] It is not surprising that there is such a desperate appeal in such slogans as "It takes a village to raise a child."

The church knows what is wrong with this world. The preacher has the word of God's Law, which acts as a kind of X-ray to detect that which is diseased about the world's condition. It is that Law which He declares to the world to call it to repentance.

The impact of the church's message is far greater than we imagine. The Gospel of Jesus Christ turned the world upside-down. Luther declared:

3 Thus Rene Descartes described himself in his *Meditations*. See Helmut Thielicke, *Modern Faith and Thought* (Grand Rapids: Eerdmans, 1990), 59.

> It is surely true that Jerusalem would still be standing if Christ had not come. Likewise, if Peter and Paul had not come, Rome, too, would very likely still be intact. But because they did come, empires tumbled. Christ says: "The Father is with Me and not with you. We told you about the misfortune that is now befalling you. You blame the Gospel for it, but it is entirely your own fault; for you reject the Gospel, crucify Me and lift Me up, and persecute Me because of it. Now you try to exonerate yourselves and pose as innocent, saying: 'Yes, if it had not been for the Gospel! It is all the Gospel's fault!'"[4]

We preach as if we know the King of the World—and we do!

The (Hidden) Lord of History

"The earth is the LORD's and the fullness therefore, the world and those who dwell therein" (Ps. 24:1). God is not only the Creator of the world, He continues to be its Lord even though the world does not acknowledge this.[5] However, He is a God "who hides Himself" (Isa. 45:15), and "His sovereign lordship of history is no transparently obvious fact."[6] And while we may not always see His footprints in history, it, too, is under His domain, for "the Most High rules the kingdom of men" (Dan. 4:25). Hermann Sasse noted a God very active in the life of Israel and her world:

> God's own Word has been put into the mouth of his prophets. This Word has not only created the world but also makes history. The fate of Israel as well as of the Eastern peoples and world empires is determined through this Word.
>
> "But now thus says the Lord, he who created you, O Jacob, he who formed you, O Israel: 'Fear not, for I have redeemed you . . . I give Egypt as your ransom. Ethiopia and Seba in exchange for you.' (Is 43:1, 3)
>
> "Thus says the Lord to his anointed, to Cyrus, whose right hand I have grasped, to subdue nations before him and ungird the loins of kings, to open doors before him that gates may not be closed. I will go before you . . . ." (Is 45:1–2)
>
> This is not just interpretation of history. This is a revelation of the deepest core of the world-historical events of that time, when the Neobabylonian Empire collapsed under Persian attack and Israel was saved. God's Word makes history.

---

4 *Sermons on John 6–8* (1531), AE 23:388.

5 LC, First Article, Tappert 413.21.

6 Martin H. Franzmann, *Follow Me: Discipleship According to Saint Matthew* (St. Louis: Concordia, 1961), 10.

> That is also true of the Word of God committed to the church. Also the fates of the peoples of modern Europe are determined by the Word of God which is proclaimed to them, is believed and rejected.[7]

Between Two Kingdoms

When we declare the kingdom of God, we speak of His reign among human beings and His lordship of the whole creation. But there is another kingdom that would establish itself in this world. That is the kingdom of Satan. He is the "ruler of this world" (John 12:31; 14:30; 16:11). The people in this world are Satan's subjects.

The kingdom of God invades this territory of Satan through His Word and Sacraments. When a person is baptized, that person is claimed for the new kingdom. No wonder it has been said about the baptism of an infant: "Today we do this child no favor, for we have made him an enemy of Satan!"[8] The preacher declares to the world that this new kingdom has come. The preacher announces to the world that the "prince of the world" has been judged (John 16:11) and will be cast out (John 12:31).

As preachers today, we dare not be shy about this message, as if speaking of "Satan" is either ridiculous and too bizarre on the one hand or too frightening on the other. The faithful pastor has the sight to see Satan's fingerprints all over the lives of his parishioners and his footprints in the world around them. There is a danger of great peril should he fail to warn the flock.

Living in Two Realms

The Christian lives *in* but not *of* the world. This causes a tension: we are called upon to renounce the world (1 John 2:15–17) and sing, "What is the world to me / With all its vaunted pleasure,"[9] while living therein for the good of the neighbor.

If the preacher is to speak to the world, what is the message? The answer may not be so obvious. Some might respond, "The Gospel, of course!" If that is intended to mean the whole Word of God, yes. But the Gospel, strictly defined, is preached to the repentant, after the Law has convicted of sin. There is a commonly held view that the church is to be involved in the world and that this involvement is part of the Gospel committed to the church. That is a misunderstanding of the Gospel, strictly speaking.

---

7 Hermann Sasse, "Article VII of the Augsburg Confession in the Present Crisis of Lutheranism," in *We Confess: The Church*, trans. Norman Nagel (St. Louis: Concordia, 1986), 49f.

8 Attributed to Luther.

9 George Pfefferkorn, *TLH* 430; *LW* 418.

The people of God live in two realms, the state and the church. The first is a realm of Law, more specifically the first use of the Law. Here God uses His authority to commend the good doer and to convict the wrong doer (1 Pet. 2:13–15; Rom. 13:1–7). The realm of the church is of both Law and Gospel. We are not to confuse the two realms and speak as if the civil realm dispenses Gospel. The Lutheran Confessions, especially the Augsburg Confession in Article XXVIII, are at pains to define quite explicitly what the power (authority) of the church is as opposed to other powers in human life. They complain that "some have terribly confused the power of the Church with the power of the State." They state: "Our teachers' position is this: the authority of the Keys [Matthew 16:19], or the authority of the bishops—according to the Gospel—is a power or commandment of God, to preach the Gospel, to forgive and retain sins, and to administer the Sacraments."[10]

The reign of God has made a visible beginning on earth. His kingship is no longer merely a reign over the history of men and nations; it is in the midst of the history of men and nations. It has, in a sense, become incarnate.[11]

We preach as if we know the end of the world—and we do!

Millennial Fears

The world (*kosmos*) knows the future, "what can happen and what cannot happen, what need not be tried, expected, hoped for. It knows the limits of God's power—this side of the grave, as we say."[12] But the world does not know what lies beyond the grave, the truly *cosmic* view of things, a knowledge that has been given to the church for her prophetic ministry. It is the view given to faith. Faith sees the signs of the end time (Luke 21:25). For we walk by faith, not by sight (2 Cor. 5:7).

But that is the problem: the world wants to *know*; it is not interested in *believing*. "The *kosmos* wants a *guarantee* before it believes . . . Its characteristic posture is the demand for a sign"[13] (John 2:18; 4:48; 6:30; Matt. 16:4). The world wants control of the future, mastery of the situation. There is a demand for explanations, the "how," a demand for the reasonable. In a sense, it is risky for us in the church to say, "We know." It is not really knowing in the empirical sense, but believing. That is, we have the certainty of faith: "I know that my Redeemer lives." The church is in danger in the world in many ways, but especially internally. "When we in the church look closely at these

10 AC XXVIII 1, 5 (*Concordia*, 58); cf. Henry P. Hamann, *Unity and Fellowship and Ecumenicity*, Contemporary Theology Series (St. Louis: Concordia, 1973), 38f.

11 Franzmann, *Follow Me*, 19.

12 Heinz, "Kosmos-Men or Men of the Kosmos," 361.

13 Heinz, "Kosmos-Men or Men of the Kosmos," 360.

Johannine theological portraits [of the *kosmos*] we recognize, against our will, too many old friends, too many of the church's men."[14]

The preacher knows the reality beyond the grave. This world lives in the face of the Judge. It is confronted by a Spirit as uncertain as the wind (John 3:8). The preacher announces these realities to the world:

- the message of judgment,
- the life without signs and explanations,
- the life without sight,
- but the life of faith, beggarly, "blind" faith.

The preacher invites the world to the new life in the Spirit of God, the new life of faith where the only assurance God gives is His Word. But that Word places God in proximity with the newborn person's condition, and that is enough. There is no more, for that is truly enough.

Jesus turns our attention from the purely *future* kingdom of God to the fact of it *today*. It is intruding into the *now*. Eschatology projects into the present and shapes the present. We preach in this end time and to this time. We preach from the perspective of the future, yet fully aware of the now.

We preach as if we know who will save the world—and we do!

Millennial Hope

The church alone has a truly cosmic view of things. It has a proclamation to the whole world, for the whole cosmos. That message is hope. The message of hope can be touchy, for it implies uncertainty—in the world. Thus the church's proclamation of hope in Jesus Christ is quite different from the hope expressed by the world—"I hope it won't rain tomorrow!" The world does not really know what is coming in the new day, the new year, the new century or millennium. While the church may not know *what* is coming, it is certain about *who* is coming in the new time. "And He shall speak peace to the nations; His rule shall be from sea to sea, and from the River to the ends of the earth" (Zech. 9:10).

The world is blessed through the church. Within a world that stands under the sign of the fall, there is built up under the sign of the cross the one community of the one Lord. The Church is the new humanity whose author is Christ. It is the new man (*kainon anthropon*) (Eph. 2:15). The new situation of the world created by the unique Christ event is a positive reality in this aeon only in the form of the Church.[15] The sermon declares that we,

14 Heinz, "Kosmos-Men or Men of the Kosmos," 360.

15 Ethelbert Stauffer, in Gerhard Kittel and Gerhard Friedrich, eds., *Theological Dictionary of the New Testament* (Grand Rapids: Eerdmans, 1964), 440.

the church of God, are here for you! We are the people of God living in your midst, for your benefit. God blesses you through us.

That the Church even addresses the millennium is a sign of her concern for the world and its fears, for the millennium *hype* is basically "pagan."[16] The Church marches to a different cadence of time and a different melody of history. For the Church there is really only one millennium at the end of which our Lord will return as He promised, "Surely I am coming soon" (Rev. 22:20).

We preach as if we know about heaven—and we do!

In the divine liturgy the Church finds itself at the threshold between earth and heaven (Ps. 96:5–6). Here we encounter heaven on earth. The church sings the Kyrie to her Lord on the occasion of His weekly (at least) *parousia*, His coming to be with us. At the altar and font and in the pulpit, God is present with His gifts. These are the most visible locations of God's presence on earth. The liturgy says that the Church is in the world, but that God is also here.[17]

Preaching is always to be *liturgical* preaching. It will always be aware of this setting. The pulpit is important, as are the altar and font, as the places where God can be found in Word and Sacraments. God's two kingdoms are heavenly and earthly. Luther described two realities in the Christian life: one is the Law, the old man, vocation, the earth. The other is the Gospel, the new man, the Church, heaven.[18] As Christ comes to us in the Gospel, He brings heaven to earth. The Church is linked with heaven. In heaven we shall experience the eternal Sabbath; on earth we also experience a Sabbath. And in that Sabbath on earth we worship as though in heaven.

The sermon is the occasion where God, actually God, speaks to His people. Here He continues His work of creation. The message of heaven is declared here. The church shows that it is aware of this by the liturgical setting, a setting of reverence, of a time and place set apart, within the world, for the sake of the world. Here God gives "explanation" or at least a meaning to all things, including the injustice in this world. To the earlier anguish of the psalmist over the prosperity of the wicked comes understanding in the liturgy, in the "sanctuaries" of God (Ps. 73:17); here he finds honor and majesty, strength and beauty (Ps. 96:6). Here the world is invited to bring its sins so that they can be forgiven. And that forgiveness is granted by God, on earth as it is in heaven.

---

16 So labeled by Hilary Jolly, whose masterful hymn "Through the Darkness of the Ages" was written as an answer to the "millennium hype." See "Hymn an Antidote to 'Millennium Hype,'" *The Christian Century* 116, no. 25 (Sept. 22–29, 1999): 894f.

17 Paraphrase of Dr. William Weinrich.

18 Gustaf Wingren, *Luther on Vocation*, trans. Carl C. Rasmussen (Philadelphia: Muhlenberg, 1957), 57.

The sermon is a unique message, the preacher a messenger from God. The sermon then is different in tone from mere conversation or even from the lecture or speech. The preacher is vested to hide his person, to give emphasis to the office (the *Predigtamt*).

Conclusion: The Refrain—"and we do"

Preaching is a risky business. Luther called the sermon the "battleground of Christ" (*Kampfplatz Christi*).[19] There is an "in-your-face"-ness about it. For when we declare that simple refrain "*and we do!*" it is the church's "in-your-face" to the world. That is not comfortable for the world. Postmodern individuals allow no one to be in their face; they demand the right not to be offended. Thus they will not have the Law "preached" at them! Even the message of forgiveness can be offensive, for it implies sin; the message of mercy implies need; the message of faith implies that we are beggars; the message of grace is undeserved. Furthermore, "the reality of grace is impenetrable to modern man, because in losing an understanding for sin he has also lost an understanding for grace."[20]

What, then, shall be the preacher's message to this world? It will, of course, be the Law that will call to repentance. This at least will not be an alien word, as was noted above. It may even be expected. The Gospel is proclaimed after repentance. It may, of course, be mentioned as the promise of God for those who repent and believe. The preacher will nevertheless be as the watchman to "the wicked" (Ezek. 3:18–19; 33:1–9, especially vv. 8–9). The preacher will address the doubts of the *kosmos* person, the doubts of justice and uncertainty. But the preacher will also allow the message to remain in all its alienness, declare the hiddenness of God and His Church, rejoice in the mystery. For ultimately it is a message not of the *kosmos*, but of heaven itself.

Preaching to the world, then, may not find a ready audience. But the preacher, under the authority of the Lord Himself, says, in those enigmatic words of Martin Franzmann, "Oh, what of that, and what of that?" How's that for in-your-face!

> Preach you the Word and plant it home
> To men who like or like it not,
> The Word that shall endure and stand
> When flow'rs and men shall be forgot.
>
> We know how hard, O Lord, the task
> Your servant bade us undertake:

19 Martin H. Franzmann, Pericope Seminar, Westfield House, Cambridge.

20 Sasse, "Article VII of the Augsburg Confession," 50.

To preach Your Word and never ask
What prideful profit it may make.

The sower sows; his reckless love
Scatters abroad the goodly seed,
Intent alone that all may have
The wholesome loaves that all men need.

Though some be snatched and some be scorched
And some be choked and matted flat,
The sower sows; his heart cries out,
"Oh, what of that, and what of that?"

Preach you the Word and plant it home
And never faint; the Harvest Lord
Who gave the sower seed to sow
Will watch and tend His planted Word.[21]

There is an alienness to this preaching and to its liturgical setting. Here the church is at the threshold of heaven and earth. In proclamation and rite, this is the place of holy drama. This is where God's gracious presence finds location, in the water of Baptism, the bread and wine of the Lord's Supper, in the Word of forgiveness given in the Absolution and in the preached Word from the pulpit. In the liturgy the church experiences a difference:

- a different sense of time,
- a different sense of locality,
- a different sense of history,
- a different sense of reality.

The sermon expresses these differences; it is part of that heavenly drama—on earth. It is the creative, living Word of God spoken among humans. The preacher says in the sermon what the church has prayed in the Lord's Prayer, "Thy will be done *on earth* as it is in heaven . . ." There is no better news for the world than that.

21 Written for Concordia Theological Seminary, Springfield, Illinois, to celebrate its 125th anniversary in 1973. *LSB* 586:1–4, 6. See Robin A. Leaver, *Come to the Feast: The Original and Translated Hymns of Martin H. Franzmann* (St. Louis: MorningStar, 1994), 74, 106f.

Liturgy and Spiritual Awakening[1]

Bo Giertz

Translator's Introduction

It is an ancient and treasured custom in the Church of Sweden that when a new bishop is elected in any diocese of the country, he writes a pastoral letter intended in the first place for the ministers of the diocese. This "Herdabrev" is usually a very personal word of encouragement and pastoral counseling which serves to introduce the new bishop to his pastors and people. Sometimes the letter is brief and can be contained in a few printed pages but frequently the letter is long enough so that it becomes a book of considerable size. Anyone who wants to make a study of the history of the Church of Sweden cannot neglect the study of these pastoral letters because in almost every instance they mirror and reflect the current state of religion and become the interpretation of the leadership of the Church of the message of the gospel for the contemporary scene. It is obvious that a man elevated to the office of bishop will take this assignment seriously and give to the writing of the pastoral letter his ablest skill. The document is intended to express the incumbent's best literary exposition of his aspirations in the fulfillment of the episcopal task of proclaiming the message and directing the activity of the Church.

Early in 1949 Pastor Bo Giertz was elected to the diocese of Gothenburg as bishop. Bishop Giertz was already known to all the church public of his country as well as to the wider public by a very large literary production, which has made him probably the outstanding writer of his time on religious questions. A series of historical novels, short stories, sermons, and monographs on various questions has issued from his pen. He is a young man whose gift of interpreting the life of the spirit is marked by uncommon brilliance and spiritual sensitivity. In his own religious development he comes out of a background of evangelical awakening and liberalism. But his spiritual pilgrimage has led him to

1 Copyright © 1950 Board of Publication of the Lutheran Church in America, administrated by Augsburg Fortress. Reproduced by permission.

an understanding and sympathetic appreciation of many of the currents of religious life in Swedish Lutheranism. He has a profound appreciation of the high-church liturgical movement as well as of low-church evangelicalism. If one should characterize the type of piety which is most congenial to his spirit, it would be as a broad evangelical orthodoxy that makes him congenial to the atmosphere of West Coast Lutheranism in Sweden.

The portion of the pastoral letter which is found in translation in this brochure is a section which deals with the place of liturgy and awakening in the life of faith. It deals with a religious question that is perennial in the church. And it is because the bishop reveals such a profound appreciation of the values of religious awakening and evangelical piety on the one hand, and of the time honored values of liturgical worship on the other, that this section has been lifted out for translation. We in the American churches will do well to ponder the problem that the bishop discusses in these pages. It is toward an understanding both of liturgy and spiritual awakening that this document is herewith published.

Clifford Ansgar Nelson
Gloria Dei Lutheran Church
St. Paul, Minnesota

Lessons from the Past

If we wish to know what true Christianity means, how the church of Christ lives and works, and how a soul is saved, we must seek to understand three great heritages of the church. We must go back first to the days of the apostles, martyrs and church fathers; then we must ponder the message of the Reformers; and lastly, bring to remembrance the blessed spiritual leaders in the last century through whom God gave the church great awakenings from which all future generations may learn.

This is the threefold heritage of which we have been made stewards and which is to be made a living possession. It is ours to preserve and to pass on. We are to learn lessons from the past that are to be a vital force in the present. It is the risen and living Lord who wrought all this in the past. To hold fast the old heritage is to abide in Him. For then it is at the same time something new, renewed by the Resurrected Christ Himself. In the measure that we live by the resources which built the church in days of old, will Christ give us clear instruction for the way we must walk today.

This, then, is our program: to learn of the past that we may be prepared to meet the coming day; to immerse ourselves so deeply in the great life stream of the church that we may be equipped to proclaim the Word of God in a new age, and to modern men and women, and to live His life in the manner which the new century in the history of the church demands.

(Closing paragraphs of the introductory portion of the Pastoral Letter in which the chapter on "Liturgy and Spiritual Awakening" appears.)

Liturgy and Spiritual Awakening

The Word of God creates the church. Already in the days of the primitive church the Word of God gave to the life of the church those forms which have continued through the centuries. This includes both those forms which seem to be more or less improvised and spontaneous and those which appear fixed and unchangeable. It is true both of that side of the life of the church which we call awakening and that which we call liturgy. Both are the creation of the Word, and both belong to that heritage which we are called to preserve.

Both liturgy and awakening were found in the apostolic church. They are spoken of already at Pentecost. "Now when they heard this, they were pricked in their heart, and said unto Peter and the rest of the apostles, Brethren, what shall we do?" That is awakening. "And day by day, continuing steadfastly with one accord in the temple" and "Now Peter and John were going up into the temple at the hour of prayer, being the ninth hour." That is liturgy.

Both liturgy and awakening have been with the church throughout her entire history. The manner in which they appear is of course very unlike. Awakening is like a flickering flame above a bed of coals. It gleams forth, spreads itself, rises toward heaven, and then seems to be gone again. Its connection with the ancient church seems to be broken by intervals of darkness. And yet the connection is there, because the Spirit is one and the same, even He who pricked the hearts on the day of Pentecost; and the Word, which lights the mysterious flame, is the same Word of power that once passed over the lips of the apostles.

The relation of liturgy to the apostolic age is obvious. It has flowed through the centuries like a ceaseless stream. It had its first deep sources in the synagogue. It is not only that a few words have remained in continuous use since that time, such as Amen, Hallelujah, and Hosanna, but the whole structural form of our order of worship shows clearly its relation to that worship which Jesus Himself shared in the synagogue at Nazareth and in which, as a grown man, he officiated when He was invited to read and interpret the Scriptures. To the ancient worship of the synagogue the apostolic church added the Holy Communion, that new creation which she received from the Savior Himself and which is the center of all liturgy. As it is celebrated still, with the traditional chants, the Preface and the Sanctus, it is essentially a contribution of the first century.

The unbroken connection with apostolic times is also revealed in the external forms of the liturgy. The altar is today the only place in our modern life where, with unbroken tradition, the vestments are still used which were worn by people in that olden day. Within the walls of the church one can still hear musical settings that preserve something of the very tones of that hymn of praise which our Lord and His disciples sang when they ate the paschal meal. The church is the one place in the modern world where one can still hear the best of medieval music and see the choicest treasures of medieval art as a living part of our culture. There is nothing in all the world today which embraces so much of an ancient culture or so many revered traditions as our chief liturgical service.

This is, of course, not the most essential consideration. The deepest significance of liturgy lies in the fact that it is a form which the Spirit Himself has created to preserve and deepen the life which He has awakened in the church.

Awakening is the fire that flames forth in dead souls. The fire burns in the breast when the sinner feels a pang in his conscience. He is gripped by an uneasiness that makes him ask, "What shall I do?" And the Spirit answers by enlightening the soul about the desperate character of sin and the boundless mercy of Christ.

Liturgy is the work of the same Spirit in preserving the flame which has been lighted. It is the means by which the awakened soul is bound together with the fellowship of the church. It is a pathway for walking in the light, a road that leads forward through the years, and the soul is ever anew called to join itself with that royal priesthood which worships before the altar of God with prayer and thanksgiving, with Communion, and with a quiet listening to the Word of the Lord.

Liturgy and awakening have often been made to stand in opposition to each other. It was not so in the primitive church and ought not to be so today. They are the work of the same Spirit, portions of the same heritage. They both have the right to exist and to fashion themselves according to their own uniqueness.

Awakening and liturgy speak each a different language, and they must do that. The instrument of awakening is the spoken Word, a word with prophetic authority, powerful to crush the hard rock of a soul and also appealing with all the inward warmth of the gospel. The language of awakening is often akin to everyday speech. God seeks the lost and condemned. The Word takes hold of him who is not at home in the House of God and probably not trained to understand the Biblical concepts. Therefore, the words of awakening do not employ such phrases as, for example, the Root of Jesse, or the Key of David. Rather do they speak to the children of the age in the language of the age about those things which have been forgotten but need to be heard again.

It is entirely different with liturgy. Its instrument is also the Word, but it is drawn out of deeper wellsprings. Liturgy speaks wisdom among those who are full grown. It uses all the richness of the Scriptures, all the meaningful symbols and prefigurements of Christ in the Old Testament. It prays the prayers of the Psalter anew, it listens to the prophecies and finds in them the deepest mysteries of the gospel. It loves exactly those hidden things that only slowly unfold themselves and that constantly give the mind something new to ponder. Just because liturgy constantly turns back to the same holy forms, it dares to make use of the hidden wisdom of the Scriptures. Therefore it also loves that music which beneath an obvious simplicity hides unfathomable depths of humble worship and joyful longing. It loves to lift its soul to God in the haunting music of the Kyrie or the reverent joy of the Preface. In all this it is very unlike the mood of awakening.

Probably we could express the difference between the two by saying that awakening is like the fire of the Lord which fell upon the water-drenched altar of Elijah. It is the incalculable, sovereign invasion of God, which reveals His power among the heathen. Liturgy, on the other hand, is that fire which burns upon the altar in the temple and about which the Scriptures proclaim that it must never be extinguished. Awakening is lightning from above that ignites a new fire. Liturgy is the flame of the Lord already burning among us, lighting and warming the faithful.

It is important for us that both awakening and liturgy be given their proper and pristine Christian place in the life of the congregation. Awakening is always needed, not only because the church must always be a missionary church and reach out after those that are on the outside, but also because there is always the need for awakening even among the most faithful members of the church. The church has exactly as many sinners as she has members. The old Adam in each one of us is prone to fall asleep, to make the Christian life a dead routine, to use liturgical form to cloak his self-complacency and impenitence. It is not difficult to fashion a form of religion that suits the ego and allows the old Adam within to become sovereign again. One may go regularly to church and Holy Communion. One may cherish beautiful church music and lovely sanctuaries. One may be honestly convinced that one possesses the correct doctrine and loves the pure preaching of the Word. And at the same time one may be thoroughly obsessed by self-love, complacent with one's self, satisfied with one's own pious accomplishments and totally indifferent to the troubles and burdens of one's fellow men, which are so apparent before one's very eyes. The Holy Spirit always needs to awaken slumbering souls, stir up the dust, push the old Adam against the wall, and blow a new breath of life into the dead bones. Awakening is never superfluous, as long as we are in the flesh.

Liturgy is just as needful. There can be no normal church life without liturgy. Sacraments need form, the order of worship must have some definite pattern. It is possible to live for a short time on improvisations and on forms that are constantly changing and being made over. One may use only free prayers and yet create a new ritual for every worship situation. But the possibilities are soon exhausted. One will have to repeat, and with that the making of rituals is in full swing. In circles where people seek to live without any forms new forms are nevertheless constantly taking shape. Favorite songs are used again and again with monotonous regularity, certain prayer expressions are constantly repeated, traditions take form and traditional yearly ceremonies are served. But it would not be wrong to say that the new forms that grow up in this way are usually less attractive and more profane than the ancient liturgy. They contain less of God's Word, they pray and speak without Scriptural direction, they are not so much concerned about expressing the whole content of Scripture, but are satisfied with one thing or another that seems to be especially attractive or popular. The new liturgy that grows in this manner is poorer, less Biblical, and less nourishing to the soul than the discarded ancient order.

Revival and liturgy, therefore, have each their given place in the church. They must go hand in hand. This does not prevent liturgy from sometimes becoming an enemy of awakening, just as awakening can be a foe of liturgy. Here is a tension that has been painfully apparent in the whole history of the church.

Awakening can actually be the most deadly enemy of liturgy. Liturgy has also other enemies, chief of which is that dull passivity which wants to hear and enjoy a service of worship instead of taking part in it. A full church is not the same as a congregation. Where hands are no longer folded and heads not bowed in prayer, where the voices, whether rough and untutored or well trained, no longer join in the singing, there is no longer a true worship. Liturgy is always an active thing. Sluggish, dead passivity is always its enemy.

Awakening can be a still more dangerous enemy. Worldliness usually knows at least that it is not more spiritual than liturgy. But the awakening that is an enemy of liturgy claims to be exactly that worship in spirit and in truth which the Father is seeking. It condemns and despises liturgy. Sometimes this may be a proper correction in prophetic spirit. If, for example, the officiant picks his nails during the Gradual hymn and turns the pages of the service book to find the General Prayer while he is kneeling at the altar after the sermon, then it is perfectly proper to speak about dead works, from which one must be converted to a right service of the one true God. But it is not thereby true that this right service consists in laying aside the vestments, in giving up the singing of the Preface in order to offer free prayers instead, and in singing the latest tunes from popular music in parish visitation. In the same way there are times when it is quite proper to quote the angry words of the Lord in the Book of Amos, "Take thou away from me the noise of thy songs; for I will not hear thy viols; but let justice roll down as waters and righteousness as a mighty stream," if, for example, the organist reads the Sunday paper in the organ loft, or the members of the choir vanish just before the sermon, or the members of the board go to their club to play poker immediately after a lovely vesper service. There is such a thing as dead liturgy—or, more correctly stated, dead hearts—that allows all the treasures of worship to pass one by without effect, or that understands how to make use of the atmosphere of the moment while at the same time avoiding everything that might possibly lead to conversion. There is also an improper and false manner of performing a rich and beautiful liturgy that makes it heavy and dragging, unnatural, marked by carelessness, or by a desire to let one's own personality shine. It is then not the liturgy that is at fault. And it is not a fault that can be righted by forsaking the good Word of God in the liturgy, which instead should be taken to heart. It is certainly true that it is better to pray a spontaneous prayer with meaning, however poorly formed it may be, than to pray the most wonderful liturgical prayer with a dead heart. It is also true that it is better to sing songs set to vulgar dance music, with the heart turned to Jesus, than pious chorals, with one's thoughts on the Sunday dinner or the latest parish gossip. But that is not to say that a cheap dance melody in and of itself is better fitted to express the Christian mood than a good, old choral melody of the church.

Awakening is wrong, therefore, when it rejects liturgy. There is often a goodly portion of self-righteousness and egocentricity in that judgment. The old Adam is an unequalled opportunist. When a man is seriously awakened, it is not very long until the old Adam makes every attempt to exploit the new situation. Naturally it has to be done with pious sentences and with a constant urging that it is for the glory of God. But even in this sham piety the old nature within will reestablish its rule. The works of the flesh begin again, not indeed in the form of "rioting, drunkenness, and loose living"—then they would be immediately recognized—but perhaps as "jealousy, strife, and contentiousness." The reasoning is very simple: since one's own awakening came in this or that manner, then that must be the proper way. The *"only* right way," adds the Old Adam to himself. Since on that occasion there was no reading of the Gospel, no Collect prayer, and no singing of the Kyrie, then such things cannot be means to salvation. The old Adam may probably add, "Besides, there is a warmer and lovelier feeling in the heart when one can pray one's own prayer, give a testimony, or sing the new songs." The conclusion of it all the old Adam does not state aloud. He only states that it is very easy to feel at home in the new clothes. If one may but hear one's own voice, talk a little about oneself, help to choose the hymns and feel soothed by their sweet melodies, which would fit well in any operetta, one can easily tolerate being called a Christian. And as added spice one can have the joy of poking fun at those who insist on liturgy and at the minister in the parish and those narrow-minded, formbound people who claim that one ought to attend the Sunday worship service regularly.

It is of course the coarsest form. But close to it is another kind of distaste for liturgy, humanly understandable but no more valid. There are people who find it difficult to feel at home in the liturgical forms. All liturgy demands the submerging of self. The individual shall become a part of a praying congregation. One must become so much a part of a fellowship with others that one can pray the same words as they, follow along in the rhythm of the worship, the Confession of Sins, and the praise, and feel the same joy and penitence as the others. Every Christian must be able to do that. He is a member of the body of Christ. He does not live to please himself, but as a part of an organism. He who will not subordinate himself in such fellowship is no Christian, because one cannot be a Christian by one's self. He who does not love his brother, whom he has seen in the church and at the Communion table, even so much that he can pray, sing, rejoice, and tremble together with him, must not imagine that he can love the God whom he has not seen, or that he can worship Him in spirit and in truth at home in his own chamber. And yet it is clear that there are forms for reverent worship which are very natural to some people, so that they immediately feel at home in them, while other people find it hard to become accustomed to them. The church must therefore be generous, open-minded, and tolerant. She must be able to give her children what they need most and what they can most readily receive, provided of course that she truly gives them the Word of God and real fellowship with God. It is self-evident, of course, that she must have a form for common worship, a place where all can meet together. That place is the Sunday order of worship. Here the church may rightly demand that all shall be present. Everyone should be able so far to conform that he enters into this fellowship as a praying and serving participant who not only demands that he receive something, but in the first place wants to make his contribution to the common worship. When people in the name of revival take up arms against the order of worship itself, they are violating the Christian fellowship. Often this is done in the name of liberty. But the freedom that is desired will mean a lack of freedom for the greater number of people. It will mean that certain pet interests shall characterize that which should be the common possession of all. One demands the right to celebrate worship according to one's own pattern. Denied this, one does not feel at home and may leave the fellowship. It is just here that the unchristian character of this attitude is seen, and it is here that every churchly movement must stand the test. When revival piety in the church is unwilling to live in the framework of the liturgy in the common service of worship, it has placed itself outside the fellowship of the church and can no longer be counted as a living movement of the church of Christ.

But outside the common worship service there must be freedom. It should not be required that all the worship and edification of the church be of uniform character. There must be full freedom also for all those forms of worship which truly serve for edification, they may be services of prayer, inner circles of fellowship, liturgical orders of devotion, and many another type of worship. It should be demanded, however, both of oneself and others, that these occasional worship patterns to which one may be attracted shall never displace or be a substitute for the great fellowship of the Sunday common service.

If liturgy has reason sometimes to complain that there is misunderstanding on the part of awakening, awakening can with equal reason say that the friends of liturgy have often failed to show it respect, or even tolerance. It is therefore proper to say a word about liturgy as a chief enemy of awakening.

Awakening, too, has a number of enemies, but hardly any that can be as dangerous as a false liturgy. Liturgy can, if it wants to do itself a disservice, become an almost impregnable armor for the old Adam. What can the Holy Spirit do with a person who goes to Communion more faithfully than anyone else in the congregation, who for an hour a day prays beautiful prayers from the Psalter or from the classic prayer books of Christendom, who reads a devotional from the Compline each evening, and bows in silent meditation after each communion, but who through all these exercises only becomes more and more convinced that he is a better kind of a person; a person, indeed, who while he seems to think that he is thus laying up an impressive reserve of merit, is at the same time careless about his daily duties and studies, neglectful of his stewardship and the nurture of his children, speaks ill of those who think differently, and loves no one except himself and his holy ceremonies? All the promptings of the Holy Spirit are usually unavailing on such an individual, as long as he moves only in his own habit patterns. The Spirit must come upon such a person as a strong wind, break down all his pious pretentions, and show him that he is a proud, self-centered, self-contained, and loveless sinner, who does not deserve anything better than to be cast away from the presence of the Lord. To do this the Holy Spirit may sometimes use a book or a human destiny that ruthlessly lays bare the religion of pious make-believe. At times the Spirit employs some sudden change in fortune that puts the homemade saint in a terrifying situation where nothing is left of his halo. But the most common method is the preaching of the Word of God, the prophetic message, in the Spirit of awakening. It is very characteristic of a false liturgy that it does not like the prophetic word, which comes as a stroke of lighting and does not respect any self-made pious rules of the game. A false liturgy would rather clip the wings of the Word of God. It loves to make the sermon itself a portion of liturgy framed in liturgical formulations and Psalm verses and spoken with disciplined carefulness in a language removed from all concretion and all specific and accusing actuality. It loves to speak the ancient truths in an esthetic and decorative way but never gives the proper name to the everyday conflicts in which the face of the old Adam is clearly identified. This false liturgy can enter into a strange alliance with that which once was awakening. It accepts the ancient pulpit language and the time honored words. But they have lost their point, and they are so far removed from everyday sins that an unrepentant heart can listen to them with great satisfaction. But if one day in the impressive hour of worship a word is spoken with the ancient power of awakening and pierces to the heart of things to reveal the true state, or if outside of the service one is confronted with a question or a personal word that shows how seriously the concern for salvation can burn in a soul, then a dead churchliness is moved to indignation and has a hundred objections to the genuine impulses of the Spirit.

Liturgy without awakening is probably the most dangerous of all church programs. It is possible to enrich and beautify the worship service, to add vestments and choirs, to plan lovely vespers, and even to arrange for more frequent communions, without a single person in earnestness asking himself, “How shall I, a sinner, be saved?” Since by nature all of us are veritable Pharisees and are so sure that we can be saved by our own good deeds, a liturgical renewal without a corresponding awakening of the conscience can mean nothing more than that a given number of people have begun to fulfill a certain number of pious exercises in the conviction that they are now making further deposits in the savings bank of heavenly merit. With such a renewal the devil himself will be very well satisfied. Certainly he will be concerned when a man begins to seek the Lord’s Supper or comes within hearing distance of the Word of God. But as long as there is preaching of such a kind that it does not awaken a sleeping sinner, and as long as the system only creates self-satisfied work-righteousness among Christians, so long Satan himself could be, officially, a church Christian. To be sure, the system has some risks for him. One does not know when a little word from the Epistle lesson or a line from a hymn will fall in good ground. The prince of darkness is not, therefore, really satisfied with any form of churchliness or ritualism. He would rather subscribe to that kind of spirituality which says that it is only a worthless habit and a dead routine to go to church and to come to the Lord's Supper.

Awakening needs liturgy. An awakening that shall have lasting value must nurture a devotional life that will live on through many a long year and that will become a heritage to be passed on from generation to generation. A sound awakening should therefore move in the direction of leading people into a regular worship life and a faithful use of the sacrament of Communion, showing them how to celebrate the common worship in a proper way and to use aright the churchly books of devotion. It is absolutely necessary that our young people, beginning at the time of confirmation, should learn to understand the service of worship at the altar, to find their way in the hymnal and lectionary, and to be able to participate in the kind of worship which is used in the local church. It is a good thing for the pastor to preach on the main themes of the catechism, but he could also with real value to the life of the soul preach occasionally upon the great words of worship, for example, the threefold Holy, the Kyrie, the Gloria in Excelsis, "The Lord be with you," and "Behold the Lamb of God," to mention a few of the chief ones.

Awakening, or revival, can also serve liturgy. When men are awakened, there is a new life in the old forms of devotion. There is new seriousness in the confession of sins, and new joy and power in the hymns of praise. Ancient, beautiful custom becomes more than custom. It becomes an expression for the life which is born again, the same life which once created the custom and which now fills it with new warmth and inwardness.

The need for awakening will one day cease. It belongs to this world, where men still sleep the sleep of death. When Christ has awakened His own on the last great day, there will no longer be any need for awakening. It will be just as obsolete and unnecessary as hospitals and the agencies of social service. But liturgy will remain. What the Scriptures permit us to imagine concerning the ineffable splendor which will then begin includes a picture of a heavenly liturgy, a holy service before the throne of God, with hymns of praise and thanksgiving making music like the sound of great waters, with golden chalices full of incense, and throngs falling down in worship before the God who is the King of kings and the Lord of lords.

Liturgy in the church is a foretaste of the eternal song of praise, an earthly expression of that which is the content of eternity and the basic melody of creation, a never ending thanksgiving to the Creator and Father of all things. Within its earthly poverty liturgy contains something of the beauty of the heavenly, the blessed sense of the nearness of the Eternal, and the joy of being privileged to sacrifice everything in order to be one with Christ.

CPSIA information can be obtained
at www.ICGtesting.com
Printed in the USA
LVOW12s2143200318
570566LV00001B/7/P

9 780758 629722